D1710395

Principles of
Industrial Facility Location

by Howard A. Stafford, Ph.D.

Conway Publications, Inc.

1954 Airport Road, N.E. • Atlanta, Georgia 30341 • 404-458-6026

Library of Congress Cataloging in Publication Data

Stafford, Howard A.
   Principles of industrial facility location.

   (Industrial development site selection handbook)
   A companion vol. to Industrial facilities planning.
   Includes bibliographical references and index.
   1. Industries, Location of. I. Title. II. Series.
   HD58.S676 1980 658.2'1 80-26737
   ISBN 0-910436-08-8

Copyright© 1979 and 1980 by Conway Publications, Inc. All rights reserved. No part of this publication may be reproduced, stored in a retrieval system, or transmitted, in any form or by any means, electronic, mechanical, photocopying, recording, or otherwise, without the prior written permission of the publisher.

International Standard Book Number: 0-910436-08-8
Library of Congress Catalog Card Number: 80-26737
Printed in the United States of America

Contents

Acknowledgements

My primary debt is to all those who have worked before me in this area of industrial location and have been so good to publish their thoughts. I could never hope to acknowledge all individually, but many are noted in the references.

Of those persons more immediately connected with the production of this volume, I wish particularly to thank Cheryl Sievering and Irene Diehl for manuscript preparation. Deborah Whitmore and Blythe Satogata for research and manuscript assistance, and Linda Liston for editing. For advice I am indebted to Harold Carter, Henry Hunker, Peter Mounfield and Howard Roepke. For their encouragement and patience, a special note of appreciation to my parents, Howard and Emilie, and my daughters, Cheryl and Emilie.

Without my wife's help, prodding and constant support, the book would never have been attempted, much less completed. Only she knows the joys of sorting out rough notes in European campgrounds. To Millie the book is dedicated.

About the Author

Dr. Howard A. Stafford is Professor of Geography at the University of Cincinnati. Since earning his doctorate in geography at the University of Iowa, he has served on the faculty at Southern Illinois University, the University of Wisconsin and the University of Wales in the United Kingdom. A specialist in economic geography and industrial location analysis, Dr. Stafford has served as a consultant on numerous development projects and is a prolific writer and lecturer in the field.

Preface

It is said among real estate men that the three most important factors in buying and selling homes are location, location and location. Every filling station operator and every grocery store owner, and every other type of retailer, is likewise aware of the importance of being in the right place. Less obvious and less pervasive is the influence of location on the successful operation of a manufacturing enterprise. In part this is because immediate access to the correct environment or to customers looms less large on the economic balance sheet of manufacturers. In part, the difference is an illusory consequence of a change in scale; whereas the retailer may reckon in terms of yards or city blocks, a manufacturer may find differences of several miles of only marginal significance. That location choice in the manufacturing sphere is more subtle makes it no less important, either to the firm choosing, or to the area chosen.

Like everyone else, manufacturers are constantly making spatial choices: where to procure supplies, where and how to ship to warehouses and customers, where to place plants, and so on. They even make locational choices in a negative sense, such as unconsciously preserving the spatial status quo. The focus of this book, however, is on the conscious act of siting a large and relatively immobile productive investment. In other words, the prime focus is on the overt act of locating a manufacturing plant. All firms do it. Large firms choose locations, using large amounts of staff time and often with abundant outside influence. Small firms also choose locations, even if only once. These decisions typically involve a large fixed investment and considerable contemplation. The choice will have long term consequences, financial and legal, social and psychological. This book discusses the ways in which the process of locational choice by manufacturers may be made more rational and the results more beneficial.

The focus is on the location of the productive facilities (plants) of manufacturing companies. It is set within the framework of relatively free, private enterprise in capitalistic economies. It draws primarily on American and British experience and examples, although specific techniques and general principles are undoubtedly applicable to a much wider field.

Manufacturers, when discussing plant location decisions, often express the thought that other manufacturers are "more sophisticated, in selecting places for factories, and perhaps next time around we will be also." One of the purposes of this book is to disabuse decision-makers of the idea that the "other fellows" are doing a better job. Another is to provide practical guidelines by which the quality of location decisions may be improved. These require discussion of how the location decision is usually made. This, in turn helps provide a better understanding of spatial patterns of manufacturing, providdng a survey of common considerations and techniques, and, finally, suggests avenues decision makers may elect in efforts to improve location selections.

The book is intended primarily for businessmen who face location decisions. It endeavors to overview the existing "state of the art," to provide practical examples and to speculate on new developments. It is a guidebook which provides insight into the essential nature of the location decision process, enables executives to share the locational experiences of others and provides specific suggestions for rationalizing and improving location decision making. These same features should prove useful to a second audience: persons and agencies interested in regional economic development. A regional development agency will be in a better position to "sell" its area to manufacturers by knowing how its prospective clients operate. The book also should be of value to economic geographers and regional economists; one important way of understanding spatial distributions is through the analysis of decisions which collectively produce the patterns. Finally, the guidebook may be of value in a variety of business administration courses and management seminars.

Part I (Chapters 1 and 2) presents an overview of the motives and circumstances of the location decision and the decision makers. Chapters 3, 4, 5 and 6 (Part II) discuss specific factors which influence the choosing of a place for a factory. The next three chapters (Part III) look at objective techniques and models for analyzing data and assessing alternative locations within the context of the overall investment strategy. Part IV (Chapter 10) presents a summarizing integration and some practical advice on how the location decision process might be improved.

This guidebook is designed as a companion volume to *Industrial Facilities Planning* (H.M. Conway and L.L. Liston, eds., Conway Publications, 1976). It provides a uniform, integrated and systematic guide through the process of industrial location analysis and decision-making and can be used independently. However, *Industrial Facilities Planning* provides a rich variety of insights, procedures and case studies from over 100 professionals in the field, and thus, when used in conjunction with the present volume, greatly enhances the value of each.

Introduction

The selection of good locations for industrial facilities is a complex process. In order to keep this book short enough to be accessible and of practical utility, the treatments of many topics are necessarily brief. The references at the end of each chapter are provided as guides to more detailed analyses as required for any given situation. To simplify even further, this introduction provides a summary of key issues and generalizations. If used with appropriate caution, this overview may provide a useful framework on which to hang the balance of the text.

Although expansions and contractions of production in existing plants are location decisions, the primary focus in this book is on the selection of new manufacturing places. The location of a new plant typically is a decision made by relatively few senior executives of the firm. It involves the objective and judgmental balancing of complex corporate goals and a variety of location factors. Conway Publications's "Checklist of Site Selection Factors" contains 1,700 listings. Gathering historic and present data on the relevant factors is an immense task; the necessity to forecast the future further complicates data collection.

The specific location factors vary in relative importance according to firm, place and time. Each situation is unique. Experience with many industrial location decisions indicates, however, that the factors most often critical are accessibility to markets and to material suppliers, transportation facilities, labor (especially availability and productivity), utilities, business services, taxes and local "quality of life." The most commonly used method of assessing the relative merits of alternate locations is to compare total cost, summing individual costs for the several factors considered. The newer and potentially powerful operations research techniques, such as Linear Programming, are underutilized, but they are becoming increasingly important.

Each specific factor demands individual attention. A group of "Friction of Distance" variables includes transportation, markets and materials access and communications. *Transportation* considerations revolve around the costs of moving the various inputs to the production site plus the costs of shipping the outputs to the various buyers. These costs depend on the distances traveled (with total charges increasing, but per mile costs decreasing with increasing distance). Costs also vary by type of commodity shipped, transportation modes utilized, the size of the shipment and commodity and freight rate structures. An Aggregate Transportation Cost Model is often used to compare alternative possible locations. A transportation costs analysis should also explicitly consider the relative merits of warehouses vs new factories.

Access to *markets* is usually the most important of all the location variables. Location nearer markets reduces transportation charges on factory outputs. Closeness to markets also tends to enable decreased delivery times and increased service to customers and to result in a higher degree of market penetration. Critical to location planning are good forecasts of future market configurations. After obtaining these forecasts, possible analytical techniques include the Aggregate Transport Model, the "Tornqvist Solution," the Market Potential Model and Linear Programming.

Access to *materials* involves transportation costs, availability and services provided by vendors. The analyst should also anticipate possible changes in the location of supplies and in the plant's product mix. Because of the greater importance of market and labor access and because most plants utilize a variety of spatially scattered inputs, materials oriented plants are relatively rare; regardless, the cost of assembling inputs must be included in a complete analysis.

Communications, the movement of people and ideas, traditionally has been underemphasized in locational planning. There is evidence that this is becoming increasingly influential, especially for business contacts, for access to current technical information and for effective management. In spite of vast improvements in passenger travel and long distance telecommunications over the past several decades, proximity is still important. Executives, especially those in dynamic industries, move away from metropolitan information networks and manage distant operations at their peril.

Another group of factors may be thought of as the attributes of areas. The most important of these is *labor.* The labor demands of the proposed plant must be consistent with the number of skilled workers available within a reasonable commuting range. An area's history of labor relations and productivity also is important. Labor is a difficult factor to analyze, but some insight is better than none. Most often, the search proceeds after first identifying the general shape of the labor market for a few areas which look reasonable on other criteria. Then, more specific data are collected via field surveys.

An area's mix of linked industries, business services, utilities, etc., (the *agglomeration* forces and *infrastructure* considerations) is also important. What groups is it important to be near? Which services should be purchased from public vendors? These considerations generally favor urban areas, but each situation is unique.

Power is not a critical locational consideration for most manufacturing plants. Historically, power has been relatively cheap and widely available; however, with price increases and regionally variable fuel shortages, some locators are now stressing future availability. Although nearness to power and fuel sources is becoming relatively more important, it probably will not become a major locational priority for most plants.

Water has not been a powerful locational force for most plants, but locators must be aware of locally inadequate supplies. Another traditionally minor factor is an area's *quality-of-life*, but its importance appears to be increasing. Quality-of-life is especially important in obtaining and retaining highly skilled labor and executive personnel.

Governmental influences are another broad area of concern. The most pervasive of these is taxes, but there is conflicting evidence on their importance in industrial location decision-making. Economic analyses tend to indicate that taxes are not, or should not, be major influences on plant location. Conversely, taxes are mentioned as important by decision-makers almost as frequently as the factors of markets, materials, labor and transportation facilities. Part of the explanation for this discrepancy may be that taxes produce emotional reactions far in excess of their monetary consequences and are often viewed as indicators of an area's "political climate," its receptiveness to manufacturing activity. Taxes are difficult to assess because they represent benefits as well as costs; they are variable over time as well as space, and they are often negotiable. It is possible to hazard a general rule of thumb: If one percent of projected sales dollars does not produce a figure in excess of other locational differentials, a detailed study of taxes may not be worth the effort.

Further complicating an analysis is that the monies governments remove via taxes they may return via *incentives*. A variety of locational incentives are constantly evolving, defying comprehensive listing. In practice, there must be assessed in terms of specific areas for specific types of operations. Usually they are not major locational forces, but rather serve to tip the balance when all other aspects are equal.

Government responses to society's concern for the *environment* have complicated the industrial location process for many firms in the past few years. Conway Publications Checklist contains over 100 items pertaining to environmental concerns. The possibility of having to file comprehensive and complex Environmental Impact Statements for major projects threatens to take manufacturers far beyond their traditional spheres of research and planning. Environmental regulations increase the time span necessary from initial planning to the operation of the completed facility and increase the costs of site selection. Although it is difficult to predict long run impacts on the overall distribution of industry, there is little doubt that for the individual firm environmental regulations make proper site selection procedures more crucial than ever.

Only after a community has been chosen should a specific building site be selected. The general region and the best town, city or metropolitan area should be selected by balancing the above location factors via the appropriate assessment techniques. At this point the scale of analysis changes to determine the best of the available sites within the selected community. There are a number of *local* factors to be assessed. A typical company agenda at the local scale might include: (1) availability and prices of sites; (2) relative site location; (3) site size (with ample allowance for possible future expansion); (4) availability and adequacy of transportation facilities, utilities and services; (5) local codes, ordinances and land use regulations; and (6) living conditions. It is important to remember that since the cost of land is usually only a small proportion of investment and operating costs, the attributes of the site are much more important than its initial purchase price.

Since manufacturers are found in a variety of types of places within an urban area, it is difficult to generalize on locational patterns at this scale; however, there is a notable trend toward choosing locations within industrial parks. The advantages of industrial parks include: (1) external economies through the common provision of such factors as utilities roads and nearby amenities; (2) land costs; (3) site readiness; and (4) pre-existing zoning and environmental approvals and permits. Conversely, industrial parks are not appropriate for every type of plant. A heavy or noxious plant is inappropriate in the typical light industrial park. Also, the usually tighter restrictions in the parks deter some companies; and since industrial parks are limited in number in any given area, they cannot offer the same variety of locations as available at non-park sites.

A number of *analytical techniques* are available to the site selector. Most commonly used is a *comparative costs framework*. Here, each relevant factor of production and transportation is costed at each appropriate scale sequentially (e.g., national, subnational, regional, local) for any number of possible locations. The *Least-cost, Weighted Criteria* approach is a useful industry-developed extension of this framework; it attempts to combine both quantitative and qualitative factors. Considering cost comparisons only is inadequate, as profits are determined by both costs and *revenues*, and revenues (demand) may be influenced by the location of the plant. This presents a dilemma since costs and revenues are simultaneously interactive. A common practical solution is to split the problem using market patterns (demand surfaces) to select the general areas within which comparative costs will be computed. Further complications include selecting the proper plant *size* and the appropriate *product mix*. Both of these influence and are influenced by location.

Operations research techniques are of potential aid in determining the optimum size of plant, the optimum product mix and the least cost transportation point. The most popular of these techniques is *Linear Programming*. Simultaneously solving a set of production constraint equations can indicate the optimal product mix for a given plant. Similarly, given an existing production and consumption pattern, new capacity can be situated via linear programming location-allocation techniques to minimize total transportation costs.

The analytical techniques so far indicated typically have three deficiencies: (1) Although a plant is a major capital investment, the results of the locational analyses are not cast in capital budgeting formats compatible with the normal investment analyses done by a firm and, thus, are less readily comprehended and compared by management. (2) The simple existence of some net profit does not necessarily indicate sufficient profit to warrant the investment. (3) Simple comparisons of total profits over the expected life of the project may lead to erroneous conclusions if the cash inflows and outflows vary over time among the locations considered. *Capital budgeting* techniques, such as Discounted Cash Flow, which take into account the time value of money, can be used to address these deficiencies. Discounting techniques, presently underutilized, may be expected to be increasingly employed; they are superior to the more commonly used pay-back criteria.

In the final analysis, locational decision making is judgmental. Good decisions depend on good research designs. They also depend on explicit consideration of *risk* and *uncertainty* and on the selection of *decision rules* consistent with the situations and the goals of the firm. There is evidence that the geography of the firm and the astute management of spatial factors are being increasingly recognized as critical elements in the well-being of the manufacturing enterprise. Keys to success include knowledgeable and *involved managements.*

This book is dedicated to enhancing the involvement in location decision-making of knowledgeable managements. All of the above topics, and more, are discussed in some detail in the following chapters.

Part I The Art Of
Industrial Location Decision-Making

I The Nature Of The Location Business

I
The Nature of the Location Business

Choosing the location for a major productive facility is one of the most critical decisions management has to make. It is a large, relatively rare investment decision fraught with complexities and uncertainties. Locational decision-making is part an art, at best an inexact science. Yet, location decisions by manufacturers must be made, and the consequences may affect the profitability, growth and even survival of the firm. This book is designed to assist managers in making plant location decisions.

There is a widespread belief that manufacturers are quite sophisticated in choosing the correct locations for their productive facilities. Most managers know that this is not the case. However, many managers seem to believe that *others* are more scientific in the location decision process. Experience with a large number of managers in a wide variety of industries shows that choosing the "right" place for a plant is an inexact process, and decision-makers are almost always somewhat defensive about the way they do it. This same experience shows that these many different location decision-makers have much to gain from each other, something they rarely have an opportunity to do. This first chapter attempts to put the industrial location decision process in the perspective of shared experience.

Figure 1-2 diagrammatically illustrates the complex "behavioral inter-relationships" of firms.[1] The primary focus of this book is on the "spatially active" firms and on the selection of new localities for new manufacturing facilities. Attention, therefore, is directed to the extreme left side of Figure 1-2.

These new, or largely expanded, facilities can be single plant opera-

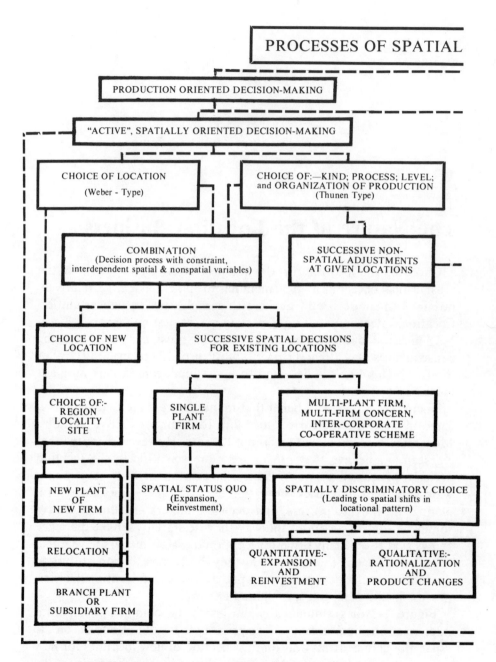

Fig. 1. Classification and flow chart of spatially relevant behavorial processes of firms.
Source: Gunter Krumme, "Toward a Geography of Enterprise," *Economic Geography,* January, 1969

Figure 1-1. Processes of Spatial Behavior Of Firms ➤

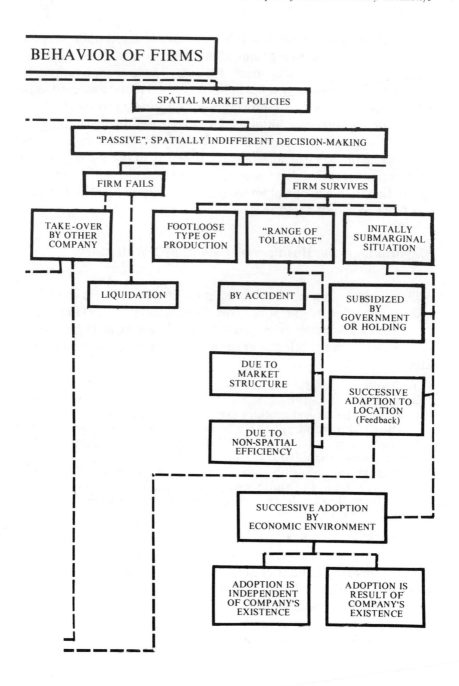

tions, but much more often will be branches of multi-plant corporations. They run the size gamut from large to small, but the basic location principles remain much the same. Precise motivations for selecting new locations will be multi-dimensional and as varied as the companies concerned. All, however, are responding to *need*, usually immediate and pressing; although factories are constructed to last for years, the planning horizon is surprisingly short. A survey of the directors/managers of real estate and property of the 700 largest U.S. corporations revealed that the usual elapsed time from first consideration to final decision of a plant location was only 13 months; the range was from 36 months to a low of one month![2]

Magnitude of the Business of Industrial Location

Investment in new productive facilities is big business, in good times and in time of economic slowdown. In one survey of 100 firms, they alone selected sites for more than 700 installations in 1977, and, on average, for each site selected examined an average of five competitive sites.[3]

Despite some idle plant capacity, a deepening recession and omnipresent inflation, U.S. business and industry has budgeted (for 1975) the largest amount ever for new plant and equipment.

The capital spending tab for business and industry is projected to reach a record $116.1 billion this year, $3.7 billion or 3.5 percent more than 1974.

Even taking inflation into account, that's a lot of billions in anybody's book. Put another way, that amount computes out to a new $10 million facility for virtually every city, town and hamlet in the nation.[4]

A late 1977 survey by the Bureau of Economic Analysis projects new plant and equipment expenditures by business to total $150.9 billion in 1978. These many billions of dollars represent a 10.1 percent increase over 1977 (unadjusted for price change). The manufacturing industries are expected to expend 45 percent of the total for all industries, with durable goods accounting for 47 percent and nondurables 53 percent of the manufacturing capital expenditures.[5]

How active is the business of industrial location? How many firms are actively engaged in either locating or relocating all or part of their operation annually? Useful data are hard to come by, but we know the number of manufacturing establishments in the

Census Division	1975 Total	1975 %	1969 Total	1969 %	1960 Total	1960 %
New England	$ 1,818	4.86	$ 1,215	5.5	$ 618	6.1
Middle Atlantic	5,290	14.14	4,075	18.3	2,056	20.4
East North Central	9,114	24.36	6,481	29.1	3,007	29.9
West North Central	2,345	6.27	1,110	5.0	518	5.1
South Atlantic	5,317	14.21	2,929	13.1	1,214	12.1
East South Central	2,645	7.07	1,428	6.4	570	5.7
West South Central	5,623	15.03	2,282	10.2	790	7.8
Mountain	1,225	3.27	447	2.0	220	2.1
Pacific	1,036	10.79	2,318	10.4	1,103	10.9
TOTALS	**$37,413**	**100.0**	**$22,285**	**100.0**	**$10,096**	**100.1**

Note: $ figures in millions

Source: *Statistical Abstract of the United States, 1977.* (Washington: U.S. Government Printing Office, 1972 and 1977).

Table 1-1. Manufacturers' Expenditures For New Plants And Equipment, By Census Division, 1975, 1969 And 1960, Total And Percentage Share

United States was in excess of 311,000 in 1967. This was an increase of 70,000 establishments over 1947. Simple arithmetic indicates that an average of 3,500 establishments were added each year during the 20-year span. While the gross number increased by the approximate 3,500 establishments noted, there is no indication of the actual number of new establishments in any given year. The fact is that more than 3,500 new establishments are placed in operation in a typical year, but there are also numerous losses of establishments due to business failures, business retirements, mergers, acquisitions and so forth. Thus, the net number of new firms remains unresolved.[6]

Table 1-1 shows expenditures for new plant and equipment for 1960, 1969 and 1975 with percentage shares by census division. Note the relative decline of the older manufacturing regions of New England, Middle Atlantic and East North Central divisions, and the increase in share by the more recently favored industrial areas of the South Atlantic, East South Central and West South Central divisions. These same trends, with an emphasis on industrial relocations, are examined in detail in an excellent article, "The Second War Between The States," *Business Week*, May 17, 1976.

The Decision Makers: Who and Why

Thus, although locating a new plant is a relatively rare event in the life of the average company, in the aggregate, industrial location is big business. By whom are these location decisions made? The *News Front* survey (1972) reports the following:[7]

Who are the 2, 3 or 4 men (by title) most involved in the decision of a company plant site?

By title:	%	By function:	%
Ch. Bd./Bd. of Dirs.	21	Administrative	142
Pres./CEO	63	Prod., Mfg., Ops.	71
Asst. to Pres.	2	Real Estate, Property	41
Exec. VP's	17	Finance	21
Group VP's	16	Engineering	18
Div. Pres/VP's	10	Mktg./Sales	14
VP's	104	Ind. Rel., Pers.	12
Treasurers	6	Planning	8
Controllers	2	Dist., Transp.	3
Attorneys	1		
Genl. Mgrs.	4		
Division Mgrs.	21		
Directors	30		
Managers	33		
Consultant	1		
Architect	1		

Average number most involved - 3.3

Who makes the final decision?

By title:	%	By function:	%
Ch. Bd./Bd. of Dirs.	24	Administrative	91
Pres./CEO	40	Prod., Mfg., Ops.	4
Exec. Com.	8	Finance	2
Capital Exp. Com.	5	Real Estate, Property	1
Exec. VP	4	Engineering	1
Group VP	6	Mktg./Sales	1
VP	8		**100**
Treasurer	1		
Div. Mgr.	2		
Manager	2		
100			

SOURCE: *Newsfront,* March/April, 1972, p. 51.

Table 1-2

We may also flesh out the previous discussion of motivation, or why a new plant site is chosen, by reporting the results of several surveys. Although different in detail from firm to firm and from area to area, in the aggregate they all tend to point in the same directions. Two survey results, one from the United States and one from the United Kingdom will suffice for illustration. *News Front*[8] asked industrialists to "please give a 1, 2, or 3 rating to the importance of the following as major objectives for planning a new location." The results were:

	1	2	3
Improvement in transportation efficiency or economy	73%	16%	11%
Availability of larger parcel of land	30	45	25
Closer proximity to resources and/or major suppliers	54	25	21
Closer proximity to company's other plants	7	30	63
Closer proximity to customers and/or distributors	75	19	6
Closer proximity to other firms in same or related industries	6	31	63
Ability to better serve new and/or expanded markets	70	24	6
Minimize competition from other plants for labor force	27	44	29
Improvement in materials handling	49	35	16
Improvements in labor cost/productivity	74	22	4
Benefit by tax incentives or holidays	16	53	31
Secure factors of location unique to a given industry (special energy requirements, waste disposal, etc.)	49	27	24

SOURCE: *Newsfront*, March/April, 1972, p. 51.

Table 1-3

From a United Kingdom survey of 531 firms who had opened a new manufacturing plant at some time in 1964-67 in an area where they had not manufactured previously, the following responses were obtained from a series of questions relating to, "What caused you to consider opening a new plant in a new location?"[9] (See Table 1-4).

These data and extensive interviews with business leaders indicate that outstanding motivations are the need for new capacity and better locations to meet increased sales. Thus, the marketing geography of the firm is often the single most important element in the location strategy. The preferred way to meet sales demands is to increase productivity within existing facilities through such measures as multiple shifts, increased overtime or more efficient machinery. The next

Was it (new plant in new location) for one of the following reasons?

Question[2] numbers		Major[3] reason	Minor[4] reason	Outstanding[5] single reason
B1-2.	To permit an expansion of output	83	8	20
B12-15.	Inadequate existing premises or site	50	11	8
B26-29.	Unsatisfactory labour supply at existing location	40	11	15
B30-31.	Inducements and facilities made available by official bodies	27	14	2
B22-25.	Opportunity to purchase or rent premises site at new location	20	8	3
B4-6.	Too far from established or potential markets	19	1	9
B20-21.	Refusal or expected refusal of I.D.C.	12	4	5
B18-19.	Town planning difficulties	11	3	4
B16-17.	Lease of former premises fell in, or good offer received	5	2	3
B33.	Desire to be in more attractive surroundings	4	8	1
B7-11.	Too far from supplies, actual or prospective, of materials or services	3	2	1
B34.	More profitable to operate elsewhere, no other postulated reason being major	1	--	1
B35.	No one outstanding reason	--	--	28
				100

[1]Questions B1-34 were asked of 531 firms—the 543 firms interviewed less 12 cases classed as enterprises new to manufacturing, for whom the questions were not appropriately worded. Question B35 was asked of 492 firms, having been added after some interviews had taken place.

[2]B3 and B32 did not postulate individual reasons.

[3]Percentage replying "major" to at least one of the questions in the group named.

[4]Percentage replying "minor" to at least one of the questions in the group named, provided "major" had not been answered to any question in the group.

[5]Percentage replying as indicated to B35: Was any one of the above reasons (B1-34) outstandingly more important than the rest in causing you to open a new plant in a new location? If so, which?

SOURCE: *Regional Development Incentives HC 85-I, Session 1973-74,* House of Commons (U.K.), p. 532.

Table 1-4. Groups of Reasons

step is an addition to the existing plant. Such in-site expansions are usually not considered as locational problems, but they should be since they constitute, however unconsciously, decisions to stay in place and not to move elsewhere. Becoming aware of this spatial dimension, not usually made explicit, is one critical step in devising an effective investment strategy. More explicitly, spatial is the next stage in meeting demands for additional capacity, the construction of a new plant on a new site.

An outstanding motivation is the desire to obtain a new, more efficient labor force. Also, there may be the necessity to protect existing markets, which may indicate the siting of a new plant. Other motivating forces may include the desire to establish a beach-head in a new area; to secure a supply of materials through proximity, especially within certain legal jurisdictions; the desire for a new, more efficient plant layout, to incorporate new techniques, and/or to establish a new product line. There may even be a negative factor wherein, for political purposes, a company decides not to enlarge its presence in a particular locality, but rather to diversify into other areas. A variety of other motivations for locating a new manufacturing facility may be quite specific and vary from firm to firm, industry to industry, and area to area.

The Nature of the Location Decision[10]

Industrial location decisions can be classed as in-site or new-site. In terms of absolute change, in-site decisions are by far the most important. Sixty to 80 percent of new manufacturing capacity each year is allocated to expansion of existing plants and only something under 40 percent to the construction of new ones.[11] In-site expansions and contractions are clearly locational decisions; they are decisions not to make these changes elsewhere. A full-fledged location theory must account for in-site location decisions.

However, for an existing firm, the construction of a new plant is a drastic response to excesses of demand over capacity, one to be considered only after every effort has been made to wring additional production out of existing facilities. Thus, in-site location decisions are usually routine, low-level, short-run decisions where location is relatively passive, with other factors of the production process being dominant. New-site decisions, on the other hand, necessarily make location considerations explicit. These decisions are made by the management for relatively longer periods of time. They are the strategic decisions.

The time span for new plant construction and the length of the amortization period that follows are significant. These factors, plus the magnitude of the investment, clearly make the decision part of the long-range planning process of the corporation. There is the conscious effort to forecast and to control the future. On the other hand, given the many variables other than location which influence revenues, and the financial resources of modern manufacturing facilities, the time period is too short for these forces to be fully operative. No doubt the majority of new manufacturing locations are both planned and non-optimal. Clearly, then, a key pattern in the understanding of industrial location patterns is an inquiry into the decision-making process.

Since new-site selection is a management decision, many persons are involved. Either maximum profit or satisfactory profit may be valid general objectives, but neither presents an operational basis for choosing among alternative location strategies. The evaluation of future states of affairs, and therefore prospective returns, would differ among the several evaluators involved in the management decision. Even if all seek maximum (or satisfactory) profit, but each concludes that it can be obtained by a different route, there is no test of rightness. There is no objective basis for judgment.[12] Likewise, multiple decision-makers tend to reduce the influence of purely personal considerations. No one person, not even the President or the Chairman of the Board, has the power to site a plant solely on the basis of a personal whim.

If maximization of profit is not entirely operational, and purely personal considerations inappropriate, what then are the key motives? We might borrow Galbraith's notion that the goals of the corporation are the goals of the techno-structure.[13] Outstanding among these is the growth of the firm. Rational, but imperfect, industrial location choices have been and are being made, and it is these which produce the spatial fabric. These are strategic, long-range investment decisions, made by top management. There are no efficiency criteria to guide judgment in the making of strategic decisions. The concept of efficiency is not relevant in the presence of the uncertainties attending decisions as to how to redeploy a firm's assets. From among a dozen possible alternative lines of action some choice is to be made. Each carries with it potentials for failure and success which can only be appraised judgmentally, which means that logic carries only so far and then gives way to some non-logical basis for decision. No marginalist calculations have any meaning in the face of uncertain magnitudes.[14]

It is likely that the location decision mechanism is objectively, if not psychologically, rather simple, because, "resource allocation within the firm reflects only gross comparisons of the marginal advantages of alternatives. Rules of thumb for evaluating alternatives provide some contraints on resource allocation, and there is no conscious comparison of specific alternative investments. Any alternative that satisfies the constraints and secures suitably powerful support with the organization is likely to be adopted."[15] Furthermore, forecasts are necessarily rather abstract; and, "as forecast needs vary from the concrete to the abstract, the importance of empirical data diminishes rapidly; also, forecasters with specialized skills must be replaced by informed generalists, capable of operating without empirical evidence but with disciplined imagination to evaluate diversified sources of qualitative information."[16]

The decision process is implemented by the individual firm's top management team, and we may postulate that a primary goal is the growth of the firm. Although precise establishment of the cost and revenue curves may be important for classic, normative economic models, the time horizon for new plant construction and the uncertainty of the future discount their influence on actual location decisions. Detailed information on the past of a firm or industry establishes a frame of reference for seeking and evaluating relevant data; but it does not answer questions about the future. Rather, the reality is that decision-makers must rely on experience, intuition, generalized trends and readily available data to guide the location decision.

Toward a Model of the Location Decision Process

There exists considerable literature in which investigators report on manufacturers' responses to questions of why they are located as they are. Much of what we know about the relative importance of the various location factors comes from such studies. By and large, such studies suffer from two common elements:

1. Such surveys almost always occur "after the fact," at which time there is the conscious or subconscious effort to rationalize and justify the location actually chosen.

2. They are structured, often *a priori*, around the standard eco-

nomic variables as decreed by economic theory, and since the decision-makers also labor under the impression that they must appear economically rational, the more subtle, but perhaps more important, decision processes are not adequately explored.

Efforts have been made to overcome these objections through:

1. The simulation of the industrial location decision process by a gaming technique wherein the decision process can be monitored as it takes place.

2. In-depth interviews of actual decision-makers, with a primary focus on the decision process.

Both of these efforts are of interest, and their convergence leads toward a general model of the industrial location decision process. Of particular interest are, of course, the economic factors involved and the techniques employed in analyzing them, and, in addition, some idea of how the large issue of uncertainty is handled judgmentally.

A role-playing game has been developed which simulates the industrial location decision process for a hypothetical metals fabricating operation (hence known as the "MetFab" Company).[17] The game is played by teams of five who, because of the flexibility of the role-playing approach, are limited only by reading ability. The players have ranged from persons of 12 years of age upwards, including professional geographers and economists as well as practicing businessmen. Although the "richness" of the game varies with the expertise the participants bring to it, the essentials of the play are remarkably consistent.

The simulation proceeds by each group of five constituting itself as the management of a new company for which, as a simplifying move, the nature and scale of the manufacturing operation itself is taken as given (previously decided). The only problem before the team at the beginning of the play is to choose the most appropriate (best) city among the 25 largest in the United States for the location of the plant. Even this problem is further simplified by postulating that this is the first and, for the foreseeable future, the only plant, thus eliminating consideration of factors such as in-plant expansion, inertia and multiple production points. Even given these simplifications, there is evidence that the game is reasonably realistic, and that the decision processes involved possess a high degree of fidelity to actual situations.

Each player chooses one of the five roles: President, Sales Manager, Production Manager, Personnel Manager or Treasurer. Each team member shares some general information about the joint adventure, and also has information, data and opinions specific only to his role. Built into these roles are data and information on locational factors such as transport costs on materials and product, labor costs and availability, locations of competitors, taxes and "personal factors." Also, conflicts of opinion over least-cost versus maximum-demand philosophies and the short run versus the long run are built in. The play consists of each member mastering his own material, then communicating his information and ideas to his teammates and, finally, participating in the arguments as to the best location for the factory.

Extensive observation of the simulation has produced a wealth of insight into the industrial location decision process. Among the significant generalizations are:

1. The uncertainties inherent in the game are deemed realistic by the participants, are accepted and "worked around." Although the players often wish for a completely, even mathematically, determined solution, they quickly come to grips with the judgmental situation.

2. The game is greatly simplified almost at the outset. Each player produces a "short list" of the better locations very quickly, based, first, on the data available and, secondly, on opinions. Considerable time is then spent ranking the short list. The full team debate is similarly simplified by first reducing the individual choices to a composite short list, whereupon things become behaviorally quite complex as debate ensues over the ultimate "best choice."

3. The final selection of the best location is based on the judgmental integration of data, forecasts and opinions. Because of uncertainties, the choice cannot be shown to be economically optimal, but is usually judged best given the circumstances. Decisions are not portrayed as "second best" or "satisfying." Likewise, the decision process is viewed as "rational" and "logical" in spite of the inability to show economic optimality.

4. If a time-shortened version of the game is used (for example, same information, less time for reflection and debate), the final decision rests much more heavily on the concrete data than on the opinions built into the roles. As the playing time is lengthened, opinions, biases and judgments, especially about the future, become more significant, eventually becoming paramount. In the latter case, the "hard" data permit the initial simplification into a relatively few "reasonable" or "viable" cities to be seriously considered; the debate about these selected cities then becomes very judgmental.

5. Primary reliance on the actual data is also associated with a short-run viewpoint. In the short-run there is a pronounced tendency to assume demand as given and to operate within a least-cost framework. Planning for the longer run tends to de-emphasize cost factors and to stress probable future variations in demand, with special focus on probable regional growth areas.

Management Interviews

In-depth interviews have been held with the industrial location decision-making executives of several manufacturing organizations which have recently located one or more new production facilities.[18],[19] The decision process revealed in these interviews is strikingly similar to processes observed in the MetFab simulations. The fact that in every case the actual locators were establishing a branch plant, rather than the one and only plant as postulated in the MetFab game, appears to be of little consequence. Likewise, although there were individual differences in the locations chosen, the location decision process was remarkably uniform, regardless of the specific nature of the firm or industry in question. And the process observed also conforms to the outline of general decision theory. Thus, generalizations based on even such a small sample appear to be of value.

Following are some general principles upon which location decision-makers seem to operate:

1. The location problem is not a common concern; rather, it most often becomes explicit when it becomes clear that additional productive capacity is necessary. The capacity problem is usually immediate, and the first solution is in-site expansion, through increasing production from existing facilities (for example, multiple shifts), and then by expansion by construction of additions to the existing plant. Only after these short-run solutions prove inadequate or unreasonable is a new facility in a new location seriously considered.

2. The majority of new plant location decisions are made in response to the need for additional capacity. Thus, the existence and location of markets are of paramount importance in the location of industries (this is true even for the so-called "materials-oriented" and "footloose" industries).

3. The speed with which a firm responds to capacity demands varies according to the quality, scope and nature of this firm's growth guide-

lines. Organizations used to expansion tend to develop specific growth plans and also tend to move more quickly from the in-site to the new plant solution to additional capacity demands than firms with more modest growth rates (or, in some cases, with larger economies of scale).

4. Decision-makers rapidly and drastically transform the infinite complexities of the optimal location problem into a relatively simple, intellectually manageable situation. This is normally accomplished by allowing the current and projected spatial demand surfaces (i.e., market maps) to be the prime determinates in defining the geographic decision space. The regional space so defined is further simplified by the judgmental selection of a finite (and small) number of specific sites for detailed consideration. At this sub-regional scale, cost factors are paramount.

5. Decision-makers also simplify and control their environment by not indulging in difficult modes of analysis when the payoffs are unclear or unsure. Likewise, they tend to avoid, when possible, implementation of any solution which entails arduous negotiation with such groups as unions and governmental regulatory agencies.

6. The ultimate decision is made and / or ratified by the highest levels of management. They view the new plant location decision as a relatively long-run solution but one which must rely for good data on relatively short-run projections. It is this discrepancy, the uncertainty of the future, which necessitates judgmental, rather than technical, decision-making.

7. Although location decision-makers make no claims for economic optimality, the decision process is viewed as logical and rational. There is no firm which cannot cite the rationale for its plant location(s). In this sense, there is no such thing as a "foot-loose" plant (or industry).

Additional Observations[20]

A small team of management people, usually less than five, makes the location decision. The decision is viewed strictly from the management side. Consequently, there is the opportunity and the tendency to maximize executive convenience, other things being roughly equal, both in the decision process and as a criterion for site selection.

Although potentially of almost infinite complexity, the location decision process is quickly and severely simplified by the decision-makers. The temporal dimension is simplified by dealing with projection of the future of only a few years, rarely more than five. This is despite the fact that managers seem to believe that the new facility and new location will help solve company problems for 10, 20 or 30 years. The spatial dimension is likewise severely simplified. Most areas of the world are never even thought of as potential sites. At the other extreme, the number of specific sites seriously considered is small, usually less than six.

Managers also pay little attention to possible temporal changes in the spatial context, such as shifts in supply or markets or moves by competitors. They have few ways of dealing with such uncertainties. The relative lack of provision for future contingencies, however, is consistent with the generalization that plants are constructed to solve immediate problems. Moreover, only a short time period is usually available for planning the new facility and selecting its site—normally only a few months.

In interviews, the more classic economic location factors are usually discussed first by the respondents. This priority reflects the basic importance of these factors. However, one suspects that managers like to see themselves as economically rational. Once the respondents are well into the interview, are relaxed and have recalled many memories, then the subjective judgmental and personal nature of industrial location decision-making becomes fully apparent.

New facilities are usually constructed to meet expanded product demand, to obtain more modern plant and facilities or to escape an unfavorable labor situation. The current findings tend to corroborate the oft-noted generalization that manufacturing firms do not establish new or expanded plants to take advantage of potential opportunities; rather, such new establishments are responses to immediate and pressing problems.

Manufacturers most often operate independently, and there seems to be relatively little explicit element of "following" any other firm in the choice of location. Of distinct importance, however, is the internal geography of the firm. There is a noticeable tendency to use what might be labelled a "spatial increment" model, wherein these relatively small plants are located far enough away from any existing facility of that firm to gain perceived locational advantages (usually labor), but no further than necessary so as to facilitate inter-plant cooperation and, especially, management contact from the home office. In one case, the search area was determined by a 200-mile radius from headquarters--

the distance the corporate jet could cover in one hour. Likewise, in a special in-depth survey of eight actual locations, six of the decision-makers were not to be personally involved in operating the new plants to such an extent that it would necessitate their living nearby; but for the two cases in which the decision-makers were designated to be also the local operators, even the then current location of their homes seemed to be a significant factor. It appears that the "information" demands of the system are severe and the requisite information/contacts cannot regularly be obtained/maintained too far from "home." This, combined with the strong desire to minimize executive inconvenience, suggests that firms will put branches as close to home as other economic conditions permit.

Of the eight plants (in the one survey), seven of the managements are happy with their location decisions and in retrospect feel that the results confirm the wisdom of their choice. The only firm unhappy with its location decision was a firm with a resident planning group, which was contending with a decision made before the group was fully operational. With the exception of the current activities of the one in-house planning group, the decision-makers characterized their location decision process as being relatively unsophisticated. They used relatively few data and no fancy analytic techniques. And they tend to think that other manufacturers probably are much better at the process than themselves.

However, those decision-makers who confessed most readily to an "unsophisticated" location decision process were those who (1) were most closely involved in the actual location decision, (2) could supply the most lucid and detailed retrospective analysis of the process and (3) seemed most happy with their ultimate location decisions. This point is especially interesting because it conforms to the basic psychological principle that the "severity of the initiation" (in this case, hard work on the actual decision) is positively correlated with loyalty to the organization (or, in this case, the correctness of the location decision). This is of practical importance because it is likely that confidence in decisions leads, in part, to self-fulfilling prophecies.

The Decision Trace: A General Model

Although each locational decision differs in detail, investigation suggests striking similarities in the decision-making process. In every case, there was a judgmental response, in the face of uncertainties, to an immediate need of the corporation. The decisions were made by relatively few persons in upper management, were seen as an integral part of the total financial decision process of the firm and were reached relatively quickly. Especially noteworthy were the rapidity and severity with which the scope of the spatial search was circumscribed and relative lack of overt, detailed feedback to the decision-makers about the correctness of the location decision after the fact.

The decision processes noted tend to conform to more general models and are examples of Chamberlain's[21] "strategic decisions," Tiebout's[22] "adaptive processes" and Krumme's[23] "spatially active" decision-making. They fit closely Townroe's decision stages of (1) development of management policy, (2) pressure for changes in space, (3) pressures for a new site, (4) the search for a new site.[24]

Strong common denominators among the eight case studies suggest the following generalized trace of the locational decision process:

1. Identification of need. New facilities are usually constructed to meet expanded product demand, to obtain more modern plant and facilities or to escape an unfavorable labor situation. The nature of corporate need influences the spatial search process.

2. Corporate preconditions. The vast majority of the world's possible locations are never explicitly considered in the search process. Most are precluded by preconditions imposed by the corporate situation. These may be subdivided into:

(i) Organizational preconditions such as, "we only consider one plant at a time" or "we are determined to escape the jurisdiction of our present union."

(ii) Spatial preconditions, such as "we avoid overseas locations," or "we have always been in Ohio," or "we already have plants in those areas."

3. The Spatial search.

(i) Selection of an area of search, at the sub-national or, more commonly, the regional scale. The preconditions provide at least vague limits to this area: it is usually centered on, or adjacent to, areas of current production and within areas of current distribution. This first spatially overt decision stage involves the rather precise, and usually arbitrary or impressionistic, delimitation of the specific area of search.

(ii) Focus on a subsection of the regional area of search. This stage is reached relatively rapidly. The decision process may involve the utilization of area development agency and utility company data, but, in general, it seems to be primarily based on the very limited regional knowledge and impressions of the part-time location decision-makers.

(iii) Selection of a set of towns. In this stage, a preliminary survey of the selected sub-region identifies those towns which promise to supply the minimum requirements for the plant, such as sufficient population size, good labor potential or adequate accessibility. The number of towns so selected for more detailed consideration is usually very small, normally less than six.

(iv) Selection of a specific town for the plant through the analysis of objective data and the subjective impressions of the decision-makers. This, and the immediately preceding stage, consumes most time and effort in the spatial decision process. Since one criterion for selecting a town is the desirability of a specific site, the town selection process very often also determines the site selection.

4. Ratification of the location decision. The location decision by the working managers normally must be ratified by the uppermost policy-makers of the firm, such as the Board of Directors and the President. So long as the location decision-makers are creditable, approval is usually routine.

5. Construction and operation of the plant. After the start of production at a given site, little thought is given to the correctness of the location decision, except when a specific decision is used to model a subsequent decision. There is also a great tendency to rationalize the decision since the location chosen is recognized as permanently fixed for a long duration. Except in extreme situations, there is an effort to amortize the building and location in spite of changes in the corporate or competitive situation which may diminish the viability of the location. The plant is adapted to change.

Corporate Goals and Strategies

The final section of this chapter is concerned with more explicit consideration of the place of the location decision within the overall corporate investment strategy. Particular attention is paid to conflicting goals and motivations and the resultant alternative locational criteria.

Deciding where to locate a large, relatively immobile facility such as a manufacturing plant is obviously a rather rare event in the life of most companies. It is a non-routine decision of considerable long-term consequence; it is a strategic decision. As such, it is an imprecise "best guess" which, at its best, considers the location decision as an important component of a firm's comprehensive investment strategies, consistant with corporate goals. It is impossible to "prove" how close a plant is to its optimal location, but egregious errors can be minimized by careful application of systematic decision-making procedures and by a conscious awareness of the inherent myopia of each of the individual decision-makers.

Much is heard about "irrational" plant location decisions. There probably is no such thing, in the sense that the decisions cannot be explained. What is really meant by the charge "irrational" is that it does not appear to meet the critics' criteria. If the issue were simply avoidance of criticism, there would be no major problem; the results could speak for themselves. Unfortunately, the difficulty is very often much more fundamental and important. The charge of "irrationality" is largely a consequence of an observer having a different set of goals than the actors who made the location decision. There are frequently, also, discrepancies between stated objectives and observed actions. In other words, the decision-makers are perhaps trying to fool the world or themselves. Good decision-making cannot proceed without clarification of motives (goals) and criteria. Too often location decision-makers begin in the middle without being explicit or gaining concensus about primary goals and concerns. At the very least, it is important not to deceive oneself.

Daggett[25] relates the story of a young engineer who insisted that his firm's plant be placed above a levee so that there would be no danger of flooding should a levee failure occur. This was in spite of the fact that such a location (in this context) would cost the firm perhaps a million dollars in extra transportation costs over the lifetime of the plant. The engineer's motive was to escape completely any future criticism through avoiding the possibility of the plant being inundated by a break in a levee. To another observer, this location criterion may seem unreasonable, or even "irrational," when it is realized that it involved, in effect, an extremely high insurance premium; but considering the engineer's motivation, the decision was quite reasonable and rational.

This is but one illustration. What is clear is that much of the confusion and many of the mistakes in locating factories can be minimized by careful consideration of corporate (management) goals.

Taking new productive investment as a given, we may begin by identi-fying the many possible motives underlying such a decision. The four most important are:

1. Make more money (profit-return on investment).
2. Have a larger firm (total revenues, more employees, etc.).
3. Work less (especially, reduce "executive inconvenience")
4. Reduce risk, uncertainty (conservative behavior; minimum regret).

Locational analyses and rationalizations typically make explicit only the first of these motives, "make more money;" but, this is a snare and a delusion. Real-world experience clearly shows that several or all of these motives are at work simultaneously. In fact, it may be argued convincingly that in many situations the profit motive is the least important of the four. Further, these different goals are usually in conflict. The decision rules ultimately utilized are dependent on which of these are in reality deemed most crucial. For example, a clear goal of profit maximization may, in the language of game theory, call for maximizing expected value. A clear risk reduction motivation on the other hand, may dictate a "minimum regret" decision rule. The resul-tant investment strategies are likely to be quite different.

At a different scale, even assuming general agreement on corporate goals, each individual executive within the firm will have a somewhat different view of the relative importance of the key issues. The follow-ing excerpts from a presentation by Betts well illustrate the differing emphases:

> The industrialist looks at a prospective plant . . . as an oppor-tunity to correct and improve all that has been unsatisfactory or marginal to him in the past . . . (but) many fingers get into this pie of idealism, all of whose intentions may be valid and meaningful and all of which must be sorted out into some semblance of value or reason. The same is true about the new location, the viewpoint depends on whom you might ask . . .
> Take the Purchasing Executive. His most important objective would probably be to get close to the major supplier of raw materials. . .
> The Salesman in the field will want the plant on a main, well-traveled highway, with a sign twice as large as the plant . . . yet he will want this factory close to his office or headquarters so that it is convenient for him to bring customers there . . .
> The Manager of Industrial Relations wants the community that

will have at least five prospective employees for each one that is needed . . .

The Engineering Manager feels differently, however, and will demonstrate his expertise in location development by demanding we be in an area close to an engineering school so his men can pursue (advanced training) with ease . . .

The Controller (wants) an opportunity to reach a cost plateau never dreamed of. Good efficient labor with a minimum of turnover, elimination of bad practices . . .

The Distribution Manager will look primarily at the cost of getting the product to the customer, as quickly and as cheaply as possible. He will plot large circles on maps showing where the customers are, and the transportation costs involved. . .

The Public Relations man would probably prefer a fairly large urban area so he could get more mileage out of his releases . . .

The Medical Director will look generally at the choice of doctors he might have and the availability of numerous clinics and hospitals . . .

The Safety Director will want The Quabbin Reservoir next door for fire protection . . .[26]

Betts then discusses the role of the "General Manager," the coordinator of the diverse talents that make up a good site selection team. He must be aware of personal preferences and biases (including his own), logically inspect the various propositions and supervise the collection of the information necessary for evaluating the relative importance of each of the locational factors. Good data are always useful and necessary, but they are never sufficient. Location decision-making is part science, part art. The process and the content are intertwined; both are important.

What are the spatial (locational) implications of the fact that managers and firms have different, multiple, conflicting motivations? In theory, we are faced with an exceedingly complex riddle. In practice, we must simplify so that practical decision-making can proceed.

The first simplification is to remove many investment decisions from the locational context. In theory, all investment decisions are locational decisions, in the sense that they have a particular, spatial context. Even routine maintenance, for example, increases the capital investment in an existing location--likewise for the installation of new machinery. It is a decision not to put the investment elsewhere, and it increases the spatial intertia of the plant. In practice, however, for many investment decisions, locational considerations are relatively unimportant and may be eliminated from our present concern. To simplify, we may consider locationally unimportant any investment decision which is of such small magnitude so as to make the alternative possibility of a new separate operation unfeasible. How small is small? This will depend on the plant's basic economies of scale, and will vary from firm to firm and industry to industry. However, all investments which fall below the critical scale, and which cannot be postponed and aggregated so to eventually achieve the requisite scale, must necessarily be made in-site, that is, in existing operations. Thus, location is given.

Conversely, all investments which are larger than the critical size may be contemplated for either new sites or as major expansions of existing sites. Under these circumstances, in-site expansion may be regarded as simply one of the many possible alternative locations.

Finally, having established that industrial location decision-making is a complex interweaving of diverse strategies and goals, are there any over-arching principles that may be advanced at this point? Three pairs of opposing forces may be recognized.

First, there is the fundamental tension between economies of scale and the friction of distance. Large economies of scale dictate larger, fewer, more widely separated plants. High friction of distance (transportation) costs dictate smaller plants located in a finer, more dispersed spatial network. Larger plants may be more internally efficient, and, in the aggregate, easier to manage, but transport costs are higher, single investments are larger, flexibility is reduced, and the risks of a poor locational choice are greater. The converse is true for a network of more but smaller plants. The trick is to balance correctly these opposing forces; the correct solution will be different for each firm and each geographical area. This topic is touched on at various points in the subsequent chapters (see especially Chapter 3).

Second, there is the analytical dilemma of deciding whether to emphasize a least-cost solution or a maximum demand locational pattern. Although in theory it is obvious that maximum profits are a function of both revenues and costs, in practice it is not easy to reconcile the two basic approaches. Once again, the trick is to get the correct balance, as discussed more fully in Chapter 7.

Third, there is the problem of planning for the short-run versus the long-run. A firm that does not plan for the future may well find itself in untenable locations far too quickly; on the other hand, if current needs cannot be met, there may be no future to worry about. This issue is discussed again in some of the subsequent chapters, and the capital budgeting techniques of Chapter 9 may offer a partial solution.

Notes and References—Chapter 1

1. Krumme, Gunter, "Towards a Geography of Enterprise," *Economic Geography,* Vol. XLV, No. 1 (January, 1969), p. 37.
2. *News Front, The Management Trend Magazine,* March/April, 1972, p. 51.
3. "Corporate Real Estate Management: An Influential and Financially Rewarding Profession," *Site Selection Handbook*, Vol. XXIII, No. 1 (February, 1978), p. 4. Atlanta: Conway Publications, Inc.
4. "Despite Some Downturns, A New Capital Spending Record," *Industrial Development.* May/June, 1975, p. 20. Atlanta: Conway Publications, Inc.
5. Woodward, John T. "Plant and Equipment Expenditures: Year 1978," *Survey of Current Business,* Vol. LVIII, No. 1 (January, 1978), p. 17. Washington: U.S. Dept. of Commerce.
6. Hunker, Henry L. *Industrial Development.* Lexington, Mass.: Lexington Books, 1974, pp. 73-75 ©1974 by D.C. Heath and Co. All rights reserved.
7. *News Front, op. cit.*
8. *Ibid.*
9. *Regional Development Incentives, HC85-I, Session 1973-74,* House of Commons, (U.K.) p. 532.
10. The next three sections are taken, with permission from Stafford, H.A., "The Geography of Manufacturers," *Progress in Geography*, Vol. IV, 1972, pp. 205-211. New York: St. Martin's Press.
11. Kuklinski, A. *Criteria for Location of Industrial Plants*, Secretariat, The United Nations, New York, p. 17.

12. Chamberlain, N.W. *Enterprise and Environment: The Firm in Time and Space,* McGraw-Hill, New York, 1968, p. 55.
13. Galbraith, J.K. *The New Industrial State,* Houghton-Mifflin, Boston, 1967, p. 171.
14. Chamberlain, N.W., *op. cit.,* p. 40.
15. Cohen, K.J. and Cyert, R.M. *Theory of the Firm: Resource Allocation in a Market Economy,* Prentice-Hall, Englewood Cliffs, 1965, p. 338.
16. Campbell, R.M. and Hitchin, D. "The Delphi Technique: Implementation in the Corporate Environment," *Management Services,* November-December, 1968, p. 39.
17. Stafford, H.A. *Manufacturing and Agriculture Unit,* High School Geography Project of the Association of American Geographers, Washington, D.C., 1966, 99 pp. (Subsequently published as part of *Geography in an Urban Age,* Macmillan, New York, 1970.)
18. Rees, J. *An Examination of People and Factors Involved in Industrial Location Decisions.* Unpublished M.A. Thesis, University of Cincinnati, 1971.
19. Stafford, H.A., "The Anatomy of the Location Decision: Content Analysis of Case Studies," *Spatial Perspectives on Industrial Organization and Decision Making,* F.E. Ian Hamilton (ed.), London: John Wiley & Sons, 1974.
20. The next two sections are taken with permission, from Stafford, H.A., "The Anatomy of the Location Decision: Content Analysis of Case Studies," reproduced with permission from *Spatial Perspectives on Industrial Organization and Decision Making,* by F.E. Ian Hamilton (ed.), pp. 182-185. Copyright ©1974, by John Wiley & Sons, Ltd., London.
21. Chamberlain, N.W., *op. cit.*
22. Tiebout, C. "Location Theory, Empirical Evidence and Economic Evaluation," *Papers and Proceedings of the Regional Science Association,* Vol. III, 1957.
23. Krumme, G. *op. cit.*
24. Townroe, P.M. *Industrial Location Decisions, A Study in Management Behaviour,* University of Birmingham (U.K.) Centre for Urban and Regional Studies, Occasional Paper 15, 1971, pp. 17-27.
25. Daggett, D.T. "How a Railroad Rep Can Best Help You," *Industrial Development,* July/August, 1975, pp. 16-20.

26. Betts, Robert E. "How the Industrialist Views New Locations," *American Industrial Development Council, Professional Notes* (AID PN #269), March, 1969.

II A Synthesis Of Case Studies

II
A Synthesis of Case Studies

Chapter 1 has pointed to the many complexities surrounding industrial location decisions. The complexities and circularities are so intractable that optimal location decisions in the classic sense of economic-geographic theory are impossible. However, it also is obvious that location decisions are made and plants are built. How do we in the real world accomplish what theory cannot resolve? The literature is replete with case studies of actual manufacturing location decisions which help answer the question and provide valuable analogs for practitioners. Some of the best and most accessible of these case studies are contained within the pages of *Industrial Development*.[1]

There is no substitute for reading good case studies in their entirety. However, there is value in attempting a summary and synthesis of selected case studies so as to note common threads, to establish a framework for assessing individual experiences and to provide a context within which to fit subsequent portions of this volume. Primarily for the sake of expediency and ready verification, the 22 case studies reprinted from *Industrial Development* in *Industrial Facilities Planning*[2] are synthesized to give an overview of the factors and techniques utilized by American manufacturing location decision-makers.

The 22 case studies include:

1. "Planning Nationwide Expansion Programs" by C.R. Vigstedt, General Manager, Armour and Co., Chicago, p. 3. (*Industrial Development*, December, 1965.)

2. "Ford Plans 'Corn Field' Plants First," p. 37. (*Industrial Development,* January/February, 1955.)

3. "Bowaters: A Practical Approach to Overseas Expansion," by A.B. Meyer, President, Bowater Paper Co., p. 91. (*Industrial Development,* December, 1962.)

4. "Science and Site Selection," by R.E. Johnson, Economist and Actuary, Western Electric Co., p. 66 (*Industrial Development,* July, 1959.)

5. "RCA Advocates Systematic Approach," by J.L. Burns, President, p. 95. (*Industrial Development,* November, 1961.)

6. "The IBM Approach to Site Selection," by R.D. Courtright, p. 100 (*Industrial Development,* July, 1960.)

7. "A Case Study in Plant Location," by K.G. Rahdert, Jet Engine Dept., General Electric Co., p. 109 (*Industrial Development,* October, 1957.)

8. "Locational Analysis and Site Selection," by E.D. Gates, Defense Systems, General Electric Co., p. 131. (*Industrial Development,* May, 1962.)

9. "How Honeywell Picked Site," by C.W. Skinner, p. 111. (*Industrial Development,* February, 1957.)

10. "Westinghouse Lists Key Factors As Labor, Community, Services, and Taxes," p. 127. (*Industrial Development,* November/December, 1954.)

11. "What Westinghouse Wants," by G.E. Garhart, Director of Real Estate, p. 119. (*Industrial Development,* November/December, 1956.)

12. "How DuPont Picks 'Em," p. 123. (*Industrial Development,* March/April, 1954.)

13. "How to Pick Process Sites," by C.H. Topping, DuPont, p. 116. (*Industrial Development,* January/February, 1956.)

14. "'Hardboiled Economics' Guide DuPont in the Selection of Sites for Plants," by F.E. LeVan, p. 106. (*Industrial Development,* December, 1959.)

15. "Chemstrand Locator Outlines Technique," by C.O. Hoyer, Director of Engineering, p. 130. (*Industrial Development,* December, 1959.)

16. "Application of Computer Technique to Specific Site Selection Programs," by Gary H. Lehman, TRW Space Technology Laboratories, p. 134. (*Industrial Development,* January, 1965.)

17. "Why Weston?" National Accelerator Laboratory, The Atomic Energy Commission, p. 137. (*Industrial Development,* March/April, 1967.)

18. "AVCO's 53-Day Wonder," by E.A. Burrus, Assistant General Manager, Charleston Plant, Lycoming Division, p. 271. (*Industrial Development,* March/April, 1967.)

19. "Evaluating Competitive Proposals,' " by P.H. Van Wert, Director, Facilities Planning, Xerox Corp., p. 136. (*Industrial Development,* February, 1966.)

20. "A Coordinated Program for Facility Planning," by M.G. O'Neil, President, General Tire & Rubber Co., p. 60. (*Industrial Development,* July, 1961.)

21. "One Approach to Facility Search, Selection and Acquisition: The Site Selection Study Sequence," by Vernon Gabe, Director, Corporate Real Estate, The Gates Rubber Co., p. 146. (*Industrial Development.* July/August, 1974.)

22. "International Shoe Thinks Through Site Selection," by H.H. Rand, President, p. 151. (*Industrial Development,* April, 1961.)

An important generalization from the survey of these case studies is that new manufacturing facilities are constructed to meet existing or near-future needs. Most often cited is the need for new productive capacity for an existing product or products; also mentioned are the necessity to produce a new product and the desire to replace existing inefficient operations. Frequently mentioned is the fact that a new plant, and a new location, are alternatives considered only after expansion of existing company facilities was for some reason deemed impractical. The decision to tap new markets or supply sources through the *location* of a new plant apparently is relatively rare. Although the presence of a plant in an area may help sales, most marketing strategies operate in a much more short-run framework, and do not explicitly allow for the redistribution of productive facilities. Another interesting observation is that only one of the case studies made the point that the location search was not confidential; all of the other firms for which this factor was noted indicated strong desires to conduct the search with as much secrecy as possible.

From a spatial viewpoint, the location search most often proceeds through three somewhat distinct phases, the first being the selection of the general region, then the selection of a specific community from a finite and rather small list of alternatives within the region (local scale) and, finally, the selection of a specific site in the chosen community.

Russell's 1953 search scenario [3] still appears an accurate depiction of the practical spatial process.

Of course, each case study presents a somewhat unique problem, with differing emphases on different locational criteria and some variation in analysis technique. The case studies also differ according to company (or division), type of product, the unique geography of the firm in question, and also according to the differing perspectives of the authors. For these reasons, the case studies deserve to be read thoroughly, and assessed in their own particular contexts. However, the overriding impression is that the case studies confirm the observations of Chapter 1 and that the "Decision Trace" presented there is a reasonably faithful generalization of the location decision process for most manufacturing firms.

To provide additional perspectives on the case studies, two tables have been constructed. Table 2-1 lists most of the location factors specifically noted in the 22 case studies analyzed, indicating whether or not a given factor was explicitly noted in each of the studies. Table 2-2 provides the same type of information for the various analytic techniques explicitly noted in the case studies. Although the tallies are thought to be an accurate reflection of what was reported in each case study, the reader is cautioned that: (1) the tallies do not necessarily reflect the judgments of the various case study authors; (2) the omission of a factor or technique does not necessarily indicate that the company analysts did not consider it, but rather that it was not explicitly mentioned in the report; and (3) the evaluation of a factor, or use of a technique, may vary between firms or even divisions within companies, even when both are noted in the same category. Thus, the primary values of the two tables are obtained by looking at the general picture provided by reading across the rows and by the row counts in the last column.

Table 2-1, "Mention of Location Factors in Case Studies," presents no special surprises. The list of spatially variable location factors is, in effect, a condensation of the well known and more extensive lists published by various authors. [4] Of most interest for present purposes are those factors cited most frequently. Accessibility to markets and material suppliers are noted in most of the cases, in accord with acknowledged business practice and industrial location theory. the markets and materials factors are most important in determining the general region for the location of the plant. Transportation facilities also are frequently mentioned; these facilities are necessary for getting

COMPANIES (date of Case Study publication in Industrial Development) / SPATIALLY VARIABLE LOCATION FACTORS	Market Accessibility	Materials (Supplies)	Labor - General	Labor - Available Skills	Labor - Wages	Labor - Laws, Unions	Accessible for Management	Locations of Competitors	Taxes (Rates, Laws)	Finance	Insurance Rates	Political "Climate"	Transport Facilities (RR, Air, Road)	Water - Transport	Water - Process	Waste Disposal	Power, Fuel	Utilities	Business Services	Size of Community	State/Local Ind. Attitudes	Community Living Conditions	Cost of Living	Zoning	Availability of Site	Climate	Topography	Soils, Bedrock, etc.	Construction Costs
International Shoe (1961)	*	*	*			*	*		*				*		*	*					*	*				*			
Gates Rubber (1974)	*	*	*				*	*	*								*	*	*						*				
General Tire (1961)	*	*	*						*								*				*					*	*	*	
Xerox (1966)				*	*	*		*					*					*	*	*	*						*	*	*
AVCO (1967)	*		*						*									*		*	*	*		*					
AEC (1967)							*						*			*		*		*	*				*				
TRW (1965)			*				*		*	*			*	*				*	*		*				*	*	*	*	
Chemstrand (1954)	*	*	*	*		*			*				*		*	*					*	*							
DuPont (1959)	*	*	*	*		*			*		*	*	*		*	*	*	*			*	*			*				
DuPont (1956)			*	*		*			*				*		*	*	*			*		*					*		
DuPont (1954)	*	*	*	*	*	*			*	*	*		*		*	*	*	*		*	*				*	*			
Westinghouse (1956)	*	*		*					*				*				*		*	*	*				*				
Westinghouse (1954)	*	*	*						*								*	*		*					*				
Honeywell (1957)			*			*				*					*		*	*	*	*	*	*			*	*	*		
General Electric (1962)	*	*	*						*								*	*	*			*			*				*
General Electric (1957)	*	*	*	*		*	*		*								*		*	*	*				*				
IBM (1960)	*	*	*	*		*												*	*	*	*	*							
RCA (1961)	*	*		*	*		*	*	*		*						*			*	*	*			*				
Western Electric (1959)	*	*		*	*	*	*	*	*				*				*		*		*				*	*			*
Bowaters (1962)	*	*	*	*		*			*				*		*	*	*		*	*	*				*			*	
Ford (1955)	*	*		*					*				*					*											
Armour (1965)	*	*	*						*				*		*	*					*								*
(Row Counts)	17	16	14	15	3	9	8	2	15	3	2	2	17	1	10	7	8	14	9	10	14	16	2	6	11	6	5	3	2

Table 2-1. Mention of Location Factors In Case Studies

materials in and products out and operate at both the regional and local scales. Adequate provisions for utilities, business services, etc., are especially, important at the local and site scales.

Labor was given extended consideration in most of the studies and was presented with the most sub-categories. Labor, likewise, is important at both the regional and local scales. Primary emphasis was not on wages, per se, but rather on labor costs as conditioned by the availability of requisite skills in sufficient abundance, the minimization of turnover and work stoppages and restrictive labor laws.

The issues of union activity and labor legislation also relate to another major theme, that of the industrial-political climate. This is reflected by the frequent mention of the importance of favorable state and local industrial attitudes and by the concern for tax rates and laws. Regarding taxes, it was frequently noted that companies were not seeking the lowest tax bill. Rather, they recognized that taxes provide necessary services and they expected to pay their fair share; but they did not want to pay more than a fair share, nor did they want to be lured to a low cost location and subsequently be billed at much higher rates.

Finally, community living conditions, size of community, etc., are important local considerations. Presumably, these are important because a "good" community to some degree equates with favorable industrial attitudes, a reasonably happy and therefore more productive labor force and an attractive setting for the assignment and retention of management personnel.

Table 2-2 provides some evidence on the various types of analytic techniques used in solving the location problem. In every case it was apparent that there was a clear sense of the research problem and that there was a rather definite procedural sequence. However, the modern "operations research" procedures were alluded to rarely, the term "systems analysis" was mentioned only once, and "modeling/simulation" techniques appear only three times.

In general, the locational investigation is undertaken after a series of prior decisions (such as specifications of need, products to be produced in the new facility and factory size) have been made. The objective portion of this simplified location search then primarily consists of alternative regions and communities. The "comparative costs" techniques were explicitly mentioned in 18 of the 22 case studies; no other

ANALYSIS TECHNIQUES	Intl. Shoe (1961)	Gates Rubber (1974)	General Tire (1961)	Xerox (1966)	AVCO (1967)	AEC (1967)	TRW (1965)	Chemstrand (1954)	DuPont (1959)	DuPont (1956)	DuPont (1954)	Westinghouse (1956)	Westinghouse (1954)	Honeywell (1957)	General Electric (1962)	General Electric (1957)	IBM (1960)	RCA (1961)	Western Electric (1959)	Bowaters (1962)	Ford (1955)	Armour (1965)	Row Counts
Comparative Costs	*	*	*		*		*	*	*	*	*	*	*		*	*		*	*	*	*	*	18
Comparative Revenues							*															*	2
Profits							*		*													*	3
Return on Investment							*															*	2
Pay-Back		*																				*	2
Weighted Criteria (point count)								*			*				*		*						4
Forecasting			*				*		*					*	*	*				*	*	*	9
Linear Programming: a. Transport Costs																			*				1
b. Product Mix							*												*				2
System Analysis							*																1
Modeling/Simulation							*										*				*		3
Map and Air Photo Analysis												*			*	*							3
Surveys/Questionnaires		*	*	*						*		*	*		*	*		*			*		10

COMPANIES (date of Case Study publication in *Industrial Development*)

Table 2-2. Mention of Specific Techniques Of Analysis

technique was even close in the tally. The "weighted criteria/point count" technique also was used primarily in a comparative cost framework.

The only other techniques with even moderate counts are forecasting and surveys and questionnaires. Most often these are used to supply present and near-future data on such factors as labor supply, prevailing wage rates, utilities costs, etc., for the comparative costs calculations, and to provide information on community living conditions, etc., for the more subjective portions of the analysis.

Table 2-2 perhaps is of most value in identifying those techniques *not* used frequently. It already has been noted that "systems analysis" did not seem to be a prevailing mind-set among location decision-makers. On a more prosaic level, there was little explicit recognition that location itself may influence revenues ("Comparative Revenues" analysis is mentioned only twice), and that both costs and revenues calculations are necessary to assess profit potentials.

It also is interesting, although the case study firms are profit oriented, that the standard accounting procedures normally utilized in other corporate investment decisions are apparently little used in location decisions. "Return on Investment" and "Pay-Back" calculations are each mentioned only twice. The "discounted cash flows" techniques are not explicitly noted at all.

The now well-established "linear programming" technique also is little in evidence. Linear programming can be useful in helping to resolve product-mix/location problems in the multiplant situation, but the whole product-mix issue was mentioned only twice. Linear programming may be especially useful in providing inputs to the transportation costs (on both marketing and materials procurement) calculus; it is even more surprising that the linear programming-transportation problem was cited but once.

Of course, it should be kept in mind that several of the case studies are over 20 years old, and the majority date back at least 15 years. Thus, they do not necessarily reflect the current state-of-the-art. In the more recent literature there are numerous examples of companies, especially those who have made fairly frequent plant location decisions, which have quite sophisticated approaches to the location problem. However, it is also probable that the firms reporting their selection procedures are, at a given point in time, among the most sophisticated; the least advanced and aware companies are unlikely to be heard from. Thus, although clearly conservative for the most able firms, the patterns revealed in Tables 2-1 and 2-2 are likely progressive relative to the majority of plant location decisions, even today.

This chapter has provided some sense of the realities of practical industrial location decision-making as revealed by a sample of case studies. The topics identified warrant further consideration. The succeeding chapters (3, 4, and 5) of Part II focus on the spatially variable location factors. The three chapters of part III explore some key techniques of analysis.

Notes and References—Chapter 2

1. *Industrial Development.* Atlanta: Conway Publications, Inc.
2. Conway, H.M., and Liston, Linda L. *Industrial Facilities Planning,* Atlanta: Conway Publications, Inc., 1976.
3. Russell, Joseph A. "Geography of Industrial Costs," *Industrial Development,* November, 1959. (In *Industrial Facilities Planning, op. cit.,* pp. 102-105.)
4. A comprehensive "Checklist of Site Selection Factors" is contained in the Appendix to *Industrial Facilities Planning,* pp. 303-309. An updated and reorganized checklist is contained in the *New Project File and Site Selection Checklist,* which presents 1,700 items to consider. Atlanta: Conway Publications, Inc.

Part II The Factors

III
The Friction
Of Distance Variables

III The Friction of Distance Variables

The many factors which influence the location of a factory vary in relative importance from situation to situation. They must be properly considered within the context of the geography of a specific firm. Nor are they mutually exclusive; they must be handled within a relevant interdependence framework. Analytical procedures are discussed in Part III. However, the purpose of this section is to examine, somewhat artificially, major factors separately before the complexities of simultaneous interaction are considered.

The location variables may be separated into two general types: 1) those relating to the friction of distance; and 2) those relating to the attributes of areas. Friction of distance variables are those which measure the costs of moving materials or products or people or ideas across space. These costs may be measured in terms of miles, or money, or time, or even psychologically as through ease or convenience. The second category is concerned not with how far one place is from another, but rather with the characteristics, or attributes, of those areas. Included are variables such as labor, agglomeration and infrastructure, power, water and the quality of life. Although for many modern companies, particularly in highly industrialized societies, the attributes of area variables may nowadays be most important, the friction of distance variables have traditionally formed the backbone of industrial location theory. For this reason alone they shall be considered first.

A. Transportation of Things

The simplest picture of a plant location problem is that of a plant located somewhere between a source of supply of materials and a point of product consumption. If in a simplified situation the only variable is the cost of transporting materials and product, and if it costs more to ship the product to market than it does to ship the materials to the plant, then the plant should be located at the market. Conversely, larger material transport costs dictate a location at the source of material supply. In such a simple model an intermediate location between materials and markets is never optimal because of added terminal costs from the extra loading and unloading (in reality, this handicap is overcome in some areas and for some commodities by granting "fabrication-in-transit" privileges.) The situation could be made more realistic, and complicated, by considering spatial distributions of markets and materials, and adding to get total access costs. But other things being equal, the principle of finding the minimum transport cost point remains the same. Of course, we could have both material suppliers and purchasers located in the same area, a not uncommon situation for many smaller manufacturers in industrialized regions. In such a situation, transportation costs would be negligible and could be safely ignored; other things being equal, the location choice is obvious. Unless psychologically important, negligible cost factors can be left out of the location calculus.

The existence or non-existence of various modes of transportation may be viewed as an attribute of an area, as discussed under infrastructure in Chapter 5. In the present context, transportation is viewed as a critical link between points of material supply and points of product distribution. Clearly then, it is necessary to examine present and projected patterns of supplies and markets and to compute total transport costs for various possible locations. The major modes of transport are water, rail and road, each with its own advantages and disadvantages. Prior decision as to the type of operation usually dictates the modes of transport to be employed, as most manufacturers have particular requirements best met by only one of the modes.

Water borne freight moves at the lowest per ton/mile rate and is especially suited to bulky, heavy and low value commodities which cannot absorb high transportation costs. Other things being equal, water is the cheapest mode for long distance transport. Many supply and market points are not served by effective water transport; those points that are usually have long, circuitous connecting routes. The long routes and the slow rates of movement for ships and barges typically restrict water traffic to standardized, non-perishable commodities.

Railroads operate on fixed routes, but obtain a fair degree of flexibility in heavily industrialized areas because of the density of the rail network. Rail transportation is intermediate between water and truck modes in many respects. It has ton/mile advantages over both for intermediate distances, but loses out to water for the very long hauls and to trucks for the more local hauls. Trains are faster than ships or barges, but usually slower than trucks. Trucks enjoy relatively low terminal costs which gives them the short haul rate advantage, and their use of the standard highway network gives them door to door flexibility. When speed rather than cost is the object, however, air freight may be the answer. The quality of these services is directly correlated with the size of the metropolitan area.

Of course, multiple mode industrial commodity movements are common, especially where trucks are used to disperse products from central rail or water terminals. In recent years, this intermodal cooperation has been fostered by the development of containerization and "piggyback" schemes. Thus, the locations of port facilities and rail terminals may be important considerations even for the land-locked, truck dependent manufacturer. Indeed, many planners are now looking for major transportation savings on the ends of trips rather than en route by seeking out well designed "bimodal" and "trimodal" sites in metropolitan areas. The development of intermodal cargo transfer points appears to be the wave of the future.[1]

The selection of a transportation mode, or a specific carrier, depends on the type of commodity to be shipped, the volume to be shipped, the length of haul, the speed required, the regularity of the carrier, and the dependability of the carrier. Generally, the more densely industrialized an area and the larger its population, then the more well developed the facilities and services, and also the greater the amount of beneficial competition between modes and carriers, producing more favorable freight rates.

The above criteria all influence the total transportation costs. The site selector must calculate the spatially variable transfer costs the proposed plant will incur. Transfer costs are more than simple freight charges. They also include such items as insurance, interest charges on capital, deterioration and damage losses and clerical costs.[2]

The transfer costs of moving commodities from point A to point B will vary, as indicated above, according to the type of carrier, or mode, utilized. They will also vary by type of commodity transported. Transfer costs vary directly with the weight and bulk of the commodity shipped. They also vary directly with the value of the commodity; this is one reason why lower value materials typically have less locational pull, other things being equal, then the higher value finished products. Special facilities required (e.g., refrigeration) will also influence costs.

More pertinent to most specific plant location problems is the variability in transfer costs of a common mix of commodities from and to a variety of locations. Assuming type of commodity (or mix) constant, transfer costs will vary according to the volume shipped to various locations, distance, competition among carriers and the geography of freight rates.

The greater the volume shipped, the lower the per ton/mile cost. Railroads charge proportionately less for car-load (CL) lots than less-than-car-load (LCL) lots; likewise, truckers can quote better rates for full truck loads. Transfer costs may be subject to considerable economies of scale. On an areal basis, the economies of scale may be expressed by lower shipping charges when there is a considerable volume of traffic in both directions. Carriers can quote lower rates when they can pick up a return cargo, rather than "dead heading" home. Furthermore, the greater the total volume of shipping in an area, the greater the competition between modes and individual carriers. For the shipper, this normally means greater flexibility, more frequent service, the availability of specialized services and facilities and lower competitive rates.

The remaining critical variable, and most important from a locational viewpoint, is distance. For a given shipment, the greater the distance, the higher the transportation cost. However, transfer costs increase at a decreasing rate with distance because the fixed charges (e.g., terminal costs, clerical expenses, etc.) may be spread over more miles. Transfer costs show a tapering effect with distance. In practical terms, this means that it costs more to ship a commodity 1,000 miles than 100 miles, but less than 10 times more. Also, plotting transfer costs against distance does not produce a smooth curve, but rather a series of increasingly lengthened upward steps. The steps are a function of freight rates zones. Finally, it may cost more to ship a commodity a given distance in one direction than it does to ship in another direction; this again is a function of the geography of freight rates.

The geography of freight rates is exceedingly complex. In the 1940s it was estimated that there were 40 million different railway rates in the United Kingdom, and that the nationalization of British railroads probably has not altered the situation appreciably.[3] This situation is common in all capitalistic economies and is certainly the case in the United States. Freight rate structures are complex in part because the economics of transportation is complex. Beyond this, however, are the bureaucratic complications resulting from carriers being in part in the public domain and thus externally regulated areal oligopolies. Freight rates have both historic and political overtones. It is beyond the scope of this volume to discuss the structure of freight rates for either rail or truck in any great detail; the serious student is directed to specialized works on the topic.[4] All that can be attempted here is to provide a few basic principles and to call attention to the factors which must be considered so that the site selector may ask the correct questions, utilize the traffic and shipping experts within the firm and have some background for understanding the information obtained from the carriers themselves.

Some of the basic principles already have been mentioned. Freight costs increase with distance, but "move upwards in a series of steps, getting shallower and longer as distance increases."[5] Rates vary with the type of commodity, especially its value, weight and bulk. Certain areas have rate advantages over other areas, in part because of volume and competitive considerations, but also because of historical inertia and political and area development influences. How are these translated into practical considerations for the site selector?

First, the type of commodity to be shipped must be specified. Each product has a specified "class rating." In theory, once the class rating is known, the line-haul transportation cost can be computed for a given destination by reference to the Tariffs published by the Interstate Commerce Commission. In practice, however, most industrial commodities do not move by class rates, but rather by "exception ratings" or "commodity rates."[6] Commodity rates, which supercede exception and class ratings, are the most common. Unfortunately, it is not a simple matter for the analyst to compute transport costs based on commodity ratings because these must be negotiated for a specific rate area after a location has been decided. Of course, the site selector can conduct his analysis by assuming that historic industry and company commodity rates will apply in any new are under consideration, but the fact that this is an assumption, subject to final verification, must be kept in mind.

Furthermore, the very process of negotiating a new commodity rate for an area can be a time-consuming inconvenience. That this sometimes may be more trouble that it is worth is illustrated by the recent rejection by a major chemical producer of its consultant's recommendation to place a new plant in a smaller city some 140 miles from the home base. Upon questioning, the incredulous consultant was informed that his analysis was flawed by his failure to consider transportation costs. He protested; indeed, he had computed anticipated transfer costs! But, replied management, the appropriate commodity rates have not yet been negotiated for the area you recommend. We never negotiate rates; rather, we ride the coat tails of Company "X" (the industry leader) and utilize the area commodity rates they obtain. Company "X" has more manpower to get favorable rates, and Company "X" is not in the area recommended. So we won't make the first move into that location.

The second major factor influencing freight costs is distance. If the applicable freight rates are uniform across space, then distance within is unimportant. For some types of commodities, the zones of uniformity encompass very large regions or even the whole country. However, most rate areas are much smaller and mileage-based freight rates are the norm for most commodities. Even mileage-based freight rates have the zonal feature because origins and destinations are grouped into relatively small rate basing areas to simplify their publication.[7] This feature and the increasing economies of greater distances together produce the previously mentioned upward shallower and longer stairstep profile of freight costs with distance.

Given the impossibility of fully comprehending the geography of freight rates, what can the practical site selector do? He can make good use of company and industry analogs. He can make good use of within firm transportation experts and the industrial location services provided by the major carriers, especially the railroads. And he can take heart. In spite of the complexity, there is a fair degree of spatial regularity. Keeping in mind that the complexities apply everywhere, the relative advantages of areas at the regional scale can be fairly well approximated in most cases by depicting transfer costs "as a fairly regular function of distance from the point of origin." [8] The more precise cost estimates required by the type of investment analysis advocated in Chapter 10 can be made after the search has been narrowed to the two or three most likely locations.

The generalized, regional scale calculation of transfer costs may utilize the *Aggregate Transport Cost Model.* If the location and volume of all markets can be specified, then the total costs of transporting finished products to markets can be computed for each alternative plant location under consideration. The cost of serving customers in a particular location from a possible plant site is calculated by multiplying the number of units to be shipped by the appropriate (estimated) freight rate. As a first-cut approximation, raw distance is often used as a surrogate for the freight rate. Making this calculation for every market point and summing produces the aggregate transport cost for a given plant location. These same calculations and summation are made for each alternative plant location considered. Symbolically, the model is expressed as:

$$A_i = \sum_{j=1}^{n} Q_j \; T_{ij}$$

"where

A_i is the aggregate travel involved in serving the market from location i, which may be measured in terms of distance or cost depending on the data applied to T.

Q_j is the quantity of the product which is sold at the market $j (j = 1, \ldots, n)$.

T_{ij} is the unit cost of transportation between i and j or, alternatively, the distance between the two points if suitable data on freight rates are not available.

If Q is an accurate expectation of sales, and if T is the actual transportation rate that will be paid, A_i will be the total cost of distributing the product to the market, and the evaluation of (the) expression for all i will provide the data from which a surface of actual marketing transport costs could be constructed."[9]

The same type of calculations may be carried out to determine the transport costs of obtaining supplies at each possible plant location. Here it is necessary to decide on the vendors to be patronized, assume that their locations are constant for some period of time, estimate the volume of each material to be obtained and ascertain the appropriate freight rates. Of course, for a picture of the relative materials transport advantages of alternative sites, only those supplies which are shipped on an F.O.B. basis must be included; there are no direct cost advantages in being near a vendor who quotes uniform delivered cost prices. Summing the transportation costs for each material to be brought into the proposed plant produces the aggregate total materials acquisition cost for a specific location. This figure, in turn, may be added to the aggregate cost of reaching markets, to produce a grand total of transportation costs, assuming, as always, that the general model is appropriate and the data are sufficiently reliable.

The Aggregate Transport Cost Model is but one of the techniques which may be utilized in comparing the relative transportation advantages of alternative sites. A similar, but fundamentally different, approach is the Market Potential Model which is discussed later in this chapter. Even more sophisticated approaches are available through some of the modern operations research methodologies. Chief among these are the linear programming techniques. The use of linear programming in transportation problems is discussed in Chapter 8.

So far the analysis of transportation costs has involved the simple situation where a single plant imports the requisite materials, does its fabrication and ships the products to markets. More often, however, the problem must be put in the context of the firm's total distribution system, including time, flexibility, inventories and warehousing. Two examples illustrate some of the possible complexities:

"The analysis of all aspects of the costs involved in manufacturing sometimes yields surprising results. An Eastern furniture manufacturer whose primary markets are in Baltimore, Philadelphia and New York employed a geographer to advise on a new plant location. The geographer recommended a place 180 miles farther away from both materials and markets than at first had seemed desirable. If the plant had been built on the seemingly more economical site, the trains that carried its products to market would have had to stop in the Potomac Yards near Washington, whereas trains from the more distant site could avoid the yards and by doing so get the furniture to the three markets two days faster. These two days reduced lead time by one week on actual delivery schedules. The reduced costs of inventory and excessive speculative manufacturing more than made up for the additional freight charges."[10]

"A Texas scrap-metal exporter had his switching charges to dockside raised from $26 to $76 per car on a yearly volume of about 50,000 cars. He turned for help to a transportation geographer, Dr. J. Edwin Becht of the University of Texas of the Permian Basin. Becht solved the problem by using 'in transit inspection' storage for the cars at an old division point for $8 per car until a ship became available to accept the scrap, then direct transfer of the cars on the usual line-haul charge. Simple arithmetic shows that this firm saved more than $2,000,000 a year."[11]

The total distribution costs faced by a firm are the sum of the transportation costs of moving the product and storage. It is not necessary that the storage or inventory function be carried out at the plant site, as implied in the simple one plant situations previously considered. The existence, or possibility, of spatially separate warehouses must be considered in analyzing the costs of overcoming the friction of distance and obtaining some degree of control over spatially proximate markets. In a short but provocative article Smykay[12] states:

"Least flexible in decision making is plant location. Most flexible in support of plant activity is re-design of distribution strategies and their attendant systems. Proper design of distribution systems frequently permits ill-located plants to extend their useful economic life, while poorly conceived distribution systems can easily cause premature economic demise of well located plants."[12]

Smykay then proceeds to illustrate the warehouse function in distribution as shown in Figure 1.

where:

OA = Plant cost of production
AFG = Direct shipping cost at small shipment size.
AHI = Consolidated shipment cost in truckload or carload quantities.
C = Warehouse location.
EH = Warehouse operating and allocated investment cost.
EF, EG = Local delivery cost from warehouse.
BD = Warehouse service territory.
OB = Plant service territory

In this simple illustration, it is obvious that customers located more than OB miles and less than OD miles from the factory at point O can

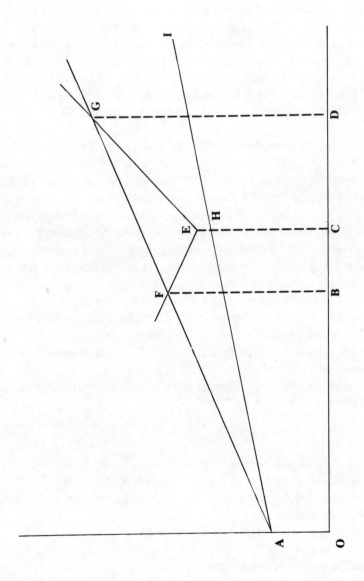

MILES

Figure 3-1. Warehouse Functions in Distribution.

be served more cheaply for small volume shipments from a warehouse located at point C. In such cases, the total delivery costs to markets will be lower with a plant and warehouse configuration than when all shipments come directly from the factory. Ideally, such possible complications should be incorporated into any application of the aggregate transport cost model by experimenting with warehouse locations and using appropriate to-and-from warehouse freight rates and shipping volumes.

The analysis of the costs of overcoming the friction of distance for "things" is too complex to be exhaustively treated here. The concerns arise in a variety of different spots and guises throughout this book. What so far has been attempted is to alert the site selector to the issue and to provide some basic principles. Beyond this, the analyst may make use of the voluminous literature on transportation and distribution planning,[13] and, certainly, make good use of within-firm traffic experts, once the proper questions are known.

Before temporarily turning aside from the topic of transportation, a chicken-egg type of question may be posed: Which comes first--the transport facilities or the demand for transportation? From a long historical, macro-spatial point of view, a good case can be made for the argument that in any area in which demand exists, transportation facilities will be developed to meet the demand. The vast majority of manufacturers, however, do not operate in a long historical context and are not sufficiently large to occasion the development of a complex transportation network on their own account. They are dependent on utilizing the facilities (which may be somewhat modified) already in place. Therefore, heed must be given Yaseen's admonition that:

> ". . . it is occasionally true that certain types of plant location site selections can be made in smaller communities with the presumption that both the required quantity of transportation services, as well as the necessary rate structures, will develop or will be created in response to shipper demand. All too often, however, this presumption cannot be made. This is particularly true for industries with customers that require so-called premium service—frequent movement of goods in small lots, short door-to-door delivery time, with a high predictability of arrival time, the requirement of minimum handling and low levels of loss and damage. In such cases, site selection usually must be narrowed down to a small handful of carefully chosen urban areas."[14]

B. Markets

For the majority of firms, the single most important factor influencing investment strategies is the marketing variable. In a capitalistic society firms who are not effective marketers are unable to remain competitive. Of all the things businessmen consider, markets are the most explicitly spatial. For location decisions the marketing geography of the firm is critical, especially at the regional scale of analysis.

Markets may hold the key to new investment strategy through one or a combination of reasons. In the first instance a firm may be locationally oriented toward its markets but is obviously unable to produce next to each customer because of the minimum size requirements of an economically sized facility. When marketing considerations are overwhelmingly dominant rational locational policy consists of siting productive facilities in the center of each sales territory so long as the territory provides sufficient sales to meet the minimum economy-of-scale requirements of a modern plant. For a given sized plant the more dense and geographically compact the sales territory the closer to the optimal is the productive geography of the firm. As new sales are developed an area previously dependent on imports may pass the minimum size threshold and warrant a new plant.

Since for most firms economies of scale will outweigh simple locational forces, the normal motive for a new facility will be that the new sales require new productive capacity which cannot be easily met by expansion within existing plants. Only in a few cases will the necessity to service customers through nearby productive facilities, rather than through sales offices or warehouses, or the high cost of transporting the finished product dictate a new plant in spite of unused capacity elsewhere within the company. The most common situation is a market oriented factory which is constructed when new sales demand new productive capacity. Of course, the siting of a new plant changes the geography of the firm and the relative location of all previously existing plants. Going from an optimal spatial configuration of, say, two plants to three theoretically requires locational readjustment of the original two. Factories are investments fixed in space for a considerable period of time; thus a new plant may well occasion adjustments in sales and supplies territories and intra-corporate communications, but the wholesale relocation of pre-existing facilities is virtually impossible. Probable future location decisions, however, should influence current decisions.

External pressures may also make markets the prime locational force even in situations where the companies might otherwise prefer to keep production concentrated at existing sites. This is a situation faced quite often by multi-national firms. Typically, companies start in foreign areas through sales. These sales may be subsequently threatened by a local government which may erect barriers such as tariffs which heavily discriminate against imported goods, or through legal requirements which require foreign companies to produce in conjunction with local interests. If sales are large enough they will be protected by construction of a plant within the country in question.

Less commonly, firms may place productive facilities in protected areas where sales are currently meager if sufficient potential is sensed, especially if by getting behind the protective curtain early they can steal the march on competitors. Unfortunately, too few firms possess the awareness or the vision to capitalize on future marketing opportunities, which makes things all the sweeter for the firms which do.

Returning to the more prosaic, and common, problem of locating a domestic branch plant, a series of basic principles must be kept in mind:

a. The best single estimate of the future spatial configuration of the market is its present spatial distribution. This involves clearly identifying, on some appropriate scale (e.g., counties), the present location and volume of demand of present purchasers. Three data arrays, or maps, should be produced: (1) the current amount of sales for the specific firm locating the new plant; (2) the amount of sales for the entire industry; (3) the firm's share of each market.

b. If the proposed new plant will produce multiple products with distinct markets, then a marketing analysis should be carried out for each different product.

c. The size of the market area served by a specific plant is a function of the economies of scale in production and the spatial spread of the market. The larger economic size of production facility, the larger the sales territory. The more dispersed the market, the larger the sales territory and the greater the cost of reaching the total market.

d. The greater the costs of transporting the products to markets, the higher the effective selling price of the commodity, other things being equal. Better located plants will have a competitive edge through lower prices or higher profits over less advantageously located plants.

e. Beyond costs, plants closer to customers usually have advantages over more distant competitors because they can provide better service, more rapid delivery and are more likely to be in frequent communication and thus more likely to anticipate customer desires. This service factor is underemphasized in locational analysis. (The Aggregate Transport Model of section A ignores it; the Market Potential Model, discussed later, however, can be programmed to account for the service/proximity factor.)

f. The location of a new plant in an area may increase the total sales expected in an area by lowering price and increasing service and may also increase the specific firm's share of the market.

g. If the locations and magnitudes of the markets can be assumed stable, then the distribution territory, or market area, can be determined for each plant in a multi-plant firm on the basis of transport costs and/or delivery times.[15]

h. The entire distribution system, or market area structure for a firm will change with the location of a new plant. The totality of alterations in the firm's marketing geography must be taken into account when ascertaining the transport cost advantages of a proposed location. Because of this, the Aggregate Transport Cost Model as presented in section A is naive; more useful are the linear programming methods presented in Chapter 8.

Even when considered in isolation of other location factors, the assessment of the influence of markets is difficult. In practice, assumptions and simplifications must be made, and one (or several) of four techniques of analysis are utilized: (1) the Aggregate Transport Cost Model; (2) the "Tornqvist Solution;" (3) The Market Potential Model; and (4) Linear Programming. Since the Aggregate Transport Cost Model is included in section A, and the linear programming approach is included in Chapter 8, the "Tornqvist Solution" and the Market Potential Model remain to be discussed in this section. However, before turning to these, it is important to note that the reliability of all four methods depends on the accuracy of the potential sales forecasts. A new plant is built not only for the moment but is a fixed investment which must be amortized over a period of future time. As always, the future is fraught with uncertainties, making forecasts for even three or five years hazardous. But a complete locational analysis requires some best estimates of the volume, timing and spatial distribution of sales, even if only for a few years into the future (in most cases, guesses for more than five years hence are so problematical that they are not utilized). How are these future sales forecasts to be made? Before proceeding, discussion of sales forecasting is in order.

Good forecasts, especially on the spatial configuration of markets, are critical ingredients in successful investment strategy. Techniques utilized in making what are hoped to be reliable forecasts range from the overly simple to the quite complex and sophisticated; from the hunch to the computerized multivariate model. The simplest techniques underutilize a company's available information. The most abstract models require extremely rare or non-existent data. For most firms the useful procedures fall in the middle range; these are discussed in this section. As is true with any analysis, the usefulness of the results must be weighed against the efforts required to produce them; also on these grounds the techniques discussed below may be recommended.

The first step in any good forecast is for a firm to systematize its internal sales information. Sales data should be collected systematically over time and stored in such ways, e.g., on file cards and computer tape, as to be readily accessible for analysis. These data should be broken down by geographic area. These spatial units are very often sales territories. Although sales territory data are useful, the units are often too gross to be used most effectively. A preferred system is to record spatial coordinates of each reporting unit, thus allowing maximum flexibility in aggregating and reaggregating data by the most useful spatial systems. In the United States, for example, it may be recommended that data are organized at the county or SMSA level of spatial resolution. Such scales are not only normally sufficiently detailed for company purposes but also have the advantage of being the units for which a variety of secondary data (e.g., population, income, manufacturing, etc.) are published.

Much of the analysis to be performed utilizing sales data can be handled best when the figures are stored on computer tape. There is, however, no substitute for the visual impact of a series of good maps, each depicting the marketing geography of the firm at a different point in time. Such maps have a dramatic appeal and greatly assist in an intuitive understanding of a firm's sales history. Maps are pictures which concisely show spatial information that would take thousands of words to express. A temporal series of sales maps, drawn according to relevant spatial subdivisions, is suggestive of what the sales pattern of the near future will look like. This is akin to, and should be, an essential ingredient in the "straight line" forecasting technique. Such maps are also extremely useful in hypothesizing variables which may be fruitfully included in more sophisticated multivariate models. It is highly recommended that a good map showing the spatial distribution of a firm's sales be drawn up at least once a year. Such a map will be useful to many and should be rather widely distributed; it will also be available as a key ingredient in the event of choosing a plant location.

Some of the more sophisticated forecasting models also require data external to the firm. Always useful is information about competitors' sales patterns and speculations about these competitors' future moves. Such data can be estimated only by those in a given industry based upon published company reports, trade journals and industry scuttle-butt. Most of the other external data required relate to patterns and forecasts, including population, incomes, and so on. These data are normally collected from documents in the public domain, most importantly government censuses and special reports. Of course, there is always the question of the cost/benefit ratio between the efforts expended in collecting data and the results derived. Especially to be guarded against is the tendency to gather data simply because they somehow seem reasonable or are easily obtainable. A logical model should specify the data; the data readily to hand should never dictate the model.

The simplest way to forecast the spatial distribution of sales is to make an overall company forecast for some future date and allocate the new total to each sub-area according to its present share. In a relative sense a new map based on such an allocation will look just like the previous map. However, an examination of new sub-area figures is warranted to determine if an area or a combination of contiguous areas may now be of sufficient size to justify having new facilities located within.

Another technique is to graph for the past several years the actual sales figures for a region and to carry on the same curve to produce a prediction. This rate-of-change method reflects the relative growth patterns of the regions and may well produce a significantly different map from a previous period. The sub-area projections may be summed to produce a company-wide sales projection, and the total may be checked for conformity with independently derived company projections.

There is a variety of statistical techniques which may be used for predicting future conditions. Unfortunately, many require data beyond the knowledge of most manufacturing companies. Conversely, information relating to the future often has such large errors of estimate as to make the application of sophisticated techniques unwarranted. No projection can be better than the data on which it is based;

as the computer people say, "Garbage in, garbage out." However, with sufficient caution, such techniques may be extremely useful.

Forecasting methods which rely only on good historical data internal to the firm may be relatively quick and easy. Furthermore, such forecasting is probably inevitable, even if done subconsciously; but it is more instructive to systemize the process. Extrapolating the future performance of a variable (e.g., sales) from its past record, however, may seem deceptively simple. In fact, extracting the best estimates of the future from a time series requires a great deal of sophistication. It is recommended that the services of a statistician competent in modern time series analysis, including the Box-Jenkins techniques,[16] be employed.

Alternatively, forecasting may proceed by building a structural model which includes exogenous variables. A useful model may be assembled by first identifying all of the factors thought to have major influence on (a) the total future sales of the company and (b) the spatial distribution of those sales. In particular, variables thought to relate to the probable fortunes of major customers should be built in; detailed industry level investigation is warranted here. More general variables may include changes in selective population groups, disposable incomes, competitors; actions, new technologies, rates of regional economic growth, movements of suppliers or customers, and so on.

The comprehensive "Checklist of Site Selection Factors" for 1978 includes nine sub-headings under "Markets" (Description, Location, Population Trends, Income Trends, Consumer Characteristics, Retail Sales Trends, Industrial Markets, Competition, Tourism in Area) which encompass 41 separate factors.[17] The list is continuously revised to incorporate the many variables necessary for meaningful market analysis. How are the many variables to be integrated and developed into a composite picture for executive decision? A series of maps, charts and statistical arrays would be useful, but integration would be difficult and excessively judgmental and individualistic. Integrating multivariate techniques, such as multiple regression analysis, have proven useful in many cases.[18]

The fact that the majority of the items listed under "Markets" are of a general nature, rather than of details specific to the industry or firm locating the plant, is likewise suggestive. It suggests that many businesses can best predict by knowing general economic trends, since both they and their customers are meshed in a system too complex to sort out on a more detailed basis, and that many analysts lack more focused, detailed information and must resort to readily available secondary data, such as that published by the U.S. Bureau of the Census and the U.S. Dept of Commerce.[19] The emphasis on trends, of course, points to the necessity of guessing the future, of forecasting.

Although the multivariate model allows for several influences, it is generally assumed that past trends are the best estimates of the future. For most variables this is the safest or only reasonable assumption, but it is not necessary to be so restricted. The model is capable of utilizing variable estimates according to any other information or strong hunches which management may care to build in. Simulations may be run under a variety of assumptions to test the limits of different locational solutions or even the viability of the investment itself.

Lest anyone be misled by the seeming precision of sophisticated arithmetic, be reminded that all projections of the future are guesses, and that managerial judgment, objectivity, vision and expertise are critical at all stages. Management must specify the techniques and the models to be used and the relevant variables to be included. Management must mine the past and divine the future to provide good data. Management must analyze the results. Management therefore, must structure itself to maximize its access to information and opinion and still have procedures for organizing data and resolving divergent opinions so that considered, judgmental decisions can be made. One suggested forecasting procedure which utilizes both management's objective and subjective expertise is the Delphi Technique. This is:

". . . a method of integrating the opinions of experts without sacrificing or compromising individuals' suggestions and ideas— as is so often the case when committees are assigned the task of compiling a long-range forecast. . . The Delphi Technique requires that a panel of experts on the subject under study be selected. These individuals are then asked to independently develop their best answers to the questions being asked, for example, to forecast changes within a specific industry or technology. In addition, they are required to make their underlying assumptions explicit and to identify any source material they would find helpful in refining and improving their answers. After their first answers are completed, each expert is given the composite replies of the group, together with the other experts' assumptions and their own requested additional information, if it is available. The names of the individual panel mamebers are not associated with the opinions provided. Successive revisions of the original forecasts are undertaken following this procedure. Finally, a composite forecast is compiled."[20]

This is but an introduction to the variety of techniques which are available. Since forecasts are so critical in the site selector's analysis, it is important that the use of the best procedures be encouraged. It is equally important for the site selector to know how forecasts supplied by management are compiled so that their reliability and applicability can be assessed with regard to the site selection analysis.

Once adequate forecasts are produced, a variety of analytical techniques are available. Two of these are the Tornqvist Solution and the Market Potential Model.

The Tornqvist Solution is an iterative approach to the general location-allocation problem. The technique may be illustrated by the transport costs to markets on the outputs of two Swedish cement block plants. The entire country is grided (at some appropriate scale) and the volume (current or projected) of cement block demand is entered for each grid. Then plants A and B are initially located in the furthest cells in space (e.g., the extreme north and south) and all other cells are assigned to either A's or B's distribution territories on the basis of lowest rail transportation cost. Then the distribution costs can be computed for A and B using the Aggregate Transport Cost Model, and the figures for A and B can be summed to produce the total distribution costs for the system. Then the search starts for locations which will reduce distribution costs. Plant A is tentatively relocated in each of the four cells to the east, west, north and south. After calculating the new marketing costs for Plant A at each of these trial locations, the cell with the lowest cost is selected as the second tentative location. Then it is B's turn to search for a better location among its adjacent cells. New tentative locations for A and B may result in a new configuration of sales territories, from which a new system total of distribution costs can be calculated. Then, the search of adjacent cells starts again, first by trying relocations for A and then for B. The process continues in an iterative fashion until neither A nor B can reduce delivered costs by moving to adjacent cells. The final solution will indicate plant locations and sales territories which minimize delivery costs. Of course, the same procedure could incorporate more than two plant locations, as many as were deemed necessary or reasonable. Likewise, other cost factors could be included. Although the amount of arithmetic is immense, and therefore tedious by hand, the operations are basically simple and easily may be programmed for high speed computers.[21]

The final market analysis technique to be here considered is the Market Potential Model.[22] This is an extension of the gravity concept where the attraction or pull of any market at location j on a possible plant site at location i is a function of the direct influence of the size of the market at j and the inverse influence of the distance from i to j. The potential of any plant at i is the summation of all the individual i to j relations. Symbolically, the market potential of point i (M_i) is given as:

$$M_i = \sum_{j=1}^{n} \frac{Q_j}{T_{ij}}$$

Where Q_j is the volume demanded at each market and T_{ij} is the distance or transportation cost between each i and j. Harris characterizes the resultant figure (M_i) as "an abstract index of the intensity of possible contact with markets."[23]

The fundamental difference between the Market Potential Model and the Aggregate Transport Model is that the potential model treats distance or transport costs as an inverse influence, in contrast to its direct influence in the latter. This means, as Smith notes, that the Market Potential Model "is more of a true demand model than the aggregate travel model because it makes allowance for the fact that sales at any market point may be a function of distance from the plant, and that plant location can affect the total volume sold and thus the total revenue earned."[24]

In any situation where it may be reasonable to assume that demand will decrease as a function of increased transportation cost, the construction of a map showing the market potentials of areas may be useful in site selection analysis. Of course, as always, the results are dependent on reliable and appropriate measures, both of market volumes and of the effect of distance. The latter is especially tricky, but through curve-fitting to existing company or industry analog data, it is often possible to derive reasonable estimates of the inverse influence of increased distance. When this can be reasonably accomplished, it is quite instructive to compare the market potential map with the aggregate transport cost map. They may be similar but not identical. The differences can be valuable inputs to the judgmental assessment of the market factor in industrial site selection.

C. Materials

Although often referred to as "raw" materials, for the vast majority of manufacturers the input materials are intermediate goods utilized directly in the production process and purchased from other manufacturers. In the simple, classic model, firms are spatially "materials oriented" if it costs more to ship materials to the plant than it does to ship products to markets. In practice, however, it is relatively rare to find a true "materials oriented firm, not only because of the variety of additional location factors but also because of the nature of materials utilization and acquisition. The fact that most manufacturing operations use a multitude of different inputs from a number of different locations reduces the locational pull of materials. Also, many of the inputs are found in areas favored for other reasons, such as market areas. Finally many vendors quote uniform delivered prices, thus reducing or eliminating their locational pull.

The first step in analyzing the materials situation is to make a list of all current suppliers and to translate these onto a map noting the precise location of each supplier, by type and by volume of materials currently purchased. The next stage would be to try to anticipate any changes in this picture over the foreseeable planning future, e.g., five years. Changes may occur either because suppliers may change, product mix may change, components necessary for the production process may change, etc. Given sufficient information, the determination of the best mix of specific inputs from various vendors can be facilitated by operations research techniques, as discussed in Chapter 8.

In addition to anticipating changes in the geographic structure of the firm's supply pattern, there are two immediate issues to be confronted when analyzing the location of new facilities relative to materials access. The first is the minimum transport point to gather the diverse products necessary as inputs to the production functions of the firm in question. This analysis, once the basic data have been obtained on the location and magnitude of supplies incoming, can be conducted by the same types of techniques as discussed under analyzing the best location for minimizing transport costs to market.

The second issue, however, revolves around the necessity of having good service from suppliers. This may take the form, for example, of necessitating quick shipment time, so to minimize warehousing problems. This may also take the form of having local representatives so that one can get superior, individualized service. Many firms have developed high degrees of loyalty to certain vendors, partly because these vendors have grown to know the firm, can anticipate needs and have good records of reliability. Vender loyalty reduces executive search time, inconvenience and uncertainty. Should these familiar purchasing arrangements be continued for a plant in a new location? What is the likelihood of vendors adjusting to the firm's new spatial distribution? These types of considerations are not easily assessed or quantified, but to the extent it is possible, they can be added to the transport costs of the materials calculations so as to best estimate the proper location of a plant regarding materials supplies, other things being equal.

The "Checklist of Site Selection Factors" contains six subheadings under "Basic Materials and Services": A. Each Raw Material; B. Each Semi-finished Material; C. Storage Facilities; D. Routine Supplies; E. General Studies; F. Technical Services. All but the first two categories concern "yes" or "no" answers about the attributes of specific areas and are more properly discussed in the "Agglomeration and Infrastructure" section of Chapter 4. Only subheadings A and B relate explicitly to the friction of distance focus of this chapter. The same six items are listed under subheadings A and B. These summarize the basic questions to be answered about materials (raw and semi-finished) access: (1) Location of Suppliers? (2) Quantity and Quality Produced? (3) Amount Produced Available to New Customers? (4) Delivery Time, Interruptibility? (5) Long-term Production Outlook? (6) Alternate Suppliers?[5]

D. Communications

Firms for which the cost of overcoming the friction of distance is a highly significant variable will have their locations largely dictated by these costs. They are commonly referred to as either market oriented or materials oriented industries; those industries for which the friction of distance is not dominant are often known as "footloose." Such characterizations, although simple and sometimes useful, can also be most misleading. It is rare to be able to consider transport costs to the exclusion of other important variables; to do so is to oversimplify the complexities of major investment decision making. There is also the danger of incorrectly inverting the logic; there are many other good reasons for a plant to be market - or materials - orientated. Finally, such terminology, as well as the mere fact of starting with transport costs as done here, carries considerable risk of overemphasizing the cost of moving materials and products. This over-emphasis is common in textbooks and in industrial location theory and among a surprisingly large number of businessmen as well, particularly those who have not had firsthand experience with location problems. Although undoubtedly of some concern to all firms, there is considerable evidence that as transport systems have become relatively more efficient over time, transportation as a friction of distance variable has declined in importance relative to other factors. Regarding the location of large multinational companies in Great Britain, it has been noted that "transport costs for the kind of high value and low weight products involved in most multinational transactions are very low. The last U.K. Industrial Census showed they totalled only about 2½ percent of total production costs. The costs of net distance (of going to Scotland rather than staying in the Southeast) are mainly a problem of persuading junior and middle range management and securing management access through frequent flight and rail schedules."[26]

The monetary and psychological costs of transporting ideas and people across space are typically underemphasized. In spite of the marvels of modern communication in moving words, data and images rapidly over long distances, there appears to be no substitute for face-to-face contact. This appears especially true among managers, and, as previously pointed out, it is the managers, not the workers, whose biases are implemented. The evolution of cheap, efficient communications has made possible the effective spatial dispersal of the various activities of a corporation. When there are other good reasons for it, the technical apparatus exists to permit dispersal. Of themselves, however, modern communications have not fostered dispersal, but rather have abetted concentration through effective centralized control of outlying areas. This seems as true for modern corporations as modern governments. More efficient communication of ideas also reinforces tendencies induced by cheaper transport of goods toward increased concentration, higher economies of scale, larger supply catchment areas and larger marketing territories. Dependence upon a few suppliers and markets thus is reduced, unless the industries from whom supplies are obtained and those which provide markets are in similar processes of rationalization.

The movement of people is another underemphasized but critical element in the location decision. Despite their numerical superiority it is not transportation of the shop workers which is important. In the location decision, labor is taken as an attribute of an area and it is the responsibility of the individual worker to get himself to and from the plant. Rather, it is the potential movement of managers which may be critical, especially between corporate headquarters and branch plants. One company, as noted previously, delimited the area of search for a branch site as within 200 miles of headquarters because, "That's how far the corporate aircraft will travel in an hour." Another manager explained that he looked at the interstate highway system first to see how long it would take him to make a visit to the branch and, secondly, to estimate truck delivery times. Overnight deliveries were sufficient, and a few hours more or less didn't matter. His time and effort he deemed more crucial.[27]

The interdependence relationships between the shipment of goods and information flows have been conceptualized by Tornqvist as three separate horizontal planes of communication:

> "On the first communications plane goods are transported. The volume of goods moved on this plane has increased enormously in recent years. Materials and goods are transported all over the region, goods are transported criss-cross between subcontractors and assembly plants, between factories and warehouses and wholesalers, and between wholesalers and retailers. Due to the concentration of retailing, the transportation effort of households also has increased considerably . . . .
>
> "One of the reasons why transportation on this plane has increased on such a scale and in such a way is that energy prices have been very low in comparison to, for example, those costs which are subject to economies of scale. It has also proven very easy to shift the burden of transport costs to other sectors, e.g., to the household sector, where no aggregated registration of these costs takes place. Finally, many decision makers have probably lost their sense for transportation and physical distance as a result of the great mobility they daily experience on the other planes of communication. It is likely that future fuel shortages and the emergence of a society oriented toward low-energy comsumption may radically change this situation. Large-scale rationalization may be necessary on this plane, and the need for research centering on the transport of goods may increase again.
>
> "On the second communications plane information is exchanged via face-to-face contracts, thereby requiring personal travel. An increased need for personal contacts has led to a vast

growth in 'organization traffic.' The intensity of this type of travel must not, however, overshadow the fact that distance exercises considerable friction on this second plane. People communicating on this plane are almost always pressed for time. They always have tight schedules; and because personal contracts require simultaneity in time and space, the coupling processes on this plane are very complicated. There appears little doubt that the increased need for personal contacts and the coupling constraints on this communications plane are among the primary reasons for large city growth during the 1950s and 1960s.

"Before proceeding any further one other phenomenon on this second communications plane should be observed. If people have to meet other people long distances away, then they have to use express trains or air services. The resulting contact system can be likened to a strongly focussed network, consisting of a set of nodes linked by fixed transport routes, which people must use for getting from one place to another. The travellers moving constantly within this network must acquire a somewhat singular view of the world around them . . . .

"On the third communications plane information is disseminated and contacts are made via various forms of telecommunications. The information exchanged on this plane is more routine in nature than the information exchanged on the second plane. Distance is of little importance. It would seem reasonable to assume that the ease and speed with which information can be transmitted and disseminated on this plane give contemporary man in a technologically advanced society the feeling that physical distance is of practically no importance. If so, this sense of distance being of no account may contribute to what, in certain contexts, probably constitutes 'uneconomic' mobility on the other planes."[28]

The increased emphasis on the importance of personal, face-to-face contacts (Tornqvist's second plane of communication) among managers leads to some interesting speculations about industrial location and urban growth. Karaska recently proposed a new theory for the reorganization of industry which "is focused upon the industrial organization or corporation. Instead of transportation costs measuring optimality in location, we now turn to information fields, contact fields and action spaces. The emphasis is not upon the manufacturing production function but upon the totality of the industry function, wherein the greatest proportion of business is management, administration, sales, services, etc. The arena for this new perspective in theory then shifts to the metropolitan center or industrial complex, wherein we observe a concentration of industrial and related services."[29] This is not a new idea, but it *is* a manufacturing-specific application of several of the metropolitanization themes suggested by several scholars, including Gottmann, who contends that "information flows are the second prerequisite of successful centrality . . . . Every quaternary activity heavily depends on the availability of diverse, accurate and up-to-date information."[30] Similarly, Pred notes that "there has been a significant burgeoning in those Metropolitan and other city system interdependencies which involve intra-organizational linkages between the headquarters offices of the multi-locational private sector organizations and their subordinate domestic units."[31]

What are the factors which account for the increasing concentration of manufacturing jobs in a large urban center, and what are the rationales for attributing these concentrations to the needs for face-to-face contact and intimate locational placement in the information flows systems? One factor is that employment as a whole in "post industrial" societies has shifted to the extent that the majority of workers are now white collar rather than blue collar. Likewise Pred notes that "In essence, the structural shifts so characteristic of advanced economies mean that the jobs controlled by multi-locational organizations, and the jobs dependent upon those organizations, are increasingly involved with the exchange and processing of specialized information rather than the transportation and processing of natural resources and semifinished goods. This changing functional orientation of jobs has considerable implications for where the jobs themselves are located. Most crucially, as will subsequently become apparent, in a variety of ways the constantly expanding consumption and production of specialized information by job-providing organizations tend to favor the growth of already large metropolitan areas and their surrounding 'urban fields.'"[32]

Another factor is that modern corporations, including manufacturers, are increasingly large, multi-functional, multi-locational and complex. These developments put a premium on intra-organizational communication and control.

A third factor is that decision-making is in the hands of a small number of executives who are inundated with information and data. They also face considerable uncertainty. The uncertainty can be best reduced by high quality information and by locations in well established urban systems. The data overload demands simplification. It is most easily obtained through consultants and specialists located in the same urban systems.

Stöhr notes that the relatively small mobility of entrepreneurial information in relation to that of capital is a concentrating factor. This factor complements external and scale economies.[33] This emphasis on metropolitan location of manufacturing activity and the associated rationales in terms of contact systems and information flows raises a number of interesting questions:

1) To what extend does the "metropolitan center-information" rationale supplant the more traditional industrial location theory which emphasizes proximity to demand centers (markets) and suppliers? Do the same empirical data support all three? Do the market and supplier factors work in conjunction with the contact systems factors to reinforce the urban bias?

2) In his 1966 book, *The World Cities,* Hall contends that industry "instead of concentration in congested centers (gained) freedom of location through improved communication"[34] How does this contention accord with the "metropolitization based on contact systems" concept? What is the empirical evidence for decentralization based upon improved communication? Might we make the opposite case: that improved communication increases the amount of information which in turn demands ready access to the more esoteric and superior information, and the sheer magnitude of available information necessitates the need for specialists to guide practitioners through the maze? Superior information which gives a competitive edge is most readily found in large urban centers.

At the more intimate level of the company, whether or not located in metropolitan areas, total geography of the firm is always an important consideration. Information flows and ease of managerial contact must never be overlooked. In *Up the Organization,* Townsend neatly capsulizes the issue:

> "If your business is in Cleveland, start or acquire an operation in Santa Barbara at your peril. Absentee management is fatal.
> "And the disaster potential is equal to the square of the distance-measured in hours—between your home base and the new plant. No matter how determined you are to visit it frequently, you'll discover that your capacity to find last-minute reasons not to go is unlimited.
> "If the new operation is in Europe or the Far East, the problems increase by cube functions. It is twenty-seven times harder to cope with an operation in Hong Kong than in Duluth."[35]

The difficulties of managing a far-flung organization lead many companies to adhere to the prudent spatial increment principle. The importance of the internal geography of the firm causes a "noticeable tendency to use what might be labelled a 'spatial increment' model, wherein these relatively small plants are located just beyond the firm's previous 'spatial sphere of production.' That is, located far enough away from any existing facility of that firm to gain perceived locational advantages . . . but no further than necessary, to facilitate inter-plant cooperation and, especially, management contact from the home office."[36] This principle and the rather large zone of metropolitan influence beyond the immediate urbanized areas may be combined to help explain the apparent contradiction between the above argument postulating increasing concentration of manufacturing jobs in large urban centers versus the results of a recent Industrial Development Research Council survey[37] which indicates that many recent plant locations are in rural areas. There are, of course, some truly rural plants, hundreds of miles from any large city. But most even so-called rural plants are found on the fringes of the more densely settled urban centers. Thus the rural designation is appropriate at the local scale, but when viewed on the national scale most rural plants are seen to be within the orbits of the major cities.

Notes and References — Chapter 3

1. "Transportation - The Key Element in Geo-Economic Planning," *Site Selection Handbook,* XXI, No. 2 (May, 1976) pp. 77-82.
2. Estall, R.C., and Buchanan, R.O. *Industrial Activity and Economic Geography,* London: Hutchinson University Library, pp. 31.
3. *Ibid.* p. 32.
4. For example, see Sampson, R.J., and Farris, M.T. *Domestic Transportation - Practice, Theory and Policy.* Boston: Houghton-Mifflin, 1971, pp. 187-206.
5. Estall, R.C., and Buchanan, R.O., *op. cit.,* p. 331.
6. Yaseen, Leonard C., *Plant Location,* American Research Council. New York: American Research Council, 1960, p. 39.
7. *Ibid.*
8. Smith, David M. *Industrial Location.* New York: J. Wiley & Sons, 1971, p. 81.
9. *Ibid.,* p. 297.
10. Russell, Joseph A. "Modern Geography: Foundation of Corporate Strategy," *The Professional Geographer,* Vol. XXIX, No. 2, (May, 1977) p. 203.
11. *Ibid.,* p. 205.
12. Smykay, Edward W. "Distribution Strategy and Site Selection," *Industrial Development,* September, 1961. (In Conway, H.M., and Liston, L.L. (eds.) *Industrial Facilities Planning. Atlanta:* Conway Publications, 1976, p. 62.
13. For a beginning, see the references in Sampson, R.J., and Farris, M.T. *op. cit.*
14. Yaseen, Leonard C. *Industrial Development in a Changing World.* New York: Thomas Y. Crowell Co., 1975, p. 23.
15. A more extensive discussion of market areas, and illustrations of their delimitation, is contained in Smith, David M., *op. cit.,* pp. 304-311.
16. The most recent and important developments in applied time series analysis are the Box-Jenkins techniques. See Box, G. E. and Jenkins, G. M. *Time Series Analysis-Forecasting and Control.* San Francisco: Holden-Day, Inc., 1976. For a simpler, but not elementary, treatment see Nelson, Charles R. *Applied Time Series Analysis - For Mangerial Forecasting.* San Francisco: Holden-Day, Inc., 1973.

17. "Checklist of Site Selection Factors;" *Site Selection Handbook,* XXII, No. 1 (1977), p. 58.
18. As an example of a multiple regression model used (in part) to project the spatial distribution of industries, see Spiegelman, R.G., *A Study of Industry Location Using Multiple Regression Techniques.* Agricultural Economic Report No. 140. Washington: Economic Research Service, U.S. Dept. of Agriculture, 1968.
19. Including the publications of the National Technical Information Service, U.S. Dept. of Commerce, such as the monthly *Survey of Current Business.*
20. Campbell, R.M. and Hitchin, D. "The Delphi Technique: Implementation in the Corporate Environment," *Management Services,* November - December, 1968, p. 38.
21. Tornqvist, G. *Studier i Industrilukaliserving.* Stockholm: Geografiska Institutionen vid Stockholms Universitet, 1963. A simplified presentation, with maps, is in Abler, R., Adams, J.S., and Gould, P. *Spatial Organization,* Prentice-Hall, 1971, pp. 546-549.
22. See Smith, David M., *op. cit.,* pp. 301-304.
23. Harris, C.D. "The Market as a Factor in the Localization of Industry in the United States," *Annals of the Association of American Geographers,* 1954, p. 321.
24. Smith, David M., *op. cit.,* p. 302.
25. "Checklist of Site Selection Factors," *op. cit.*
26. Holland, Stuart. "Multinational Companies and a Selective Regional Policy;" memorandum in *Regional Development Incentives,* Trade and Industry Sub-Committee, Expenditure Committee, House of Commons, Session 1973-74. London: Her Majesty's Stationery Office, 1973, p. 685.
27. Stafford, H.A. "The Anatomy of the Location Decision: Content Analysis of Case Studies;" reproduced with permission from *Spatial Perspectives on Industrial Organization and Decision-Making* by F.E. Ian Hamilton (ed.), p. 183. Copyright 1974, by John Wiley & Sons, Ltd., London.
28. Tornqvist, G. "The Geography of Economic Activities: Some Critical Viewpoints on Theory and Application," *Economic Geography,* Vol. LIII, No. 2, (April, 1977), p. 157.
29. Karaska, G.J. "Metropolitanization, Corporate Structure, and Industry Location," text of a paper presented in the Working

Group on Industrial Geography, International Geographical Union, Novosibirsk, U.S.S.R., July, 1976, p. 12.
30. Gottmann, J. "Urban Centrality and the Interweaving of Quaternary Activities," *Ekistics,* Vol. XXIX (Jan. - June, 1970), p. 329.
31. Pred, A.R. "On the Spatial Structure of Organizations and the Complexity of Metropolitan Interdependence," *Papers of the Regional Science Association,* 1975, p. 121.
32. Pred, A.R. *Major Job-Providing Organizations and Systems of Cities,* Commission on College Geography, Resource Paper No. 27. Washington: Assn. of American Geographers, 1974, p. 3.
33. Stohr, W.B. *Interurban Systems and Regional Economic Development,* Commission on College Geography, Resource Paper No. 26. Washington: Assn. of American Geographers, 1974, p. 16.
34. Hall, P. *The World Cities,* World University Library. New York: McGraw-Hill, 1966, p. 24.
35. Townsend, R. *Up The Organization.* New York: Alfred A. Knopf, 1970, p. 65.
36. Stafford, H.A., *op. cit.,* p. 183.
37. Conway, H.M., and Liston, L.L. *A Composite Case History of New Facility Location.* Atlanta: The Industrial Development Research Council, 1978.

IV
Attributes Of Areas

IV
Attributes of Areas

Several of the most important industrial location factors do not vary over space in any systematic manner as a consequence of distance. Rather, they are the economic, cultural, physical and political attributes of specific locales which may change rather abruptly over short distances, from one community to another. The key area attributes examined in this chapter are (A) Labor, (B) Agglomeration Economies and the provision of Infra-Structure, (C) Power, (D) Water and (E) Quality of Life.

A. Labor

After computing the least cost transport point, the traditional simple location model then considers labor costs. If savings in labor costs are sufficient to compensate for increased friction of distance charges, then a move from the optimal transport cost point is warranted. Labor costs may vary over space and thus can be an important factor in the locational calculus. Labor costs do not vary directly with distance; they are properly considered attributes of areas and may change rather abruptly over short distances.

Conceptually, the simplest approach to dealing with labor as a location variable is to compare various potential sites according to best estimates of probable labor costs. Assuming that the number and character of workers required are given by prior decisions regarding the type and scale of investment, then labor costs are composed of three elements: 1) wage rates; 2) labor availability; and 3) productivity. Wage rates may be computed for each locality by ascertaining from governmental sources or manufacturers already in the area the prevailing wages for each revelant job classification.[1] Multiplying each rate by the projected number of workers in each category and summing provides a useful estimate of costs. Ideally, the cost of the average fringe benefit package will be included in the original figures. If fringe benefits are not originally included but are of approximately the same magnitude for each area they may be ignored. If there are significant spatial variations they must be included.

As with almost all aspects of the investment decision, the unknown future poses major complications. Spatial variations in wage rates can change over time through labor force migration from less favored areas to more favored areas or through the actions of other employers who may bid up prices. Such changes are constantly taking place and may be quite rapid locally. Such is the exception rather than the rule, however, and for most regions the size of counties or larger, wage rates remain remarkably stable relative to other areas over a number of years.[2] More likely to cause change in the spatial advantages enjoyed by a plant is union activity. Projecting the likelihood and consequences of such activity may be an extremely important factor in discounting the labor advantages enjoyed by one place over another. Of course, if there is companywide or industrywide bargaining with identical rates for all relevant sites then wages may cease to be a spatial variable and may be thus eliminated from the location problem. However, even with company or industrywide bargaining, regional differentials may still exist as actual job classification systems vary between areas.[3]

Even more important to many firms is the availability of labor. Sheer numbers of available workers may be an issue; more likely critical is the availability of specific skills. This is one reason why firms locate in metropolitan areas in spite of higher wage costs. The size and flexibility of the labor pool in an industrial area offers important advantages.

If available, data on spatial variations in labor productivity would be a most useful measure of the labor factor. Unfortunately, productivity is an even more elusive measure than the other two. The adage, you get what you pay for, applies to the employment of labor as well, and managers usually prefer to pay more and get more, rather than the converse. Official estimates of labor force productivity broken down by small enough areal units are virtually nonexistent. Crude indexes fashioned from available data are so conceptually and empirically weak as to be virtually useless.

In attempting to compare labor productivity among major industrial sectors, the Conference Board notes: "Productivity can be defined as the amount of goods and services that can be produced from a given level of inputs. The basic, underlying change in productivity—as measured by its long-run trend—defines how much more can be produced from the same level of inputs. Total productivity relates total production to all resources—labor and capital. Partial productivity relates the level of production to only one input source, more commonly to the amount of labor used. Measuring productivity, however, is not as straightforward as it might appear. Labor productivity would be defined most accurately by how many units of output are produced from each unit of labor input. That measure would be accurate if only one type of output were produced, but in reality many different kinds of goods and services are made available. The next best measure is to reduce all production to dollar amounts—their exchange value. Measuring labor input also entails some modification. Optimally, the number of hours worked by people with an equal level of skill in producing output would be used, but workers do have different skill levels. One alternative method is to weigh the hours worked at the wage paid per hour worked. This method implies that people are compensated for higher levels of skill. Another complexity is that the number of hours paid for is not equal to the number of hours actually engaged in production because of paid sick leave, holidays and vacation time. These hours paid for—but not engaged in production—account for as much as 4.5 percent of total paid time for the economy as a whole. In some sectors, such as mining, manufacturing, transportation and public utilities, it might be as much as seven or eight percent."[4]

Another thorny issue is the degree to which wage levels are related to productivity levels. Some observers say there is a positive relationship, while others deny a general connection. In spite of a great deal of attention, there appear to be few valid conclusions.[5] It is obvious, however, that labor stability is a factor in average labor productivity. Again, this is difficult to measure, but Yaseen contends that it is linked to local industrial attitudes and that:

"there *are* certain strong indices of community attitude that should influence its selection. Perhaps the most crucial question that can be asked about a community is 'What is its *past* history?' . . . While the past record of a city offers no *guarantee* of what is going to happen in the future., there is reasonable certainty that given continued sound management, a community which has had industrial peace should prosper better than its neighbor with a lengthy history of labor strife . . . In the plant with a healthy labor-management 'climate' it is entirely normal and expected that employees will occasionally be absent or late for work—an absentee rate of 3% is typical. When employers in the community report, however, that such rates are double or triple the average for work comparable to that of the proposed new plant, a potentially volatile labor situation may exist . . . Full knowledge of all influences affecting specific industries is necessary before any conclusions can be drawn. A monthly net turnover rate in the average manufacturing concern of over 5% can definitely be construed as a cause for alarm, but in such industries as logging or shipbuilding, separation rates of 11% to 24% are not uncommon."[6]

For a specific plant, the plant locator must largely rely on his and other firms' previous experience in similar areas when attempting to assess the amount of work likely to be produced per dollar by the average work force.

Both the locational significance of labor and the difficulties of assessing the factor are noted by Hunker:

"Whereas few location factors receive greater attention than does labor, few decisions involve generally less reliable data and more prejudice than those relating to this factor. Undoubtedly, the principal condition of labor most intriguing to those responsible for the location decision is labor costs. Several general observations can be made in so far as labor costs are involved:

1. Labor may be a major cost of production, hence total labor costs may be a critical factor in the location decision.
2. Evidence suggests that for most industries the location decision does not appear to be strongly affected by wage levels.
3. It is difficult to determine accurately true costs of labor and to obtain meaningful comparative data relative to wages as between regions.
4. Regional variations continue to exist in labor costs (the idea that the South is a cheap labor region) but are being equalized.
5. Increasing unionization is a significant contributing factor to decreasing regional variation even as the absence of unions may serve to attract some industries.
6. Increasing mechanization and automation have reduced the advantages that traditionally accrued to the unskilled and to areas of labor surplus further reducing regional variations.
7. Improved educational opportunities and training and re-training programs aimed at upgrading labor have helped to reduce cost variations by regions.

8. Increasing worker mobility, both geographically (as between cities or regions) and occupationally (as between jobs types) characterizes U.S. labor and hence reduces regional variation in wages, skills, and supply.
9. Fringe benefits of one sort or another are increasingly important in an analysis of labor costs and thus reduce the effect of wage levels as a criterion.

The cost of labor varies according to the amount used and to the type. The first point is self-explanatory. But the type of labor involved may be skilled or unskilled, experienced or inexperienced, or may vary by task performed as among several types of manufacturing jobs or between manufacturing and clerical jobs. Census data reveal that labor costs for 12 of the 20 SIC (Standard Industrial Classification) groups account for one-fourth or more of the total value of shipments. For some industries, labor costs may be high and form a significant share of production costs; in others, the opposite is true. To the extent that labor is a major cost, it is important as a factor affecting the location decision . . ."[7]

Similarly, Smith notes that:

"The overall influence of the labor factor on plant location is thus difficult to evaluate. Increasing mechanization, automation, and the tendency to substitute capital for labor may well be reducing the importance of labor in the modern industrial nation. But significant local advantages with respect to cost quantity and quality still exist. The increasing sophistication of industrial processes is reducing the need for unskilled labor in many industries, but the presence of workers with special technical skills can now give some areas big labor advantages. And on a world scale there are still many areas where the low cost of labor is the main competitive industrial advantage, particularly in the developing countries of Africa and Asia."[8]

Smith then concluded that:

"The problem of obtaining a precise estimate of the wage rates that a new entrant should expect to pay in any locality is virtually insoluble . . . The fact that there is a certain prevailing level of pay in a city for a given occupation, or in a given industry, is no guarantee that a new firm can get the number of workers required for the same expenditure."[9]

So, what to do? Regardless of the difficulties in measuring spatial variations in labor costs, so long as data are utilized judgmentally, some information is better than relying solely on hunch or bias. A practical first step is to try to simplify the process as much as possible. If, for example, other locational considerations, such as markets and materials factors, dictate a general region then it makes little sense to search beyond. Of course the actual spatial scope of the search will depend on the importance of labor as a location factor relative to other factors. The same techniques utilized in a very restrictive search can be applied, with consequent time and expenditure penalties, to a far ranging search if such an extensive search is warranted. The same reasoning applies if the analysis can be simplified by focusing on the type of area desired, such as rural or urban, large or small community, etc. In almost all cases, such as a priori decisions are industry and/or company specific and must be decided in light of past experience and anticipated needs. The major danger is that some quite acceptable areas will be excluded simply because they are not the types of areas ordinarily chosen; however, if the decision makers are alert and open-minded at the outset, then the simplifying process may proceed rationally and produce substantial search economies.

In spite of the difficulties in utilizing general labor cost maps of large regions, such overviews may be useful in narrowing the search and thus simplifying the analysis. An example of such a map is given in Fig. 4-1.[10] For similar computer drawn maps see Smith's *Industrial Location.* [11] Of course, for a specific industry it is best if maps are created from carefully selected data most appropriate to the case in question. In addition to proprietary industry data, useful secondary data sources for the United States include *Area Wage Surveys* for 105 areas and the more extensive occupational wage and related benefits studies for 82 other areas throughout the United States. (Both are produced by the Bureau of Labor Statistics, U.S. Dept. of Labor. The regional BLS office can give more information on these and other Bureau publications.) Also useful are the *U.S. Census of Manufacturing and County Business Patterns.* Information also can be obtained from many state and local industrial development agencies. Indeed, the careful location team will seek information and advice from all legitimate sources, while at the same time maintaining control over the interpretations of the imputs and being alert to quality, level of detail and inherent biases.

Once again, be reminded that any labor data must be viewed with caution. As an example, Smith quotes a disclaimer of the British *Ministry of Labour Gazette* regarding some published earnings data:

"In view of the wide variations as between different industries, in the proportion of skilled and unskilled workers, and in the opportunities for extra earnings from overtime, night work and payment-by-results scheme, the differences in average earnings shown in this table should not be taken as evidence of, or as a measure of, disparities in the ordinary rates of pay prevailing in different industries for comparable classes of work people employed under similar conditions."[12]

Recognizing both the difficulties and the need for some procedures for narrowing the search, Yaseen offers some advice and generalizations:

"Let us assume that you are now that manufacturer seeking a stable unskilled labor reservoir. Before time is wasted in expensive and time-consuming field investigation, it is advisable to eliminate as many localized areas as possible for due and sufficient cause. The general rules that follow are the result of actual experience gained in locating over 1,600 industrial plants.

1. Caution is advised in evaluating the labor potential of resort and vacation areas. Many workers, temporarily available off-season, will leave full-time employment for the allure of high-paying seasonal work. This is true to a lesser degree in areas where canning, packing and agricultural production prevail.
2. It is not necessarily true that a large city will have more of a permanent labor surplus than a small town. The number of people in a community is only important in relation to the *number of people gainfully at work* in the community.
3. In semi-urban and rural areas, population and work force figures should be applied county-wide. The county seat, for example, may have a population of only 4,000, yet the county itself may easily have 10-fold that population. In many areas the county seat is the natural shopping orbit, school, social and recreational center. Area residents naturally graviate towards it. Do not make the common mistake of precluding examination of a town because its size does not initially indicate sufficient manpower for your needs. In this connection, the density of the population, public highway transportation, commuting patterns and shopping habits have all have significance.
4. The most desirable community is the diversified community where industry, commerce and services are well-balanced. Care should be exercised in considering a community where employment in manufacturing is more than 50% of aggregate employment, trade and service.
5. A self-contained, independent labor supply is vital to long-term success. Anticipating the recruitment of a large percentage of the necessary work force beyond a twenty-mile radius may be hazardous. Constant shipping and utilization of workers by

RELATIVE HOURLY EARNINGS
MANUFACTURING PRODUCTION WORKERS
SEPTEMBER, 1973

BY STATE

☐ BELOW NATIONAL MEDIAN

▨ NATIONAL MEDIAN WAGE
$4.10 per hour

▧ ABOVE NATIONAL MEDIAN

BY SELECTED URBAN AREAS

▼ 15% BELOW NATIONAL MEDIAN
▽ 1-15% BELOW NATIONAL MEDIAN
○ 1-15% ABOVE NATIONAL MEDIAN
● 15% ABOVE NATIONAL MEDIAN

Source: V. Roterui and T. Szot, "Map Showing Wage Levels Permits Area Comparisons," *Arizona Revival*, December, 1974

Figure 4-1. Relative Hourly Earnings Manufacturing Production Workers

MICHIGAN

1 Muskegon-
 Muskegon Heights
2 Grand Rapids
3 Kalamazoo
4 Lansing
5 Jackson
6 Ann Arbor
7 Bay City
8 Saginaw
9 Flint
10 Detroit

NEW YORK-NEW JERSEY

11 Buffalo
12 Rochester
 a Monroe County
13 Syracuse
14 Utica-Rome
15 Elmira
16 Binghampton
17 Albany-
 Schenectady-
 Troy
18 Poughkeepsie

19 New York SMSA
 a New York City
 b Rockford County
 c Westchester County
20 Nassau-Suffolk SMSA
21 New York-Northeastern
 New Jersey, Standard
 Consolidated Area
 a New York and Nassau-
 Suffolk SMSA
 b Jersey City
 c Newark
 d Peterson-Clifton-Passaic
 Perth Amboy
22 Trenton
23 Camden
24 Atlantic City

PENNSYLVANIA

25 Philadelphia
 SMSA
 d Delaware Valley
26 Allentown-
 Bethleham
 Easton
27 Reading
28 Lancaster
29 York

30 Harrisburg
31 Wilkes-Barre-
 Hazelton
32 Scranton
33 Williamsport
34 Altoona
35 Johnstown
36 Pittsburg
37 Erie

CONNECTICUT
38 Stamford
39 Bridgeport
40 New Haven
41 Waterbury
42 New Briton
43 Hartford
RHODE ISLAND
44 Providence-Pawtucket-Warwick

45 Fall River
46 New Bedford
47 Brockton
48 Boston
49 Lawrence Haverhill
50 Lowell
51 Worchester
52 Springfield-
 Chicopee-Holyoke

0 100 200 300 400

Scale of Miles

September, 1973

       incoming plants in such contiguous areas can eventually deplete the labor resources of the central area.

6. In considering the over-all work force, investigate and eliminate those persons who are listed as residents, but are confined to mental or other hospitals, prisons, or similar institutions. (In an extreme case, a recent survey in a New York State county revealed 11,000 persons so confined out of a total reported population of 70,000.)

7. In suburban communities adjacent to large metropolitan areas, thoroughly investigate the commuting population. Do not consider the commuting population as potential recruits for an industrial work force. In most cases it is difficult, in fact well nigh impossible, to persuade the white collar worker to accept industrial employment.

8. For those concerns utilizing female labor, it is important to ascertain the average *family* income in the area under investigation. Generally the need for *supplementary* income draws females into the labor market. Estimates of female labor supply must be based on the correlation between primary and secondary (or supplementary) income.

9. A partial index to the female labor market is the availability of domestic help. Whenever the demand for female labor exceeds the supply, domestics are virtually unavailable.

10. In general, areas tending to attract migratory labor of the "flotsam and jetsam" type (large ports, for example), should be avoided by certain types of manufacturing operations.

The recommendations outlined above are only a few suggestions that can be amplified by the manufacturer in the light of his own special requirements, forming the basis of his preliminary 'at home' investigation."[13]

After the search has been somehow narrowed to a manageable few alternative locations, then detailed current information may be gathered. The most common procedure is to conduct on-the-spot field surveys. Before conducting a survey, another prior question must be answered: How large a territory will the survey encompass? In other words, what is the expected commuting range, or "Daily Urban System"? The best answer can be obtained only with reference to the type of plant to be constructed, and especially its labor requirements, and to the type of area to be surveyed. However, some useful rules of thumb include: (1) the spatial shape of the potential labor market is a downward sloping distance-decay function; that is, the probability, other things being equal, of obtaining labor decreases with distance from the plant; (2) the effective spatial extent of the potential labor market varies according to type of area; (3) in an urban area it is necessary to look at its specific commuting patterns, or Daily Urban System; (4) in rural areas it is usually advisable to conduct a search on the county scale; (5) although conditioned by factors such as the attractiveness of the employment offered, the congestion of the area, and intervening employment opportunities, the effective outer limit for the majority of comuting workers is rarely much more than 20 miles.

Once the general shape and extent of the potential local labor market has been established, the detailed field surveys can be conducted. First, data on work force specifics relative to the needs of the planned facility should be gathered from local and state development agencies, employment agencies, chambers of commerce and local utilities. Next, interviews with executives of other local manufacturers will both help to establish good rapport and will be valuable in interpreting the previously collected data. After the location decision has been narrowed down to a few sites, say three, it is not uncommon for the interested firm to conduct very detailed surveys in each of the localities. These surveys may be run by consultants or by the company managers. Some firms, for example, simply advertise specific types of potential job openings in each local newspaper and invite inquiries. The number and type of inquiries are then used as crude, but probably accurate, measures of interest and availability. Although expensive, current information for key localities is important as specific labor data may go out of date rather quickly, thus reducing the decision-maker's ability to rely on previously collected statistics. However, Yaseen notes that such "labor registration" techniques normally work best in smaller communities, and "should be used sparingly and only when there is reasonable certainty that positive action will be taken to construct the plant in the community should the registration prove favorable."[14]

Although a much utilized common sense approach, Reifler notes several pitfalls in the "labor registration" or "census technique." He states that it is likely that:

> ". . . the investigator would find, at the outset, job classifica-
> tions and rankings totally dissimilar to the ones he was seeking.
> In some cases the actual jobs he is looking for do not appear to
> exist. There is no way to tell by this so-called 'census' method
> whether or not these jobs exist and are being carried on under
> some other title or do not exist at all in the area . . . .

> The task of comparing 40 to 70 job descriptions of 30 to 50 firms is formidable, particularly when many firms haven't even written out these descriptions . . . .
> This method leaves no provision for estimating the potential impact of the locating company upon the local labor market . . . .
> Such a method, a pure census of an area, combined with an attempt to match job classifications of different meanings, can run into surprisingly high statistical errors (as high as 8%-12%), too great to be used as a basis for a location decision."

Instead, Reifler advocates "purposive sampling" of easy-to-compare, representative jobs. The underlying assumptions are that the scarcities, productivity, skills, etc., of a given area impact on all segments of the labor market, and that the proportionate differences between jobs are consistent from one area to another. Thus, it is possible to utilize analogs to construct for a given firm its usual labor cost structure. It is also possible to construct rather easily a general labor cost structure for an area utilizing easily obtainable, fairly standard data. Using a semi-log scale to preserve the proper proportionality, easily compared, company specific charts are pared for each area under consideration (Fig. 4-2). This basic system is further refined by adjusting for the available labor supply (e.g., unemployment rates) and for the size of plant to be located relative to the total labor force. Although at first seemingly complex, Reifler's technique is in reality rather simple and has the great advantages of allowing for good use of secondary data and avoiding some of the cost of surveys, and the confusion of too much detail. His claimed statistical error of only 2.50 to 4.25 percent certainly makes the technique worthy of serious consideration.[15] The conclusions are particularly powerful when the results of Reifler's "classification structures," the more standard assessment of secondary data, and the details of a labor registration all converge. Conversely, when they do not, extra judgmental caution is advised.

Of course, in all cases sound executive judgment is necessary. The assessment of labor, perhaps more than any other key location variable, is subject to management biases. For example, consider the interesting economic and social implications of the *News Front* finding that "by the eye-opening ratio of 94 to six percent . . . those queried felt an antipathy to moving into the 'central city of a metropolitan area.'"[16] Although there are no doubt a variety of reasons for this avoidance, executive biases almost certainly play a part. Such an antipathy toward the older, more troubled central cities is consistent with Maccoby's observation that:

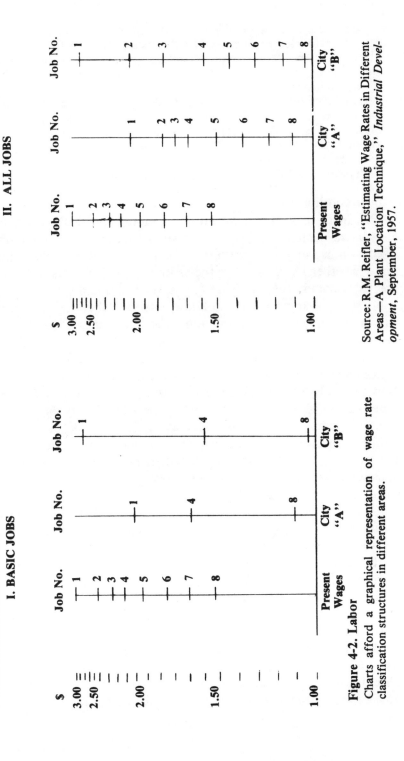

Figure 4-2. Labor
Charts afford a graphical representation of wage rate
classification structures in different areas.

Source: R.M. Reifler, "Estimating Wage Rates in Different
Areas—A Plant Location Technique," *Industrial Development*, September, 1957.

"Corporate managers do not hear the cries beause they have created protected enclaves where they can separate themselves. These enclaves, these isolated villages, grow up wherever there are large corporations. Indeed, corporations move out to the suburbs in order to build enclaves . . . .The enclave protects a person from himself and the world. Many an American manager has moved from city to suburb to leave the violence and decay, taking no responsibility for improving the city. Because he lives in an enclave, he continues fearful of those outside the walls who may be envious of him. Isolated from the poor, he lacks understanding (not to speak of compassion) about why they are poor and how the corporate system isolates them and insures their continued poverty."[17]

This in turn is consistent with the importance of the "executive convenience" factor in location decisions.[18] A president of a modest sized firm in a major midwestern city commented that he really didn't know whether his move from the central city to a far eastern suburb created a commuting hardship for most of his employees. He never really thought about it. He did know, however, that the new site was within two miles of his own home and the homes of his two vice presidents.

The antipathy toward the central city also has implications for a firm's social responsibilities. In discussing the urban desolation that is New York City's South Bronx, the *Wall Street Journal* recently noted that "job hunger is so great that this spring when the city took applications for temporary summer jobs paying $50 a week, thousands of young people camped out all night at the application centers to get first crack at the jobs . . ."[19] To what extent do firms both intensify social ills and overlook potential manpower pools by not dealing directly with their own inherent biases?

Finally, to end this discussion of the labor factor in industrial location, two very practical points should be emphasized. First, because of the usual lack of good, recent comparable data and because of the emotionalism involved, it is mandatory that the site selection team be as open and objective as possible; suggestions on being "objectively judgmental" are contained in the final chapter. Second, when compiling labor cost data, the ideal solution is to factor in not only wage rates but also fringe benefits (which may account for 25 percent of the total labor costs), and to adjust the figures for productivity (including anticipated output per man-hour, work stoppages, absenteeism, etc.). Total labor costs not only allow for meaningful area-to-area comparisons, but, perhaps even more importantly, allow the labor factor to be more directly compared with the other relevant location factors. As always, labor is only one factor in the locational matrix; techniques for assessing it in context are explored in Part III.

B. Agglomeration and Infrastructure

Agglomeration is an umbrella term which applies to the economic advantages which accrue to a firm by locating in an area which contains a number of related industries, and/or in a large city or metropolitan area. The former are sometimes called "localization economies," and the latter are commonly termed "urbanization economies." These advantages result from sufficient magnitudes of activity within an area to permit the continued existence of specialized beneficial activities external to the firm, thus they are termed "external economies" Although generally more critical for small plants which find it impossible to provide many essential services themselves, all manufacturing facilities are to some extent influenced by external economies.

The localization economies resulting from location near similar or related industries are neatly summarized by Smith;

> "The advantages to a new firm of a location among other firms engaged in the same activity are fairly obvious. An existing industrial concentration may contain a pool of labor with particular skills, or special educational institutions geared to the needs of the industry in question, both of which will help the firm to reduce the cost of training its workers. Firms may also join together to develop a research institute, a marketing organization and other collective facilities that individual manufacturers would be unable to provide for themselves. In addition, a city or region specializing in one industry will often have machine makers and repairers, suppliers of components, containers and so on, and other industries ancillary to the main one and providing goods and services for it. All these benefits of agglomeration, when added together, may offer a firm considerable cost advantages over alternative locations."[20]

The urbanization economies are generally positively related to city size. The larger and more well developed the urban complex, the more likely it is to offer a complete and competitive infrastructure. The most critical infrastructure elements are transportation facilities, including roads, trucking firms, railroads and airports; utilities; specialized business services; and also "more favorable insurance and capital supply costs, . . . the economies inherent in the larger size of public facilities, and in the broader base of instutions, including schools, technical training centers, research institutions and cultural organizations, that the larger urban area can provide."[21]

On a local and regional scale manufacturers are strongly attracted to areas which possess a good industrial infrastructure. It is the rare firm which is large enough to supply very many of its own external facilities such as water, sewer, electricity, roads, railroads or major fire protection. Even more rare is the firm that wishes to provide these facilities. The vast majority find subscribing to communal facilities through taxes and rates more economical. Planned areas in which such facilities are conveniently grouped and scaled for industry are especially attractive to small-and-medium-sized plants. These groupings, plus adequate land use planning and requisite zoning, explain the popularity of industrial parks. An assessment of the quantity and quality of the local infrastructure should be concomitant with the consideration of local tax loads.

Although it is normally true that the more activity in an area the more agglomeration advantages it will enjoy, this is not always the case. There are *dis*-economies of scale. As possible disadvantages of too large a community. Hunker notes traffic congestion, overcrowding and inter-industry competition for sites, labor and supplies, all of which may act to drive up costs.[22] Similarly, Smith comments that "the forces of 'deglomeration' are leading many firms to leave the inner city for what they consider to be better sites outside."[23] From a study of the intraurban locations of new plants, Cameron states:

". . . that new plants as a whole tended to settle farther away from the core of the central city, (and) it has also been shown that for any given industry, there was a strong likelihood that the new plants would replicate the pattern of their parent industries with regard to access to the center. The most plausible explanation of these findings is that the average new establishment in a centrally located industry is unable to compete for the highly limited supply of available space against the average existing user of space within the same industry and against other users of centralized space. However, the economic advantages of the locale of the parent industry are such that new plants, on average, seek to be as close to this locale as possible. The corollary also follows. New establishments in industries which are already decentralized and/or scattered repeat this pattern and avoid the high rent cluster in and around the central core. We are therefore forced to reject the conclusion that new activity locates in a random fashion. Similarly, we are forced to eject the crude notions that all new plants locate in low cost decentralized locations, or that all new plants require the external economies of a central cluster."[24]

Another unwelcome attribute of over centralization is pollution. Both Smith[25] and Hunker[26] comment on the public policy problem of private industry passing on some of its real costs to the community at large. Equally important, however, is that high densities, especially of industry and automobiles, tend to overwhelm the abilities of the natural air and water systems to cleanse themselves. The old dictum; "the solution to pollution is dilution," cannot hold in densely populated areas. Increasingly, manufacturers are going to be required to limit their effluents and pay their share of the costs of enhancing and maintaining the physical environment.

While the external economies (and dis-economies) of scale are very real, it is virtually impossible to offer generalizations of much use to a specific site search. It is incumbent upon the locating firm to study its normal modes of operation and the projected modes for the proposed plant to identify those facilities and services (1) which will be provided by the firm itself (internal economies), (2) those which must be provided externally, by the community and (3) those which may be provide either internally or externally. Most critical are categories (2) and (3). A simple matching of the mandatory external facilities and services with those provided at the alternative locations under consideration will indicate those places which are viable. More tricky is trying to decide the magnitudes of any costs penalties involved in supplying internally or importing any services not provided in an area. Here it is necessary to operate by company analogs if available and to try to share the experiences of other manufacturers. Caution must be exercised since firms often underestimate the real costs of internalizing services. When contemplating the importation of services (or, sending jobs outside the region), careful consideration must be given to increased transportation costs, predictably slower delivery, storage costs and less personalized attention.

C. Power

The location of industry is less dependent on the location of power sources—water, wind, fossil fuels, atomic energy—than it was 100 years ago. Even 100 years ago, most manufacturing was not located primarily with reference to access to local power sources; rather the market, labor and technology factors which mainly influenced the location of industry caused local power sources to be intensively utilized. On a world or national scale there are far more water power sites or good coal resources which have never attracted industry than those which have become heavily utilized in manufacturing processes. In short, the locational influence of power sources traditionally has been over emphasized. Since inanimate energy is an essential ingredient in manufacturing, the clear conclusions are that (1) power is relatively ubiquitous over space, and (2) power and fuels move to manufacturing points located primarily by other criteria. Of course, the future may be different, especially if access to premium fuels, such as natural gas, is critical, but the second is the more normal situation for most plants.

In the latter half of the 20th century, externally generated electric energy is the most important inanimate power source for the vast majority of industries. Within the United States the electrification of virtually the entire country, the interlocking distribution grids of the electric utility companies, and the low-cost of transporting electric energy have combined to make power a relatively minor location variable.

Of course, there are some industries which use such large amounts of energy that the availability and costs of power have always been important location factors. Aluminum refineries, electro-chemical processes and synthetic fiber plants are examples. It is also true that there are spatial variations in the quality of electric service and in the costs of purchasing power. Thus, even firms for which power is not a key location factor find it important to calculate the variable costs of energy. Without these calculations, the cost/profit analysis of a proposed investment is incomplete. Conway Publications' "Checklist of Site Selection Factors" contains 31 items to be considered when assessing energy.[27]

It is beyond the scope of this volume to provide examples for specific industries or a detailed map of the geography of purchased power costs. Power requirements and costs are relatively easily measured, so site seekers are much better advised to utilize plant specific analogs than to rely on generalized figures. Since for most manufacturing processes purchased power is not a key location variable, the analysis is simplified by allowing the more important variables to specify the viable alternative locations. Then, the checklist can be filled in with the cooperation of the utility companies in those relatively few locations under serious consideration.

So much for the situation as it now exists for most manufacturers, and, indeed, as it has existed for the past several decades. The traditional emphases have been on costs (rates) and quality of service. But what of the future? Although there is considerable debate over causes,[28] the national and world-wide "energy crisis" is very real. The probability of interruption is becoming the critical quality calculation; and for many nervous about the future, availability supersedes costs. Indeed, continuity and availability considerations are making power a much more important locational variable than ever before.

The manufacturing sector consumes over one-quarter of all the inanimate energy produced in the United States. The primary sources of this power are the traditional fossil fuels—coal, petroleum and natural gas— and there are few indications that the dependence on these sources will diminish in the near future. The alternatives of hydropower, solar energy, geo-thermal energy, etc., are simply not presently viable, either because of spatial maldistribution, or excessively high costs, or technical difficulties. Nor has the bright promise of the 1950s of ubiquitous power based on atomic energy been fulfilled. Large scale generation of nuclear power in areas of demand faces formidable technological, safety and environmental hurdles which may or may not be solved. Certainly, nuclear energy offers no short-term solution.

Petroleum is a modestly abundant fossil fuel. Although many predict that at present rates of consumption the world will run dangerously short of oil within the next 100 years, the future is clouded by debates over accurate measurement of reserves and by the possibilities of finding new fields. It is possible to adopt a more limited, selfish point of view wherein 100 years in the future is too far away to worry about. Such a stance, however, does not even solve more immediate problems. Many of the problems of predicting industrial expansion based on petroleum stem from the fact that petroleum supply is more determined by politics than economics. Within the United States the intertwining of petroleum and politics has a long history; examples include trust busting, production quotas, depletion allowances and taxation policies. Equally important is the fact that almost all major industrialized nations are net importers of oil. The exporting nations, through the development of a strong cartel, greatly influence the prices and availability of petroleum supplies in most manufacturing areas. It is almost certain that petroleum prices will continue to rise, both as natural reserves are depleted and as existing supplies are manipulated, and that continuity of shipments will become increasingly uncertain. Also, it is quite possible that in the longer run there will be pressure to limit the utilization of petroleum for manufacturing power so to take advantage of its portable character in transportation uses.

Although natural gas rarely enters inter-national commerce, its production and consumption is also strongly influenced by political forces. Within the United States the price regulation of gas which enters interstate commerce has discouraged exploitation of reserves, produced spatial supply and demand imbalances and encouraged utilization within producing states. We now have the situation where some manufacturers have deliberately opted for the higher prices in gas producing states to ensure adequate service. However, even if federal deregulation should provide a temporary respite, there appears little doubt that natural gas is a relatively scarce resource. Natural gas is a preferred fuel for both industrial and domestic uses because of its transportability, efficiency and cleanliness. There will be increasing pressure to curtail its utilization for ordinary industrial functions so to preserve it for "higher" uses. Equally certain is an increase in cost.

Coal is the most abundant of all the fuels. A corner stone of United States energy policy is a return to coal as the primary energy source. The increased utilization of coal, however, also faces major obstacles. In the short run, industry conversion costs will be high, affecting productivity, competitiveness, costs and inflation, and the coal industry will take considerable time to significantly increase production. Furthermore, coal remains a bulky, expensive to ship commodity. For the longer run, we are faced with the dilemma that our most abundant reserves are high-sulphur coals which, while containing a relatively good thermal potential, are at the same time heavy contributors to air pollution. If the negative environmental consequences of increased coal utilization (including both air pollution and strip-mining effects) can be ameliorated with reasonable costs, then the nation's coal producing regions will be more attractive industrial areas. To the extent that the coal resources are transformed into easily transported electric energy fed into a national grid, then we are likely to have a continuation of current conditions wherein power is not a major industrial location variable. But the future is by no means certain.

While the site selector is cautioned not to overreact to the energy crisis, there is no doubt that procurement of an uninterrupted power supply is an increasingly important consideration. "Already, utilities in some parts of the country have been forced to discourage new industrial investments in which large consumption of energy raw materials—natural gas especially—would take place."[29] The three articles in *Industrial Facilities Planning* which most explicitly deal with energy considerations illustrate the changing emphasis. Richardson's 1962 article[30] places emphasis on actions utilities should take to attract and hold industry. In contrast, the 1975 Puerto Rican example[31] emphasizes conservation, and Rossiter's 1973 article suggests ways of dealing with petroleum shortages. Rossiter's recommendations are worthy of note. Site selectors should strive for:

(1) "Fuel Flexibility—A plant that can interchangeably use several types of energy forms will be best equipped to live through periodic shortages of any given type. The capability of utilizing a combination of two or three of the following sources would be desirable: Gas, light fuel oil, heavy fuel oil, high sulfur fuel oil, coal slurry and crude oil ...,"

(2) "Receiving Flexibility—A facility that is capable of receiving its petroleum supplied by a large number of methods is, likewise better able to cope with any temporary shortage. Here we are speaking of truck, rail, water and—in some cases—pipeline ...,"

(3) "Increased Storage—It also follows that a facility which can accommodate larger individual receipts can better ride out shortages. This additional investment should be worthy of your consideration.

(4) "Proximity to Supply—The closer to the source, the more secure the supply ...,"

(5) "Commitment—longer term contracts—if you can—with multiple suppliers in," and

(6) "Shipping Flexibility—As with receiving flexibility, if your facility is located such that its products can be shipped via several transportation means, it can enjoy some additional measure of security from petroleum shortages."[32]

Under government pressure, many companies are now converting from oil and gas back to coal as a plant fuel. This costly conversion process has many significant implications for the structure and operating procedures of U.S. industry, but the short-run locational effects are likely to be small. In the longer run, however, the expense of coal-fired plant construction could halt the trend toward the dispersal of small plants and encourage the development of fewer, larger facilities. This will also have area development impacts, and hurt small towns' drives for industry.[33] Hunker concisely summarizes the unsettled status of power as an industrial location factor:

". . . the energy crisis threatens to reshape certain established locational practices, due to (1) the lack of a necessary and traditional energy source in a given region, (2) the need to relocate industry in order to obtain more efficiently an alternative energy source, and (3) the need to change production processes (uses) to adjust to changing energy supplies with resultant increased costs of operation. Behind the scenes is the concern of the environmentalist whose pressures relative to questions of environmental degradation have affected the location of power plants and new industrial facilities. How the nation achieves balance among its energy needs, industrial growth, and the goals of the environmentalists for a cleaner and healthier society will have considerable impact on the future distribution of economic activity in this country."[34]

D. Water

Water, like energy, traditionally has not been a major locational variable in industrial location. This is not because water is unimportant; precisely the opposite. Because water is an essential ingredient for all life, locations otherwise attractive to industry also have had adequate water supplies. The vast majority of manufacturing plants can be satisfied by the ubiquitous water supply and sewage disposal systems concomitant with any industrially developed area. The historic (and continuing) problems urban areas experience with water supply and effluent disposal primarily have been problems of underinvestment in facilities rather than absolute water shortages. Spatial variations in water costs are usually insignificant in the locational calculus.

Even for those industries which require huge amounts of water for processing and waste disposal, or those dependent on water transportation, water, like energy is commonly a permissive factor. Either the required stream flow or harbor facilities are available, or they are not. The locational process is simply one of eliminating all areas without the necessary characteristics. Water cost differences among viable alternative locations are usually insignificant.

This is not to say that water costs can be completely ignored. They must be included in a complete investment analysis. Water and sewage rates should be compared; variations in plant treatment costs to incoming water due to areal differences in quality, and variations in effluent treatment costs must be factored in. The "Checklist of Site Selection Factors" list 36 separate water and waste disposal items for consideration under the subheading of (1) Regional Water Situation, (2) Local Water Supply, (3) Surface Water-Streams and Lakes, (4) Ground Water-Wells, (5) Sewage Disposal and (6) Solid Waste Disposal.[35] It is significant that only four of the 36 items are concerned directly with costs; the majority relate to adequacy, relability, quality and legal regulations.

Again like energy, water is becoming a more important locational attribute. The key concerns are (1) the future adequacy of regional water supplies and (2) water pollution problems. The situation of the metropolitan Washington, D.C. region may serve to illustrate the first of these two issues.

The nation's seventh largest metropolitan region, including the District of Columbia and large adjacent areas of Maryland and Virginia, has sustained steady and often rapid growth. Although the region abuts the Chesapeake Bay and receives an above average annual rainfall (over 40 inches), it faces severe water shortages. The problem is not the mere existence of water, but rather easily accessible water of the right kind at the right time. The problem is that the present system is taxed by too many people and too many activities.

The U.S. Army Corps of Engineers still argues, as it has for years, that the water supply problems of the Washington area could be alleviated by the additional construction of upstream reservoirs. Although no doubt of potential benefit, the Corps scheme runs afoul of some environmental concerns, would be costly in terms of time and money and would only be a short run solution. The simple fact is that the major water source, the Potomac River, has a limited capacity. Water is a renewable resource, but the total amount in the world is fixed, finite. Only so much can be extracted from surface or underground sources before steam flows are reduced to dangerously low levels or the ground water table is so depleted that a host of related environmental problems emerge.

Although the depletion of water supplies is normally a slow, insidious process, the dependence of modern society on central water systems can be dramatically illustrated by an unusual event which occurred in the Maryland suburbs of Washington on July 6, 1977. On that Wednesday morning there was a fire in the pumping station which supplies water to virtually all of populous Prince Georges and Montgomery counties. Residents were urged to practice conservation, and outside water uses, such as lawn watering and car washing, were forbidden. Perhaps even more important from the viewpoint of facility planners was that many firms and offices were ordered closed for several days, both to conserve water and because of inadequate fire protection. In time of environmental stress, the burden of conservation always falls first on factories and offices; limited resources are reserved for residential consumption. The dollar value of the lost time is incalculable.

The key lesson for the site selector is that an inadequate water supply in a region spells trouble. The prudent investigator will assess present facilities, investment policies and plans (including the thorny political jurisdiction issues which may impede development), alternative supply services, the ratio of use to supply ("reserves") and regional growth trends. Some areas may face slow growth policies due to supply problems. The Washington, D.C., area is but one example of an area which may face such restruction. Many others, including the southwestern United States and especially southern California, appear even closer to imposed growth restructions.

The second major issue of increasing concern is that of water pollution. Firms which traditionally had to make modest investments for treating incoming water are finding increased expenditures necessitated by declines in water quality. Firms which had normally considered waste disposal into streams an almost free good, are now faced with considerable effluent treatment expenditures. The impact of the increasingly stringent environmental protection policies, of which water is but one part, are examined more fully in Chapter 5. For the moment, suffice it to note that there are wide spatial variations in the severity of environmental problems and natural resource availability. Generally, the severity of the problem (but not necessarily the solution) is directly related to the density of population and industry and the rapidity of regional growth.

E. Quality of Life

The legendary industrial baron, and his associated labor force, endured the dirty, overcrowded manufacturing city as a price willingly paid for industrial growth and relative prosperity. As the industrial economy has matured and affluence has increased and spread, the tolerance level has declined. Increasingly, the local living environment has become an important consideration in attracting and holding a productive, stable and loyal work force. The quality of the living environment perhaps has even more influence on decision-making managers. For example, the policy of one of the world's leading corporations of never locating a manufacturing plant in a town of under 30,000 population is directly related to the company policy of promoting managers from within the firm. They consider the amenities normally available in isolated small towns to be incompatible with the needs of managers sufficiently sophisticated to eventually rise to top level positions.

Thus, for many reasons, quality of life emerges as a locational criterion of some importance. Unfortunately, it also is an emotional, value-laden issue which defies precise definition and measurement. One person's amenity is another's boredom. Furthermore, there are very sharp local variations; there is no region that does not have within it both relatively desirable and undesirable areas. Dollar calculations of quality of life are virtually impossible.

Regardless of the difficulties, variations in quality of life are of sufficient interest to warrant serious attention. A first step is to identify the appropriate ingredients. Most commonly employed are statistics on labor force participation, unemployment, income and poverty, educational levels and facilities, health care, marriage and divorce rates, cultural and recreational facilities, and crime. A good example of these "indicators" is published annually in the *Site Selection Handbook*.[36] The Midwest Research Institute of Kansas City, Mo., presents another view of state quality of life rankings based on 117 individual measures grouped into the nine major components of (1) Individual Status, (2) Individual Equality, (3) Living Conditions, (4) Agriculture, (5) Technology, (6) Economic Status, (7) Education, (8) Health and Welfare and (9) State and Local Governments.[37]

Griffin and Dee offer an interesting procedure for qualifying the intangible which they argue is more comprehensive than the statistical quality of life study produced by *Harpers Magazine*.[38] Their study is noteworthy for several reasons, including: (1) it focuses on a metropolitan area rather than a state; (2) it utilizes easily obtainable data; (3) it is replicable and statistically sophisticated; (4) it relates volatile social, economic and environmental data to more constant, prosaic and easily measured physical characteristics. The procedure is summarized as follows:

> "The index is based on seven quality of life indicators and is developed through using a Principal Components Analysis. This index is then related to the physical characteristics of a city. Nine physical characteristics are used to describe a city. Six of these characteristics are urban land uses; the other three are city size, population and population density. The relationship between the quality of life and these physical characteristics is determined using a multivariate analysis technique called AID. The results are displayed graphically in a Quality of Life Nomogram which can then be used to determine the quality of life of other cities.

> As noted, the objective of this paper is to determine the relationship between quality of life and a city's physical characteristics. To accomplish this objective, it was necessary to develop a methodology to measure quality of life and to determine which physical characteristics of a city best determine various levels of quality. A four-step methodology was developed and included:

> —Determination of quality of life indicators;
> —Reduction of indicators to a composite quality of life index (QLI) using Principal Components Analysis;
> —Identification of physical characteristics of a city; and
> —Determination of relationship between QLI and physical characteristics".[39]

Although certainly provocative and perhaps potentially useful under controlled conditions, the Griffin and Dee procedure produces its own set of problems. As always, the results are controlled by the selection and measurement of the component variables; are these really significant? The procedure relies on statistical relationships and binary classification; are important nuances obscured? The total "character" of a city changes more rapidly than its physical characteristics; are the physical measurements sufficiently sensitive? Is the city as a spatial frame sufficiently detailed? How are the normal advantages of smaller cities, such as ease of access, to be balanced against the advantages, such as a major symphony, which can only be offered in large metropolitan areas? Finally, as with all indexing and classification schemes, individual results are debatable; certainly there are many who would not easily accept, for example, the very low ranking of Los Angeles, relative to the top ranking Allentown, Pa.

The quality of life in an area remains intangible, impossible to measure to everyone's (anyone's?) satisfaction. Statistical indicators and composite indices may provide a framework, but this should be tempered with sensitive field investigation. While in the field, caution also must be exercised against being taken in by the inevitable town boosters, or being put off by those equally inevitable souls who always find the grass greener somewhere else. Finally, and most importantly, assessments of variations in quality of life must be put in context with the other relevant location variables. Sophisticated judgmental decision making is required.

Notes and References—Chapter 4

1. See, for example, Yaseen, Leonard C. *Plant Location.* New York: American Research Council, 1960, p. 62.

2. Chintz, Benjamin, and Vernon, Raymond. "Changing Forces in Industrial Location," *Harvard Business Review,* January-February, 1960, p. 136.

3. Yaseen, Leonard C. *Industrial Development in a Changing World.* New York: Thomas Y. Crowell Co., 1975, p. 39.

4. The Conference Board, "Labor Productivity," *Road Maps of Industry,* No. 1792, October, 1976.

5. Yaseen, Leonard C., 1960, *op. cit.,* p. 65.

6. *Ibid,* pp. 71-74.

7. Hunker, Henry L. *Industrial Development.* Lexington, Mass.: Lexington Books.© 1974 by D.C. Heath and Co. All rights reserved., pp. 113-114.

8. Smith, David M. *Industrial Location.* New York: John Wiley & Sons, Inc., 1971, p. 52.

9. *Ibid.,* p. 292.

10. Roterus, Victor, and Szot, Thomas. "Map Showing Wage Levels Permits Area Comparisons;" *Arizona Review,* December, 1974, p. 9.

11. Smith, David M., *op. cit.,* pp. 48-49 and pp. 290-291.

12. *Ibid.,* p. 46.

13. Yaseen, Leonard C., 1960, *op. cit.,* p. 47.

14. *Ibid.,* p. 58.

15. Reifler, Ronald M. "Estimating Wage Rates in Different Areas - A Plant Location Technique," *Industrial Development,* September, 1957, pp. 5-10.
16. "Perspective on Plant Location in the U.S.," *NewsFront,* March/ April, 1972, p. 50.
17. Maccoby, Michael. *The Gamesman.* New York: Simon and Schuster, 1976, pp. 200-201
18. Stafford, Howard A. "The Anatomy of the Location Decision: Content Analysis of Case Studies." Reproduced with permission from *Spatial Perspectives on Industrial Organization and Decision-making,* F.E. Ian Hamilton (ed.), p. 182. Copyright © 1974 by John Wiley & Sons, Ltd., London.
19. Simpson, Janice, and Reveron, Derek. "On Gutted Kelly Street, Vandalism and Arson Aren't Anything New," *The Wall Street Journal,* July 20, 1977, p. 24.
20. Smith, David M., *op. cit.,* p. 83.
21. Hunker, Henry L., *op. cit.,* p. 155.
22. *Ibid.,* p. 156.
23. Smith, David M., *op. cit.,* p. 87.
24. Cameron, Gordon C. "Intraurban Location and the New Plant," *Papers of the Regional Science Association,* Vol. XXXI, 1973, p. 142.
25. Smith, David M., *op. cit.,* p. 88.
26. Hunker, Henry L., *op. cit.,* p. 156.
27. "Checklist of Site Selection Factors," *Site Selection Handbook.* Vol. XXII, No. 1. Atlanta: Conway Publications, 1977, p. 64.
28. For example, see: Hines, Lawrence C. "Energy-A Contest Between Demand and Supply," *Environmental Issues.* New York: W.W. Norton & Co., Inc., 1973, pp. 165-194; Zarb, Frank "The Seven Truths of Energy," *The Wall Street Journal,* September 10, 1975; "The 'Energy Crisis' Explained," *The Wall Street Journal,* May 27, 1977; "We Have Energy . . . Or Do We?." *Site Selection Handbook, op. cit.,* Vol. XXII, No. 2, 1977, pp. 98-100; Odom, Howard T. "Energy, Ecology and Economics," *Industrial Development,* January/February, 1974 (in *Industrial Facilities Planning, op. cit.,* pp. 229-236).
29. Hunker, Henry L., *op. cit.,* p. 99.

30. Richardson, P.L. "Purchased Power-Its Importance in Site Studies," *Industrial Development,* February, 1962. (In *Industrial Facilities Planning, op. cit.,* pp. 166-168).

31. "Puerto Rico's Uncommonly Good Energy Conservation Checklist," *Industrial Development,* September/October, 1975. (In *Industrial Facilities Planning, op. cit.,* pp. 160-166.).

32. Rossiter, John S. "Petroleum Shortages and Facility Planning," *Industrial Development,* September/October, 1973. (In *Industrial Facilities Planning, op. cit.,* pp. 155-159).

33. Winter, Ralph S. "Industry Shifts to Coal as Government Forces Oil, Gas Conservation," *The Wall Street Journal,* August 15, 1977 p. 1.

34. Hunker, Henry L., *op. cit.,* p. 101.

35. "Checklist of Site Selection Factors," *op. cit.,* p. 64.

36. *Site Selection Handbook, op. cit.*

37. "Western States Have Edge on 'Quality of Life'," *Industrial Development,* March/April, 1974. (In *Industrial Facilities Planning, op. cit.,* pp. 226-228.)

38. Louis, A. M. "The Worst American City," *Harpers Magazine,* January, 1975.

39. Griffin, John N., and Dee, Norbert. "Measuring the Intangible: How to Quantify Quality of Life," *Industrial Development,* September/October, 1975. (In *Industrial Facilities Planning, op. cit.,* pp. 219-225.).

V Governmental Influences

V
Governmental Influences

A manufacturing company operates within a business environment which is composed of customers, suppliers, competitors, employees, stockholders, machinery and technology. It also operates within a wider societal context which includes a multitude of diverse, and often conflicting, influences over and above the more immediate concerns of the market place and the means of production. The societal concerns are most explicitly expressed through the larger society's primary mechanism of control, government. Governmental influences on the location of manufacturing may be conveniently classified into the categories of costs, incentives and regulations. Because they reflect the complexities and contradictions of society, governmental influences are impossible to chart in any comprehensive and coherent way. Accordingly, this chapter attempts only partial coverage of the more prominent governmental influences on plant site selection. It is hoped that site selectors will be reminded of the important issues and have some useful insights which may be transferred and elaborated in a specific planning context.

A. Taxes

A primary way in which society, through its governmental agencies, impinges directly on the cost of doing business is by levying taxes. Even the variety of taxation schemes is confusing, including types directly of concern to business, such as the property tax on facilities and inventories, corporate income and franchising taxes, various licensing taxes and severance taxes. Also of potential concern are the less direct levies, including personal income and sales taxes.[1] Adding to the confusion is that various taxes are collected by the hierarchy of governments—local, state and federal. Furthermore, business taxes must be viewed not only as dues paid to support society's multitudinous activities but also as fees paid for services rendered. It seems to be beyond the wits of either business or government to precisely calculate the specific benefit/cost ratios of the governmental provision of collective services (e.g., roads, sewers, employment agences, education, etc.) which businesses either cannot or do not provide for themselves.

Conway Publications' annual "Checklist of Site Selection Factors" lists as items to be considered under Local Taxes the following: Property Taxes (including tax rates for last five years, method of tax assessment and equalization, balance between tax loads on industrial, commercial and residential property, amount of tax-free property in area, local tax revenue per capita); School Taxes; Local Sales or Use Tax; Local License Taxes; and Comparison of local tax load with services rendered. State tax items to be checked include: Personal Income Tax; Corporate Income Tax; Sales, Use or Payroll Taxes; Unemployment Compensation Tax; Workmen's Compensation Tax; Inventory, Machinery and Equipment Taxes; Franchise and Incorporation taxes; Gasoline, Liquor and Tobacco Taxes, and Vehicle and other license fees.[2] This is a formidable list, the details of which can only be specified for a particular locality.

The difficulties in sorting out the labyrinth of taxes and taxes laws, and in measuring the place-to-place variations in the benefit/costs relations between services provided by the tax bills makes the locational influence of taxes as much an emotional issue as a financial issue. Although there is general agreement among experts that taxes should not be a major locational factor, in actual case studies taxes are very frequently mentioned as important variables. This conflict between theory and reality is indicated by the selections included in *Industrial Facilities Planning*.[3] Of the 22 case studies (summarized in Chapter 2 of this book) taxes are specifically mentioned as a location variable in 15. In terms of sheer count, this places "taxes" as a first rank factor, along with markets, materials, labor, transportation facilities, utilities and community living conditions. On the other hand, there is only one article included which delves into the complexities of comparing tax loads, and even here the conclusion is that "the prospective manufacturing firm . . . must still do its own homework . . . In the long run, factors such as weather, working conditions, labor supply, sources of raw materials and transportation costs, may, after all, play a much more significant part."[4]

Indeed, the "manufacturing firm must do its own homework." It is difficult to even guess with any degree of precision the tax loads of a manufacturing operation without knowing such specifics as type and size of plant, materials needed and products produced, scheduling and inventory, operating financial statements and the actual location of the facility. Given the variations between firms and between localities, plus the complexities of tax laws, any observations applicable to industry in general are especially hazardous. Regardless, some tentative generalizations may be instructive:

1. There is a natural human tendency toward a negative view of taxation. To be fair to both government and to itself, business must take the positive view that taxes are fees for services provided. They are the costs associated with the advantages of agglomeration. In general, higher taxes are indicators of more and better public services. The critical question is whether a higher cost location has commensurately higher benefits. Unfortunately, this is an exceedingly difficult question to answer.

2. Taxes may be an important business cost and should be included in a complete financial analysis to determine if a proposed project will provide an adequate return on investment (as in the capital budgeting framework of Chapter 10).

3. Regardless of their magnitude, taxes which do not exhibit spatial variation are unimportant in deciding between alternative locations. For example, if all the prospective sites are within the United States, then federal taxes are not locationally significant. This is true for state level taxes if all prospective sites are within the same state. Generally, variations in local and state taxes are locationally most critical. Always, the key locational issue is the *differential* from place to place.

4. Taxes are not always what they seem. There are a variety of exceptions to the nominally legislated tax rates. These concessions vary from place to place and take the forms of tax moratoriums, special exemptions, tax credits, discretionary devices and differing assessment procedures. Determining tax rates is somewhat akin to negotiating freight rates, and an accurate picture cannot be obtained without knowing the specifics of plant, locality and timing. (Prudent site selectors will interview manufac-

turers already in localities of interest to determine prevailing local practices.)

5. Tax types, rates and methods of assessment change over time. For example, although the property tax is now the largest single business tax in most areas, it is predicted that its relative importance will decline.[5] Also, because taxes are legislated, they are sometimes especially vulnerable to change in the prevailing political climate. Thus, tax advantages should be discounted to some degree, especially in areas with a volatile history. Investor beware!

6. There is some tendency for tax burdens to balance out. States with higher stated rates on certain items (e.g., property tax) may provide for more exemptions. Localities in high tax states may have low municipal taxes, and vice-versa. It is essential that a potential location not be ruled out because of relatively high taxes at one level; the complete tax burden (e.g., state plus local) must be calculated for adequate assessment.

7. Although tax differentials normally account for a very small proportion of business costs, they tend to loom unduly large in the public and business consciousness. This is because taxes are emotional issues, hard to quantify and compare, and because they are decided in the public arena. Politicians often use them to attract attention. Business sometimes publically complains because they are one of the few business cost items over which the public has any direct control.

8. Hunker reports that "Maurice Fulton, of the Fantus organization, indicates that industrialists often use taxes as rationalization for their opposition to labor unions and other costs, real or imagined, in a region. They tend to associate all of these with an unsatisfactory regional image. Despite this, Fulton goes on to state, based on his company's studies, that 'it is apparent that in every case state taxes are the least significant of all factors.'"[6] If taxes are taken as indicators of an area's "political climate" for industry, then their importance as a locational decision variable is much increased; whether such "indicators" are of any real value is a highly debatable question, about which there is little supporting evidence. Regardless of the propaganda value of taxes to area developers trying to lure new industry, or to manufacturers trying to influence the public, site selectors at least must try to be honest with themselves.

9. In spite of what manufacturers like to think, the location of a plant is not an unmixed blessing to the community chosen. Net fiscal impact (the difference between the new plant's contribution to local government revenue and the costs to local government attributable to the new plant) may be positive or negative. One study found that "the establishment of new manufacturing plants in five rural towns in Kentucky during the period 1958-63 had a negative net fiscal impact on most of the affected local governmental units".[7] Most susceptible to a negative impact were school districts, closely followed by city governments. As Cumberland and van Beck have noted, there is "sufficient evidence to challenge the widely held view that 'industry pays its way.'"[8] Site selectors insensitive to the possible negative impacts of their project will not understand a more perceptive community's caution. Insensitive firms will not contribute to good communities, for others or for themselves.

In spite of the difficulties of comparing tax burdens and benefits, studies have been done which shed some light on the subject. One example is the previously noted study by Foster. After setting out a series of assumptions, Foster traces his procedures in some detail and provides realistic data for a hypothetical metal fabricating firm with plants in two states, each plant employing approximately 300 workers. The hypothetical corporation has total annual net sales of $11.7 million and total assets of $9 million. Calculations are based on the firm's fifth year of operation to obtain the relative tax burden of an ongoing company. State taxes are the primary focus, but local variations are incorporated by sampling eight different localities in each state to arrive at a state average. Dealing with levies and exemptions, Foster computes expected taxes for eight different states. Using maximum property tax exemptions, he finds for the total of state and local taxes a range of $47,837, from the Ohio high of $102,605 to the low for Mississippi of $54,768. This $47,837 maximum spatial variation represents 0.4 percent of net sales, 4.3 percent of net income before taxes, and 8.2 percent of net income after federal taxes.[9]

Smith summarizes a study by the Pennsylvania Economic League which attempted to determine the relative tax position for an imaginary corporation in 82 municipalities within a radius of 75 miles of Philadelphia. The firm employed 1,000 workers, had gross sales of $13.9 million and net income before taxes of $2.5 million. The study included state taxes, local taxes and local charges for water and sewage-disposal services. The summation of these at 1959 rates, produced a range from $31,000 to approximately $155,000, or a variation from the highest to lowest tax cost municipality of approximately $156,000. This maximum spatial variation represents 1.1 percent of sales and 6.2 percent of net income before taxes.[10]

Another example is provided by a study conducted by the Wisconsin Dept. of Revenue. After setting out limiting assumptions, and noting the rather large potentials for error, the department computed property tax, state income tax, sales tax, franchise/filing fee, and total state and local taxes for each of six different types of hypothetical manufacturing plants in each of 15 states. The total state and local taxes for a paper products plant varied from $973,873 in the highest tax cost state to $372,512 in the lowest. This spread represented 1.7 percent of the paper products plant's sales and 17.4 percent of net income before taxes. The comparable range for a fabricated metals products plant was $264,680 to $106,719, with the spatial variation representing 0.9 percent of sales and 9.2 percent of net income before taxes. Corporation #3, a machinery manufacturer, had a maximum state-to-state range of $335,673 to $136,921, the spread representing 1.1 percent of sales and 9.0 percent of net income before taxes.

A scientific instruments manufacturer was the fourth hypothetical firm considered. Here the range in total state and local taxes was from $220,572 for the highest tax cost state to $84,876 for the lowest. This spatial variation represented 1.3 percent of sales and 7.7 percent of net income before taxes. The fifth corporation, involved in food manufacturing and processing, would have faced a maximum between state tax range of $98,267 to $39,942, with the spread representing 0.4 percent of sales and 10.4 percent of net income before taxes. Calculations for a printer-publisher produced estimated total state and local taxes ranging from $1,392,996 to $560,768, with this difference representing 1.1 percent of sales and 10.8 percent of net income before taxes.[11]

What can be made of such studies? Obviously, estimated tax load variations depend on the type and size of company, the places chosen for comparison, and the methods and assumptions used in obtaining the estimations. They are all subject to considerable error. Regardless, the total amount of taxes to be paid runs into a sizable amount, especially if the even larger federal taxes are added to the state and local taxes. Likewise, spatial variations in tax loads, the crucial aspect when deciding between alternative locations, may be considerable. The

Wisconsin study noted that "the magnitude of variance of corporate tax liability among states is quite pronounced with the highest taxing state levying an average of 2.5 times more taxes than the lowest taxing state."[12]

On the other hand, the spatial variation in state and local taxes, that is, the amount of tax monies that could be saved by locating in the *lowest* tax area rather than the *highest* tax area, averages only about one percent of total sales. Furthermore, this one percent spread is likely to overstate the actual savings since at least some of the additional taxes may be expected to be returned via better services. Thus, a rule of thumb might be advanced. If one percent of projected sales dollars does not produce a figure in excess of the many other locational cost differentials, then a detailed and time consuming comparative study of taxes is not worth the effort in assessing locational advantages.

B. Incentives

What governments take away they also can give back and not necessarily in proportion to the taking away. In other words, for reasons such as maintaining a viable economy, shoring up economically distressed regions, national security, etc., governments at all levels may provide incentives to induce manufacturers to locate, or stay, in particular locations. These incentives most often take the form of (1) special tax relief, (2) government provision of special infrastructure (e.g., roads, utilities, etc.), and (3) subsidies, either direct as, for example, by building a plant, or indirect as, for example through lending money at less than market interest rates via revenue bond financing.

Conway Publications annually produces charts on "Financial Assistance for Industry," "Tax Incentives for Industry," "Special Services for Industrial Development,"[13] and "Industrial Revenue Bond Financing."[14] Those special provisions and services available are indicated for each state.

"Financial Assistance for Industry" notes such items as whether there is a state supported industrial development authority, state/county/city loans for building construction and/or for equipment and machinery, loan guarantees and special incentives for establishing industrial parks. Examples listed under "Tax Incentives" are corporate income tax exemptions, excise tax exemption, tax exemptions or moratoriums on improvements, inventories and goods in transit and tax stabilization agreements for specified industries.

The "Special Services for Industrial Development" chart indicates which states, for example, allow state financed speculative building, free land for industry, state funds for a variety of city and/or county projects, state recruiting, and screening of industrial employees (all do), help in training "hard-core" unemployed, and state assistance in bidding on federal procurement contracts.

The "Industrial Revenue Bond Financing" chart represents a category that has attracted much interest in recent years. The post World War II phenomenon of industrial development bonds, now legislated in most states, enjoyed dramatic growth in the 1960's as a means of financing facilities. The obvious attraction of IDB's is the "tax exempt nature of the bonds and the resulting interest rate differential between IDB's and conventional securities . . ."[15] Although growth slackened after the limits imposed by the 1968 Revenue Control and Expenditure Act (Peck and Swartz argue for modifying the present limitation[16]), the IDB may still be an important location variable. Just how important is debatable. The title of Lamberson's report on 119 Arkansas firms who used IDB financing perhaps best sums up the general position: "Industrial Development Bonds Can Tip The Balance in Site Selection." He concludes "that while the availability of IDB's many not be a strong consideration in selecting the geographic region for a plant, they definitely influence the firm's decisions in selecting a specific community within that region."[17] Also noted is that "one-third of these firms probably would not have located in Arkansas without the availability of industrial bond financing."[18] Conversely, of course, two-thirds would have. Perhaps of most interest to the site selector is Lamberson's observation that "it is unlikely that the users of IDB's have an important competitive advantage over nonusers."[19] This is because many firms using IDB's are required to or voluntarily make contributions in lieu of property taxes, and, more fundamentally, because IDB savings "when spread over the large numbers of units of output, would reduce unit costs by such a small amount that the effect on price would be non-existent."[20]

The complex and changing world of state and local incentives defies a comprehensive listing. As far as the site selector is concerned, these incentives properly should be viewed as attributes of areas. They can be assessed only in terms of specific areas and specific types of operations. Because it is difficult to ascertain precisely the values of the various inducements, and the complex trade-offs between areas, it is important that the site selector have a good idea of their real importance before becoming emotionally involved in any negotiations. The tail of governmental incentives must not be allowed to wag the dog of sound location principles. Even when incentives are attractive, it is necessary to try to balance the short-run and long-run advantages. Over the life of a factory, an area's programs encouraging retention and expansion of existing industry may be more important than one-shot incentives to initial location. Although a few areas, such as Baltimore, Maryland, have developed industrial retention plans, the general situation, unfortunately, "appears to reflect a conviction that full scale industrial retention activities with their associated costs are not a necessity for municipalities."[21]

How effective are the various area development schemes in attracting and holding industrial activity? There is no conclusive evidence to answer the question. Effectiveness varies according to types of incentives, areas and industries. In a sophisticated study of the Southern Georgian Bay Region of Ontario, Yeates and Lloyd concluded that, according to the criteria of increased productivity and demand for the region's output, the Area Development Agency program of the Canadian Dept. of Industry "can be considered highly successful."[22] On the other hand, regarding the post World War II industrial growth of the Southeastern U.S., Greenhut suggests that the economic development of the area might as well be explained by "natural growth" as by special incentives,[23] and Lee notes that many industries which utilized incentives would have located in the South in the absence of subsidies.[24]

Perhaps the most comprehensive study of regional industrial development incentives (and restrictions) has been conducted by the British House of Commons Trade and Industry Sub-Committee. Although there are some wide variations between types of industries and areas, two general conclusions are of particular interest: (1) "The proportion of smaller firms or projects influenced by financial incentives appeared to be higher than that of large firms," and (2) "The main advantage of regional financial incentives, at any rate as seen by larger firms, was to help offset the higher costs of locating in an assisted area, or improve profitability; they constituted a marginal bonus rather than a vital element."[25]

Area development agencies trumpet their governmental incentives. But like all advertising, this has to be judged with caution, in the context of the total locational calculus. Government incentives do not change the basic configurations of markets, materials or labor. The incentives are limited in magnitude, and the competition between areas reduce the relative advantage of any one. For these reasons, government incentives generally become locationally important only after the more major decisions are made. They then may "tip the balance" when "other things are equal," or be a "marginal bonus."

C. "Political Climate"

Giovanni Agnelli, Chairman of Italy's giant Fiat Group, was asked, "What about free enterprise?" His response was "What does free and independent mean these days? I'm not free any more. My prices, the technical characteristics of my autos, the locations, the settlements with unions—all are decided, or at least influenced by the state. My own judgment is a diminishing factor."[26]   Likewise, Estall & Buchanan state that "in no country now are industrialists completely independent of political decisions in making their own decisions about location."[27]

Because industrialists must operate in a political as well as economic context, inordinate amounts of worry are sometimes expended on questions of whether a given area has a political "climate" conducive to location or expansion of production. Of course, such worries may be quite legitimate. Foreign investments are particularly prone to political influences, such as ownership rules, supply and production constraints, duties and tariffs and threats of expropriation; *political instability* increases uncertainty and investment risk. Although normally less volatile, domestic politics also may pose important considerations. Thus, manufacturers look for "clues" to society's attitudes toward industry. The rates and structures of taxes and incentives are scrutinized. So too are existing legislation and legislative trends.

Keeping up with the complexities of legislation which has impacts on industrial location and production is difficult. Numerous business publications contain reports on the current status of legislation, especially at the federal and state levels. Virtually every issue of more specialized publications such as *Industrial Development*[28] contains such reports; *Industrial Development* includes an annual survey of "The 50 Legislative Climates," and its companion publication, *The Site Selection Handbook*[29] produces a "Geo-Political Index" issue which attempts to tell the site-seeker in which states, counties and cities the "welcome mat is out for new industry."

How important "political climate" should be in selecting sites is open to considerable debate, but there is evidence that these "issues of principle" do have an impact. For example, there is no conclusive evidence that "Right-to-Work" states necessarily have major locational advantages, but "The National Right to Work Committee has compiled statistics from the Dept. of Labor which show that the 19 (now 20) right-to-work states gained nearly a million new manufacturing jobs during the past decade, while the 31 compulsory union states lost nearly three-quarters of a million manufacturing jobs . . . California was the only compulsory unionism state in the top five (in increases).[30] As another example, Idaho's relatively fast growth in industrial employment is in part attibuted to its favorable "business climate," including not only a productive work force, but also a relatively low rate of unionism, a state university system that provides vocational and technical education, and taxes that are "among the lowest in the nation."[31]

What are the lessons for the site selector? Among the several possible suggestions, perhaps the first should be that an ill-defined, non-quantifiable issue such as "political climate" can easily become emotional, and caution must be exercised not to overemphasize its importance; a favorable political climate may facilitate business operations, and may even lower some costs, but it cannot change basic patterns of markets, materials and labor. Second, there is competition between areas for new industry so negotiation is possible; inquire before rejecting. Third, each industry, each firm and each area is to some extent unique; do not put too much faith in generalizations. Fourth, keep in mind that politics can be a dynamic game; as a small example consider the *Wall Street Journal* headline which proclaimed "California Gov. Brown Shifts Position, Begins to Woo New Business."[32] Finally, actions really are more important than words, and many small conveniences may be more important than one "super program;" a government agency which simplified paperwork to allow one form to take the place of 10 separate forms may be giving a clearer signal than an expensive advertising campaign.

D. The Environment[33]

Of all governmental actions which influence business, the most recent, perhaps the most complex, and with the most, as yet unknown, potentials, are those which deal with the protection of the environment. Concern for the environment, and legislative solutions, are not new, but the pace and scope have dramatically increased. The pacemaker for American concern for the environment is the 1969 National Environmental Policies Act.[34] It requires all agencies of the federal government to "include in every recommendation or report on proposals for legislation and other federal actions significantly affecting the quality of the human environment, a detailed statement by the responsible official on—

(i) the environmental impact of the proposed action.

(ii) any adverse environmental effects which cannot be avoided should the proposal be implemented.

(iii) alternatives to the proposed action.

(iv) the relationship between local short-term uses of man's environment and the maintenance and enhancement of long-term productivity, and

(v) any irreversible and irretrievable commitments of resources which would be involved in the proposed action, should it be implemented."[35]

The National Environmental Policies Act (NEPA) has no direct enforcement provisions. It derives its powers from two sources: 1) NEPA operates under the Office of the President and thus carries the weight of any influence the Executive Branch cares to exert; 2) any concerned citizen or group may bring suit to force federal agencies to comply with the intent of NEPA, and thus the courts and the judicial processes become major enforcement avenues.

Although NEPA is directly applicable only to federal agencies or projects requiring federal licenses, its influence is surprisingly pervasive. Not only projects done directly by federal agencies, but any major project utilizing federal funds, even in part, must prepare an Environmental Impact Statement. NEPA may also affect private businesses through the jurisdiction exercised over them by federal agencies. For example, "a federal judge has ordered the Securities and Exchange Commission to make new rules that will require corporations to file Environmental Impact Statements in their annual reports. The rules would affect the 11,000 companies whose stock is publicly held and who are subject to SEC jursdictions. They would have to publish evaluations of environmental changes that might result from planned plants or new products. The suit charged that the SEC, as a federal agency, was not conforming to (NEPA) requirements since the agency had not amended its corporate disclosure rules to make them responsive to environmental needs."[36] The U.S. District Court for the District of Columbia, while noting that NEPA does not *mandate* that substantial environmental disclosure requirements be imposed, later judged that the SEC's decision not to impose additional rules was insufficient and not in compliance with the spirit of NEPA.[37] The U.S. Court of Appeals, District of Columbia Circuit, subsequently reversed the order of the District Court, but not because environmental concerns are unimportant. Among other reasons, "this Court is mindful of the difficulty of agency decision making in such contexts, and when an agency indicates a need for a further opportunity to study or act, in circumstances like this, we will generally accord its position considerable deference."[38]

Also of note is the encouragement given to state and local environmental policies and planning. Under NEPA, the Council on Environmental Quality (CEO) was established to review Environmental Impact Statements for the construction of facilities involving federal funds. Now the emphasis has changed, and many states have established their own policies for an EIS. Formats for those state plans are not fully developed, but it is expected that they will be similar to the federal guidelines.[39]

Closely related to NEPA is the federal Environmental Protection Agency (EPA), a separate federal agency which sets pollution standards and does have both direct and indirect enforcement powers. EPA's major areas of pollution concern and controls are air, water, noise, mobile sources, solid wastes and land use. Through the enforcement of direct local, state and federal environmental standards, and through indirect controls, all major industrial expansion and new construction now must give some considered thought to the environmental consequences of its actions.

Practicalities. That environmental issues are now major considerations in locating and expanding manufacturing is nowhere better illustrated than in Conway Publications' annual "Checklist of Site Selection Factors." The section on "Environmental Factors, Amenities" has now expanded to more than a full page of small type, containing over 100 separate items.[40] This is a basic list of what may have to be considered. Insights into actual regulations and clues as to how to begin to gather information and data are provided by the 1977 *Site Selection Handbook* issue on "Environment, Energy and Industry." Listed here are "Energy Suppliers and Environmental Agencies;" "What the States Regulate;" and "State Pollution Control Incentive and Financing Programs."[41]

In a more discursive mode, *Industrial Facilities Planning* contains several articles which offer conceptual and procedural advice. Holbrook describes how B.F. Goodrich Chemical Co. has organized itself to discharge its environmental obligations.[42] Reilly discusses how "Tax Exempt Bonds Ease Industry's Pollution Burden."[43] That "Environmental Protection Criteria Should Balance Benefits, Risks" is argued by Moolenaar of Dow Chemical.[44] Also, the "IDRC Airs Views on Environmental, Land Use Controls,"[45] and another article offers advice on "Charting a Path Through the Regulatory Jungle.[46] Finally, in a tightly reasoned article, Odum argues for a position not always found in the industrial development literature: that a "high qualify of life . . . may be more closely approximated in steady state than in growth periods."[47]

Regardless of one's views, there is no doubt that increasingly manufacturers will have to document their impacts on the environment. Not all firms will be directly affected, but most will. The extent to which they are affected will vary with their type of operation and type of area, but increasingly firms will be caught in the network of federal, state or local regulations. Of the two—EPA and NEPA—the Environmental Protection Agency regulations are more direct and specific, and the required planning and action are more clear. Most firms affected by EPA regulations already have experience with compliance; the future promises changes in degree more than in kind.

The possibility of having to file comprehensive and complex Environmental Impact Statements threatens to take manufacturers far beyond their normal spheres of research and planning. The basic ingredients of an EIS are those five areas listed at the outset of this section, and diagrammed in Figure 5-1, for which "detailed statements" by the "responsible official" are required under NEPA. The "Checklist of Site Selection Factors" amplifies these. The site selector, however, should be aware that this listing was meant only to illustrate the types of questions to be answered through the use of scientific data and not to provide a statement outline. As Wood notes, the Council on Environmental Quality guidelines for the preparation of EIS suggest ". . . agencies should make every effort to convey the

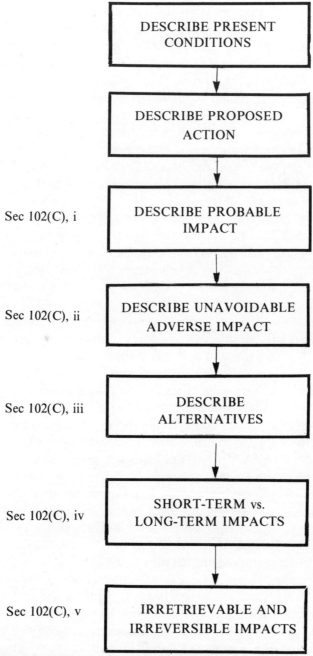

Sec 102(C), i — DESCRIBE PROBABLE IMPACT

Sec 102(C), ii — DESCRIBE UNAVOIDABLE ADVERSE IMPACT

Sec 102(C), iii — DESCRIBE ALTERNATIVES

Sec 102(C), iv — SHORT-TERM vs. LONG-TERM IMPACTS

Sec 102(C), v — IRRETRIEVABLE AND IRREVERSIBLE IMPACTS

SOURCE: Lewis Hopkins, *et al, Environmental Impact Statements: A Handbook for Writers and Reviewers.* (Chicago: Institute for Environmental Quality, 1973.)

Figure 5-1. Typical Outline For Current EIS

required information succintly in a form easily understood . . . giving attention to the substance of the information conveyed rather than to the particular form or length, or detail of the statement."[48] An alternative general outline espoused by many authors is that developed by Hopkins, et. al.,[49] and shown on Figure 5-2. If the EIS is to be an integral part of the decision between alternatives, then the sequence of Figure 2 may be preferable. If only one or two sites are to be evaluated, then the basic NEPA format (Figure 5-1) might be most appropriate.[50] Of course, other approaches may be even more suitable in specific circumstances.

It is far beyond the scope of this volume to delve into the intricacies of filing environmental impact statements or complying with Environmental Protection Agency regulations. Each situation must be assessed individually. However, there is a rapid growing literature, both conceptual and practical, which is most useful. For starters there are Dickert and Domeny's *Environmental Impact Assessment: Guidelines and Commentary,*[51] and *The Environmental Impact Handbook* by Burchell and Listokin which contains an extensive annotated bibliography.[52] A recent publication with an engineering orientation is Canter's *Environmental Impact Assessment,*[53] and one with an urban policy focus is *A Primer on Industrial Environmental Impact.*[54] At the federal level there are a variety of government publications, including the Council on Environmental Quality's monthly *102 Monitor.*[55] Likewise, the Environmental Protection Agency produces many documents. A useful EPA-oriented compendium is the continually updated looseleaf *Environment Regulation Handbook.*[56] Also highly recommended is Quarles' "Federal Regulations of New Industrial Plants."[57] State level documents and regulations may be accessed by writing to the appropriate state agencies as listed in the *Site Selection Handbook.* Inquiries at the local level may be initiated through the state agencies, and followed up in those specific communities of special interest.

Impacts. It is difficult to predict the long run spatial implications for manufacturing of America's increased concern for, and control of, the environment. The regulations are too new and are still evolving. Manufacturers must deal with a plethora of regulations and a complex hierarchy of local, state and federal bureaucracies. In some instances the regulations or their effects are contradictory. Regardless, it is of interest to speculate on the consequences of the new environmental regulations with regard to: 1) Agglomeration and deglomeration

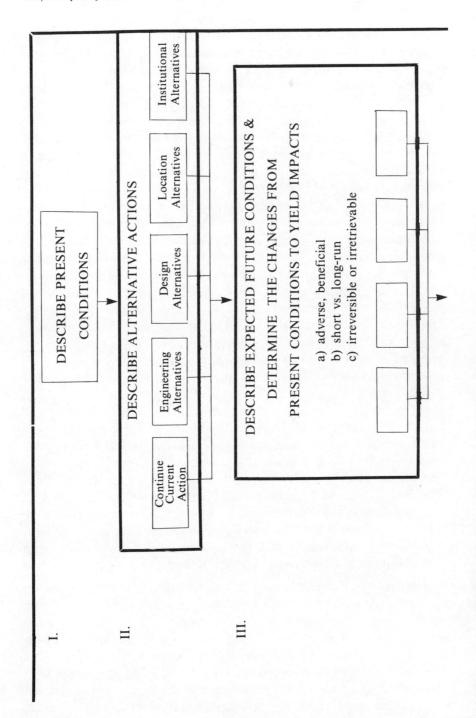

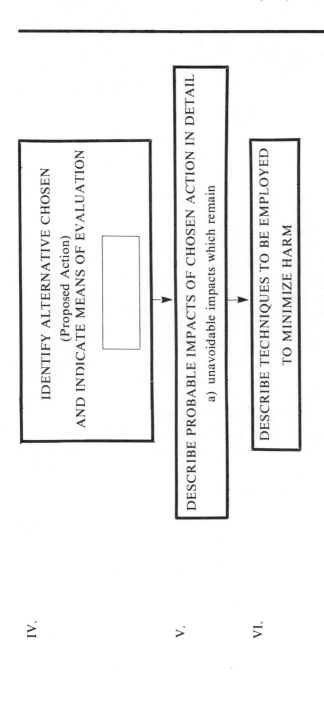

IV.

IDENTIFY ALTERNATIVE CHOSEN
(Proposed Action)
AND INDICATE MEANS OF EVALUATION

V.

DESCRIBE PROBABLE IMPACTS OF CHOSEN ACTION IN DETAIL
a) unavoidable impacts which remain

VI.

DESCRIBE TECHNIQUES TO BE EMPLOYED
TO MINIMIZE HARM

SOURCE: Lewis Hopkins, *et al.*, *Environmental Impact Statements: A Handbook for Writers and Reviewers*, (Chicago: Institute for Environmental Quality, 1973).

Figure 5-2. Proposed Outline For An Environmental Impact Statement: Lewis Hopkins, et al.

tendencies, especially in regard to expansion in place versus new plant locations; 2) shifts in industrial development potentials among regions; 3) alterations in the industrial location decision process; and 4) the greatly increased corporate and public awareness of space and spatial systems.

In-Site vs. New Site. Manufacturers typically would prefer to expand production in existing facilities by employing more labor or machines, or by multiple shifts, or via construction of an addition to the plant, before they would invest in new facilities in a new location. The new environmental regulations may well reinforce this natural tendency toward in-site expansion, for several reasons: (a) Larger operations can more easily absorb environmental control costs due to economies of scale in waste disposal;[58] (b) it is probably easier to get permission to expand production in an area where one is already operating; (c) because any additional pollutants would be a smaller percentage increase than in a new area; (d) because the change in social and economic characteristics of the area are incremental rather than drastically different; (e) because environmental controls, searching for alternatives, delays, etc., increase the cost of locating a new facility; and (f) because they increase uncertainty, this uncertainty can be most easily reduced through expansion of an existing operation.

Running counter to increased pressure to expand in-site production are several forces. There may be absolute restrictions on expansion in already heavily polluted or very densely populated areas. Absolute restrictions necessitate the location of new productive capacity in new locations. Akin to this are differential standards which place greater restrictions on some areas than others. For example, the EPA has placed the nation's 247 Air Quality Control Regions into three classes. Class I includes areas where any air quality deterioration would be considered significant; Class II includes regions where air quality deterioration that normally accompanies moderate, well-planned growth would not be considered significant; Class III applies to regions where intensive major industrial growth is permissible. Currently, of the 247 AQCR's, 186 are categorized in terms of non-attainment for at least one of the five criteria pollutants. It is estimated "that development would be barred or severely restricted under current regulations, if implemented, on as much as 70 to 80 percent of the land area in the U.S."[59]

On a different scale, in some densely populated areas, and within SMSA's, potential air pollution studies must be carried out before the construction of a parking facility of over 1,000 cars or before the expansion of an existing facility by more than 500 car spaces. In contrast, the respective figures for non-SMSA areas are 2,000 and 1,000 car spaces. In areas with *severe* pollution problems EPA parking management regulations apply to lots with over 250 car spaces; these regulations are now applicable to 19 metropolitan areas.[60] Parking is but an example. To the extent that some areas are especially tightly controlled, we may expect an increased tendency toward either undersized projects to escape the regulation limit or avoidance of the areas.

Variations in Local and Regional Development. As suggested, for example, by the EPA Air Classification System, it appears probable that the most stringent standards and restrictions will be placed on locales and regions at the ends of the economic development continuum. Already heavily, intensely developed areas will probably find significant new development increasingly difficult. Conversely, presently clean, pristine areas may have little latitude for industrial development due to the requirement that no significant deterioration of the quality of the environment will be permitted. Under these conditions it appears likely that the areas most readily available for additional industrial development are those "intermediate" types of areas which are neither pristine nor close to saturation.

At the local scale, these lines of reasoning may argue for expecting, within heavily industralized areas, encouragement of the existing trend toward the *suburbanization* of manufacturing. Possibly running counter to this are increasingly stringent controls, at the local, state and federal levels, on the development of new industrial parks.

It is possible that certain areas of the country, e.g. states, may project a more favorable image for industrial development vis-a-vis environmental controls and may be somewhat more liberal in their interpretation and enforcement of standards. To this extent it might be expected that those states which are neither highly industrial nor which trade heavily on the natural beauty of their environment (e.g. tourist areas) would continue to be most encouraging to the development of new and expanded manufacturing. A recent survey of private industrial developers indicates that the states in the Southeast and South Central sections of the United States were viewed most favorably in terms of their industrial development activities, while the states of the North Central and eastern industrial belt and New England, Florida, Colorado and the West Coast were the least encouraging.[61] Differential environment standards and enforcement could reinforce these images.

However, running counter to this is that state and local regulations are coming more and more to resemble the federal regulations and standards. Currently, "regional differences are generally not taken into account. Pacific Northwest Pulp and Paper Mills, discharging waste into Puget Sound—a deep, fast moving body of water with great assimilative capacity— must meet the same technological standards as pulp and paper mills located on small inland streams."[62] This trend might be expected to continue, perhaps to the point where there are no significant state to state variations, leaving degree of regional development (e.g., heavily industrialized) as a critical spatial variable. However, if the focus is shifted to the costs of waste control operations, it can be argued that "even if identical standards of control are enforced everywhere, the location of plants and industries is likely to be affected."[63] This argument rests on (a) regional variations in site costs for waste storage space and the length of haul for each plant, (b) variations in waste disposal economies of scale, especially due to agglomeration and sharing of facilities, and (c) alterations in product and input mixes which will change the relative cost structures among regions.

It is also important to remember that the greatly increased emphasis on the environment in no way obviates the traditional influence of the standard industrial location factors. Those states and regions already relatively heavily industrialized should continue to be favored.

Alterations in the Location Decision Process. There is evidence that environmental factors are now powerful influences on the location of manufacturing. A 1967 survey of electric utility area development executives did not place "environmental considerations" in the top 10 primary factors of industrial site selection; a similar 1972 survey placed environmental considerations first.[64] Aside from the more technical and explicit environmental controls, there are more subtle, but, perhaps in the long run more profound, influences on industrial location decision-making. NEPA and EPA, and their state and local progency and counterparts, demand scale and procedural changes in the locational decision making for most activities. Environmental controls require explicit concern for the interrelationships between the many elements of the interlocking system. Manufacturers are, perforce, required to indulge in some regional systems analysis, as distinct from the all too common pattern of fragmented, local analysis.

On a conceptual level, Beyers and Krumme argue that "owing to regional dimensions associated with pollution regulations, and spatial characteristics of pollution processes, an integration of environmental output relationships into locational models should be more than a mere afterthought."[65] They suggest that "residual disposal costs many influence the slopes of iso-revenue and iso-cost functions, in such a way that the mix of products and factors may be altered . . ."[66]

Another interesting dimension is that manufacturers may be affected by the locations of others in new ways, quite aside from the traditional concerns for the locations of competitors, material suppliers, and markets. Beyers and Krumme state that "given local pollution control standards, the optimal decision of one decision-maker with respect to his optimal level of production and the combination of inputs and outputs including pollution outputs will depend on how other polluters might act or react."[67] Similarly, Kohn argues that "an efficient allocation of urban land would require that each firm's maximum bid price for a parcel of land be reduced by the abatement costs which its emissions at that location would impose on others."[68] Of even more practical concern to manufacturers are EPA's new regulations that "outline a trade-off policy the agency is now using to permit industries to locate in Class II, areas, i.e., non-pristine air quality areas, if sufficient reductions in air pollution are realized elsewhere in the area to offset the new industry's pollution,"[69] and an EPA operating principle that "sources in any area must be sited so that they will not use up an adjacent area's increment."[70]

Another significant shift of emphasis is that the probability of obtaining the required construction and operation permits is much harder to predict than ever before, and at all levels of government— local, state and federal. Typical pre-1969 zoning and land control laws were local, with outcomes rather well known at the outset. The newer environmental regulations more often demand impact analysis, and the results, which can only be guessed at prior to the analysis, play a significant part in securing the necessary construction approvals. Also, at this point, concerned citizens opposed to the facility in a specific location may challenge it through the judicial process. Many developments are being challenged through the courts. In almost every case the developer is faced with considerable delay and cost as he researches and presents his case, listens to counter arguments and awaits the judgement. Win or lose, the manufacturer must contend with greater uncertainty, increased site selection costs, and a longer time frame.

Certainly the entire process increases the cost of site selection. The uncertainty attendant upon site selection and the consequent executive inconvenience produce significant real and psychic costs. Conceptually, it can be argued that environmental regulations greatly increase the complexity of solutions to the problem of "optimal" location decision-making. Beyers and Krumme suggest that" . . . preference for a more 'adaptive' approach to the problem of locational optimization is reinforced by the lack of direct solutions to the theoretical location problem."[71]

As cost increases, so does the tendency to consider fewer alternatives in detail; but this, in spirit at least, is counter to the necessity in environmental impact statements of presenting alternates. As uncertainty increases we should expect more spatially restricted search behavior because information gathering costs are very real, and lack of knowledge and lack of contacts tend to increase the economic and perceived distances beyond existing locations. A likely consequence might be more detailed consideration of alternative locations (usually six or fewer in any case),[72] but with the alternatives chosen from a more restricted regional space adjacent to existing nodes of operation, "close to home," in familiar territory.

Environmental regulations rather significantly increase the time span necessary from initial planning to the operation of the completed facility. This suggests that manufacturers will be less able to construct new capacity quickly to meet immediate and pressing production needs. "Instead of being able to pick a plant site in three to six months it could go to two or more years easily. By that time you might not need the plant because it is too late to get into the market place with the product."[73] With the necessity to meet current production demands forced somewhat away from their traditional central role, it might be expected that new capacity decisions could be considered more carefully, that the investment decisions would be more clearly strategic. Kohn notes that "in the long run, there is a trade-off between two categories of pollution control, technological abatement and locational choice."[74] Certainly, space and place will assume hitherto unknown importance in corporate decision making. A business writer echoes the concern, even while overstating the case: "Now, with the flux and fury of modern corporate business, and vital supporting services, with the incredible corrosion of our environment, with new meaning given to words like mobility and competition, a portentous choice must be appended, not 'shall we move?', not even 'where shall we move?', but 'where *can* we move?'"[75]

Increased Awareness of Space. Combined, these forces suggest a great enhanced role for place and space considerations in industrial location decision making. The "where" becomes both more important and more explicit. We have even reached the point of involving the legal profession. The American Bar Assn. has issued a report entitled *Industrial Development and the Environment: Legal Reforms to Improve the Decision-Making Process in Industrial Site Selection.*[76] We might well expect spatial and regional considerations to have enhanced stature, not only in the context of the geography of the firm but also in terms of the economic geographies of regions and the nation. Spatial considerations will assume a much more important role in the overall investment strategies.

What has so far happened may be relatively insignificant compared to what might happen in the near future. The United States is on the brink of enacting extensive and coherent land use controls. Land use controls largely are a spin-off from the environmental movement, and indeed some existing environment regulations "back-in" to land use control through the necessities of dealing with an interlocking system. Even now, it is expected that "whether the proposed legislation is adopted, or whether the EPA regulations are finally enforced, industry will be subject to land use control of the most limiting sort."[77]

The national Congress is now on the verge of considering, with some favor, direct land use legislation. That lawmakers sense a public receptivity to some land use controls is revealed by the fact that two major proposals are sponsored by recent presidential aspirants (Henry Jackson and Morris Udall).[78] If enacted, land management will have an impact on every manufacturer in the country. It will help guide the location of large new plants, new towns and other significant developments. "Thus land use planning and legislation, traditionally the domain of local governments since 1962, when Massachusetts Bay Colony restricted industry to specific districts, is becoming ever more centralized in state and federal governments. While comprehensive land use planning laws have yet to pass Congress, the effect of 20th century technology overtaking 19th century sovereignty is apparent in the adoption of a multiplicity of federal and state laws that are affecting land use control at the local level."[79]

Although the consequences of environmental protection measures on the location of manufacturing are not yet highly visible, significant potentials remain. Trends toward ever more comprehensive and powerful land use planning and control reveal an increasing awareness of the importance of places and spatial interrelationships.

Notes and References—Chapter 5

1. Hunker, H.L. *Industrial Development.* Lexington, Mass: Lexington Books.© by D. C. Heath and Co. All rights reserved. p. 137.

2. "Checklist of Site Selection Factors," *Site Selection Handbook,* Vol. XXIII, No. 1, February, 1978. pp. 60-61. Atlanta: Conway Publications.

3. Conway, H.M., and Liston, L.L. *Industrial Facilities Planning.* Atlanta: Conway Publications, 1976

4. Foster, W. "The Complexities of Comparing State Taxes," *Industrial Facilities Planning, Ibid.,* p. 181. (Reprinted from *Industrial Development,* November/December, 1975.)

5. Hunker, H.L., *op. cit.,* p. 142.

6. *Ibid.,* p. 139.

7. Garrison, C.B. *The Impact of New Industry on Local Government Finances in Five Small Towns in Kentucky.* Agricultural Economic Report No. 191. Washington: U.S. Dept. of Agriculture, 1970, p. iv.

8. Cumberland, J.H., and van Beck, F. "Regional Economic Objectives and Subsidization of Local Industry," *Land Economics,* Vol. XLIII, No. 3, August, 1967, p. 260.

9. Foster, W., *op. cit.,* p. 177.

10. *Comparative Tax, Water and Sewer Costs for Philadelphia and 81 other Municipalities in Pennsylvania, New Jersey, Delaware and Maryland.* Philadelphia: Pennsylvania Economic League, 1960. Summarized in Smith, D.W. *Industrial Location.* New York: J. Wiley & Sons, 1971, pp. 292-295.

11. *Comparative Tax Burdens on Selected Manufacturers in Fifteen States.* Madison: Wisconsin Dept. of Revenue, June, 1974.

12. *Ibid.,* p. 11.

13. *Site Selection Handbook, op. cit.,* Vol. XXII, No. 2, 1977, pp. 114-119.

14. *Industrial Development, op. cit.,* November/December, 1976, p. 9.

15. Peck, J.E., and Swartz, T.R. "Industrial Development Bonds: The Economic Impact of their Limits," *AIDC Journal,* Vol. XI, No. 2, April, 1976, p. 53.

16. *Ibid.,* pp. 53-68.

17. Lamberson, M. "Industrial Development Bonds can Tip The Balance in Site Selection," *Industrial Development,* January/February, 1977, p. 16.

18. *Ibid.,* p. 17.

19. *Ibid*

20. *Ibid.*

21. Springate, D.J. "Industrial Retention Practices of Local Governments," *AIDC Journal,* Vol. XI, No. 4, October, 1976, p. 14.

22. Yeates, M.H., and Lloyd, P.E. *Impact of Industrial Incentives: Southern Georgian Bay Region, Ontario,* Geographical Paper No. 44. Ottawa: Policy and Planning Branch, Dept. of Energy, Mines and Resources, 1969, p. 64.

23. Greenhut, M.L. "An Explanation of Industrial Development in Underdeveloped Areas of the United States," *Land Economics,* November, 1960, pp. 371-379.

24. Lee, M.E. "Tax Incentives and the Industrialization of the South East," *Proceedings of the Fifty-fourth Annual Conference on Taxation-1961.* Harrisburg, Pa.: National Tax Assn., 1962, pp. 168-174. (Quoted in Cumberland, *op. cit.,* p. 263.)

25. *Regional Development Incentives,* Second Report from the Expenditure Committee, Trade and Industry Sub-Committee, House of Commons, Session 1973-74, London, U.K., 1973, p. 11.

26. "A Tycoon Faces the Future," *Newsweek,* June 17, 1974, p. 44.

27. Estall, R.C., and Buchanan, R.O. *Industrial Activity and Economic Geography.* London: Hutchinson University Library, 1970, p. 122.

28. *Industrial Development, op. cit.*

29. *Site Selection Handbook, op. cit.*

30. *Industrial Development,* May/June, 1977, p. 21.

31. Libman, J. "Idaho Starts to Prosper as Companies, People Escape Urban Stress," *The Wall Street Journal,* October 17, 1977, p. 1.

32. Wong, W. "California Gov. Brown Shifts Position, Begins to Woo Business," *The Wall Street Journal,* July 12, 1977, p. 1.

33. A substantial portion of this section is from Stafford, H.A., "Environmental Regulations and the Location of U.S. Manufacturing: Speculations," *Geoforum.* Vol. VIII (1977), pp. 243-248. Oxford, England: Pergamon Press.

34. Precursors of the 1969 National Environmental Policies Act which were especially important for industry include the Water Pollution Control Acts and Amendments of 1948, 1956, 1961, 1965 and 1966, and the Federal Air Pollution legislation of 1955, the 1963 Clean Air Act and the Air Quality Act of 1967.

35. NEPA, P.L. 91-190, Sec 102(2) (c).

36. "Legislative Measures Promise Heavy Impact on Industry," *Industrial Development,* March/April, 1975, p. 14.

37. "National Resources Defense Council v. Securities and Exchange Commission," U.S. District Court for the District of Columbia, C.A. No. 409-73, May 19, 1977. In *Federal Securities Law Reporter,* Commerce Clearing House, Inc., June 2, 1977,—96,057.

38. National Resources Defense Council, Inc., et. al., v. Securities and Exchange Commission, et. al., U.S. Court of Appeals, District of Columbia Circuit. No. 77-176, April 20, 1979. In *Federal Securities Law Reporter,* Commerce Clearing House, Inc., May 2, 1979,—95,356.

39. Barbaro, R., and Cross, F.L., Jr. *Primer on Environmental Impact Statements.* Westport, Conn.: Technomic Publishing Co., Inc., 1973, p. 38.

40. "Checklist of Site Selection Factors," *op. cit.,* pp. 62-64.

41. *Site Selection Handbook, Environment, Energy and Industry.* Vol. XXII, No. 3. Atlanta: Conway Publications, September, 1977.

42. Holbrook, W.C. "How One Company Organizes to Meet Its Environmental Responsibilities," *Industrial Facilities Planning op. cit.,* pp. 28-31. (Reprinted from *Industrial Development,* March/-April, 1971.)

43. Reilly, F.X. "Tax Exempt Bonds Ease Industry's Pollution Burden," *Industrial Facilties Planning, op. cit.,* pp. 183-185. (Reprinted from *Industrial Development,* September/October, 1974.)

44. Moolenaar, R.J. "Environmental Protection Criteria Should Balance Benefits, Risks," *Industrial Facilities Planning, op. cit.,* pp. 208-210. (Reprinted from *Industrial Development,* September/-October, 1974.)

46. "Charting a Path Through the Regulatory Jungle," *Industrial Facilities Planning, op. cit.,* pp. 215-218. (Reprinted from *Industrial Development,* January/February, 1974.)

47. Odum, H.T. "Energy, Ecology and Economics," *Industrial Facilities Planning, op. cit.,* p. 231. (Reprinted from *Industrial Development,* Jan./Feb., 1974.)

48. Wood, R.B. "The Organization of Environmental Impact Statements," *AID Journal,* Vol. IX, No. 4, October, 1974, p. 58.

49. Hopkins, L., et. al. *Environmental Impact Statements: A Handbook for Writers and Reviewers.* Chicago: Illinois Institute for Environmental Quality, 1973. (Distributed by National Technical Information Service, Washington, D.C.)

50. Burchell, R.W., and Listokin, D. *The Environmental Impact Handbook.* New Brunswick, N.J.: Center for Urban Policy Research, Rutgers-The State University, 1975, p. 41.

51. Dickert, T.G., and Domeny, K.R. (eds.) *Environmental Impact Assessment: Guidelines and Commentary.* Berkeley, Calif.: University of California, Berkeley, 1974, 238 pp.

52. Burchell, R.W., and Listokin, D., *op. cit.*

53. Canter, L. *Environmental Impact Assessment.* New York: McGraw-Hill, 1977.

54. Greenberg, M., Belnay, G., Cesanek, W., Neuman, N., and Shephard, G. *A Primer on Industrial Enviornmental Impact.* New Brunswick, N.J.: Center for Urban Policy Research, Rutgers-The State University, 1979, 299 pp.

55. Council on Environmental Quality. *102 Monitor,* Executive Office of the President, Washington, D.C.

56. *Environment Regulation Handbook.* New York: Environment Information Center.

57. Quarles, John. "Federal Regulation of New Industrial Plants." *Environment Reporter,* 10, No. 1, May 4, 1979.

58. See, for example, Shriner, R.D., "Pollution Control and Plant Location," *AIDC Journal,* April, 1972, p. 41.
59. "Air Classification System May Determine Site Locations," *Site Selection Handbook, Environment, Energy and Industry.* Vol. XXI, No. 3, September, 1976, p. 256. Atlanta: Conway Publications.
60. EPA's "indirect source regulations remain shelved, with no funding, until September 1977 or until a clearer congressional mandate is received," *Industrial Development,* January/February, 1977, p. 12.
61. "IDRC Airs Views on Environmental, Land Use Controls,"*op. cit.,* p. 213.
62. "Some Factories Gain by Abating Pollution," *The New York Times,* January 20, 1977.
63. Shriner, R.D., *op. cit.,* pp. 39-42.
64. Lynch, A.A. "Environment and Labor Quality Take Top Priority in Site Selection," *Industrial Development,* March/April, 1973, pp. 13-15.
65. Beyers, W.B., and Krumme, G. "Multiple Products, Residuals and Location Theory;" in Hamilton, F.E.I. (ed.), *Spatial Perspectives on Industrial Organizaton and Decision-Making.* London: J. Wiley and Sons, 1974, p. 79.
66. *Ibid.,* p. 99.
67. *Ibid.,* p. 89.
68. Kohn, R.E. "Industrial Location and Air Pollution Abatement," *Journal of Regional Science,* April, 1974, p. 55.
69. "Business Borrows Time From Legislative Control," *Industrial Development,* January/February, 1977, p. 12.
70. "Air Classification System May Determine Site Locations," *op. cit.* p. 258.
71. Beyers, W.B. and Krumme, G., *op. cit.,* p. 100.
72. Stafford, H.A. "The Atatomy of the Location Decision: Content Analysis of Case Studies." Reproduced with permission from *Spatial Perspectives on Industrial Organization and Decision-Making,* by F.E. Ian Hamilton (ed.), p. 182. Copyright© 1974, by John Wiley and Sons, Ltd., London.
73. *Industrial Development,* May/June, 1975, p 10.
74. Kohn, R.E. *op. cit.,* p. 62.
75. "Perspective on Plant Location in the U.S.," *NewsFront,* March/- April, 1975, p. 50.

76. American Bar Assn., Special Committee on Environmental Law. *Industrial Developments and the Environment: Legal Reforms to Improve the Decision-Making process in Industrial Site Selection.* Chicago, 1974.

77. "Air Classification System May Determine Site Locations," *op. cit.,* p. 258.

78. "Round Three: Jackson, Udall Offer a Brace of Land Use Bills," *Industrial Development,* May/June, 1975, p. 3.

79. "Land Use. Introduction," *Environment Regulation Handbook, op. cit.,* p. 1.

VI Local Site Selection

VI
Local Site Selection

Yaseen emphasizes it. After—and only after— a community has been chosen should a specific building site be selected.[1] The general area and the best town, city or metropolitan area should be selected by carefully balancing the location factors of Chapters Three, Four and Five via the utilization of some of the assessment techniques of Part III. Then the scale of analysis changes to determine the best of the available sites within the selected community.

General Patterns

Before proceeding to discussion of specific site factors, it may be instructive to take a brief look at general industrial location patterns at the local scale. If general locational patterns can be discerned, then these may provide clues to the considerations which other manufacturers find important; lack of generality may suggest that industries are relatively "footloose" at the local scale, and that a specific manufacturer should pay more attention to his unique requirements, rather than to any norms, when selecting a specific site.

Although industry locates in all sorts of environments from rural to urban, most plants are located in medium to large urban areas. Hence, attention is here focused on intrametropolitan industrial location. Surprisingly, in spite of numerous case studies, there is relatively little systematic knowledge of intrametropolitan industrial location patterns. Nor are the more academic urban land use models of much value. At the outset, this suggests that most industries can, and do, survive and prosper in a wide variety of urban environments.

This lack of consistency in urban industrial location patterns is neatly summarized in a recent study by Struyk and James. They were unable, even after a search of the literature plus detailed intrametropolitan industrial location patterns and change studies (1965-68) for four cities (Cleveland, Boston, Minneapolis-St. Paul and Phoenix), to advance specific generalizations. Of their conclusions, seven are worthy of note in the present context (italics added):[2]

1. There is a high degree of mobility of manufacturing employment among sub-districts within urban areas. Establishment births, deaths and relocations were equal to 37 percent of the number of establishments at the beginning of the observation period. Struyk and James note that these high mobility rates "imply that industry location may be much more amenable to direction and change through public policy than has heretofore been thought." For the manufacturing site selector, these high mobility rates suggest that matching specific site requirements to specific site characteristics at a given point in time is more important for many plants than is location in a particular type of sub-region within the city.

2. Manufacturing tends to be decentralizing, away from the central city. Conversely, however, in every city studied there were some central city areas which increased their share of manufacturing employment. Once again, site selectors should look at specific site characteristics; every city will have a somewhat unique industrial geography, and decision-makers should not be automatically biased toward a suburban or rural location.

3. Struyk and James found little systematic variance in the spatial incidence of establishments going out of business, and no evidence that core area establishments are more likely to die. This reinforces the observations above.

4. "The incubtor hypothesis, which states that new manufacturing establishments are attracted to centralized locations because of essential services provided there (e.g., rentable production space), was tested . . . (but) was *not* supported . . . The lack of support seems to be explained by the availability of sites with sufficient *external* economies for new establishments at decentralized locations."

5. There is some evidence that low-wage industries are being attracted to intrametropolitan areas where large pools of low-skilled workers reside. So, too, are "nuisance" industries (e.g.,

chemicals, petroleum and primary metals). It is not clear, however, whether the nearby low-wage labor is a locational factor, or if other area characteristics primarily influence such locational patterns.

6. Although industry tends to be found scattered through metropolitan areas, every specific industry type showed significant spatial concentrations. This "strongly suggests the importance of *external economies* in the locational decision of manufacturing enterprises."

7. Struyk and James also state that their data "support the hypothesis that the spatial clustering of establishments and the employment characteristics of an industry continue to influence the locational behavior of firms in that industry." This suggests that firms of similar type tend to cluster, perhaps to be near common suppliers or markets, to share similar localized facilities (e.g., transportation, utilities) and/or in response to zoning or other institutionalized land use patterns. The importance of these locational factors must be assessed individually by each manufacturer in a specific urban context.

Checklists of Factors

As with all location searches, local site selection should proceed systematically. At the outset, a list of site requirements should be drawn up, supplemented by a secondary list of desirable characteristics. These then form a checklist of items for which information should be gathered and upon which decisions should be based. Although the specifics of any checklist will vary according to type of plant and industry, there are several published general checklists which are sufficiently comprehensive to satisfy the needs of most decision-makers. Among the best is Conway Publications' annual "Checklist of Site Selection Factors."[3] Scattered through this "Checklist" are several factors which are important at both the regional and local scales, and which have been discussed in previous chapters. Examples include Labor (Chapter 5), Local Government and Taxes (Chapter 6), Transportation (Chapter 4), Utilities (Chapter 5), Environmental Considerations (Chapter 6) and Community Qualities (Chapter 5).

Beyond the factors which operate at several scales, the "Checklist" identifies, under Section XXII, 43 items which should be evaluated for specific individual sites. The 11 major subheadings are: (1) Requirements; (2) Type of Site; (3) Topographical Considerations; (4) Geologic Considerations; (5) Accessibility; (6) Utilities; (7) Cost of Extending Utilities and Responsibility of Bearing Cost; (8) Intangible Considerations; (9) Legal Check-Points; (10) Cost of Land; and (11) Vacant Buildings.

There are many other published "checklists," each somewhat distinctive in emphasis, but sharing many characteristics. For example, Chicago's Continental Bank lists "49 Things to Check Before You Locate and Build Your Plant." Of these, most relate explicitly to local site selection. They suggest checking: (1) the professionalism of the real estate brokers, architects and contractors you choose; (2) enforcement of industrial park covenants; (3) other firms to determine if there are any major problems; (4) locations of suppliers; (5) trucking services to a prospective site; (6) the legalities of necessary rail spurs; (7) mail delivery system; (8) water run-off; (9) police and fire protection; (10) availability of local amenities (e.g., banks, restaurants, clubs, hospitals, libraries, shopping) in the vicinity; (11) availability of natural gas and alternative fuel sources; (12) gas pressure; (13) whether a source of electricity or gas adjoining property can be tapped; (14) water supply, pressure and quality; (15) location and elevation of sewers; (16) waste disposal; (17) local labor supply and wage structures; (18) availability of public transportation; (19) traffic flows to and from the site; (20) work shift schedules of other firms in the area to minimize traffic problems; (21) installation of proper safety devices; (22) needs for special foundations; (23) county and local zoning ordinances; (24) vehicle parking regulations; (25) pollution control standards; (26) space for future expansion.[4]

Many of the studies included in *Industrial Facilities Planning* make mention of local site selection factors. A summary of local scale checklists from three is presented to round out this discussion and to illustrate how they may vary from firm to firm.

DuPont is reported to first set up a list of requirements, then to select, in turn, a general area and a specific city. Then local site selection involves gathering detailed information on such factors as: (1) availability and prices of sites; (2) relative site location; (3) rail, highway, water and public transportation; (4) water supplies; (5) fuel supplies; (6) waste disposal; (7) regulating codes; (8) ordinances and regulations; and (9) living conditions. These and other factors are then weighed and combined via a point-count system for input into the final location decision.[5]

Ford Motor Co. prepares a detailed brochure for each prospective site. Included are items such as: (1) ownership and land acreage; (2) land cost; (3) comparative site development costs; (4) recurring costs; (5) topography and grading; (6) soils and foundations; (7) drainage; (8) water supply; (9) sanitary sewer; (10) gas and power; (11) geographical area; (12) zoning; (13) visibility; (14) roads; (15) railroads; (16) encroachments; and (17) general comments.[6]

A more compact list is provided by an AVCO example. Their site guidelines included: (1) availability of labor; (2) cost to buy or lease; (3) proximity of residential areas (wanted to avoid because of possible noise complaints; many other firms, of course, wish to locate near appropriate residential areas); (4) character of local business community; (5) room for expansion; and (6) convenience to truck and air transportation.[7]

Checklists oriented toward area industrial development also may be used profitably by site selectors. It is of interest to note the factors thought by area developers to be important to locating new (or existing) manufacturers. The site selector may gain considerable insight through the exercise of inverting the focus from the factors important in attracting industry to the factors attractive to industry. Of even more value are completed industrial development surveys for regions and communities of specific concern. In addition to the data contained, it is sometimes possible to gauge a community's industrial development sophistication and receptivity by comparing the categories used against some "standard" outline of useful community information.[8]

It should be noted that in-depth investigation of any of the factors may, in turn, generate an even more specific list of items to be checked. As one example, consider Sowers discussion of foundation investigations for industrial sites. In summary, he notes that the information required includes; (1) the depth, thickness and properties of the soil strata; (2) the depth to rock and the character of the rock; (3) the location of ground water and its seasonal variations; (4) possibilities of mineral exploitation beneath the site. Gathering the information should proceed in three basic steps, a reconnaissance stage, the exploration stage and a final detailed examination stage which provides the necessary engineering data.[9]

Even if it was not apparent at the outset, the site selector should be aware that a thorough site investigation at the local scale may involve a considerable amount of time and detail and require the services of other specialists. Indeed, the potential expense of proper site evaluation makes it doubly imperative that the proper regional location be determined *before* specific sites are appraised. Good sites can be found somewhere in any general area; to expend a considerable effort on local details before the proper region is selected will at best be a waste and at worst may lead to a great site in the wrong place.

It is also obvious that the almost infinite complexities of actual site selection preclude detailed discussion. The individual requirements of a specific plant plus the individual characteristics of a specific site produce unique combinations which defy generalization. At the same time, however, some additional general comments about a selected few of the local scale site selection factors may be useful. Following are brief commentaries on: Parcel Location, Size and Cost; Land Use Regulations; Industrial Parks; and Research Aids.

Parcel Location, Size and Cost

In spite of the many variations, the selection of a specific industrial site is most influenced by its availability, in terms of existing land use regulations (especially zoning) and in terms of its relative location regarding such factors as transportation, utilities, labor, and so on (as indicated in any good site selection checklist).

Next must be considered the size of the appropriate and available parcel of land. To purchase (or lease) too much land is to tie up scarce capital, rendering it unproductive, at least for the short run. The converse, however, is even more dangerous. Obtaining too small a parcel of land may hinder operations at the outset, and almost certainly will impede necessary future growth. Yaseen suggests that "generally a site of not less than five times the actual size of the plant is considered minimum to allow for sliding, loading platforms, truck ingress and egress, parking facilities, storage area and future expansion. If possible, open land should be available on two or more sides to allow for future site expansion."[10] While the land requirements for a specific plant can only be determined within its own unique context, it is important to remember that the old rules of thumb are probably too conservative. Increasingly stringent land use regulations, especially those relating to the environment, will make in-site expansion even more attractive in the future; thus, the attractiveness of adequate room for expansion is enhanced.

Only after appropriate and available parcels of land have been identified should questions of land cost be entertained. Obviously, it is never desirable to pay more than the land is worth, and there is always the necessity for hard-headed bargaining. Unfortunately firms too often engage in hard bargaining over the wrong parcels of land. To get a "good price" on an unsuitable site is really no bargain. Remember that the real value of a site is only partially determined by the local land market; it is also determined by its value to the specific manufacturer. Since the cost of land is usually only a very small proportion of the total investment, and an even smaller proportion of operating costs, the "correctness" of the site is always much more important than its cost. Furthermore, land purchased becomes a permanent company asset, and good sites are likely to show more appreciation over time and thus be worth more if and when resale is advisable. So, don't be cheap!

One potentially significant cost factor, listed separately in the Conway "Checklist" is local taxes. Whereas taxes are generally recognized as minor influences on industrial location (see Chapter 5), they may be relatively more important in local site selection. This is because "in a single metropolitan area the cost of most other inputs may vary from place to place only to a minor degree (which increases) the significance of differences in taxation levels. And if substantial variations in the cost of labor and land, for example, do exist these are likely to reinforce the trend indicated by the taxation figures rather than oppose it. Differences in the level of business taxation, with or without the assistance of other cost variations, are likely to favor the decentralization of industrial activity within the major metrpolitan area."[11]

While good industrial land is likely to appreciate in value, industrial buildings and facilities will depreciate. The more purpose-built the facility, the less its value on the open market and the faster its depreciation. This cannot be helped and, like taxes, must be viewed as a cost of doing business; once again, having the correct "tools for the job" is more important than their cost. However, if an existing building is purchased, its price should reflect its depreciated value.

The basic rule is to be willing (and able) to pay what is necessary to obtain the correct size of land parcel in the right location. The desirability of precisely determining the specific plant requirements before entering into any purchase negotiations will likely become even more important in the future. It is predicted that increasing pressures for public disclosures of corporate intentions at the beginning of the permit process will force a change in the current practice of seeking sites anonymously.[12] The firm that knows its needs will be a stronger bargainer for its most appropriate site, be better able to withstand "public" pressures and avoid some fruitless debate.

Land Use Regulations

There are a variety of land use regulations which impinge on the suitability of a site for a given type of operation. These vary by state and community and by type of plant. It is important that assurances be obtained prior to purchase of property that the intended uses are compatible with the public regulations.

Building codes and zoning codes are the most common and long standing types of land use regulations, and must be explicitly considered in almost any area of interest. Building codes and permit processes are best checked at the local level. Advice from a competent local industrial realtor and contact with local governmental agencies are necessary. The same is true for zoning compliance.

In an interesting article on industrial zoning, West points out that "during preliminary site investigations, short-range consideration is given to sites with a zoning classification compatible with the company's industrial processes and products. If the classifications are not compatible, the investigator rates the sites according to their possibilities for appropriate rezoning and/or for amending the zoning ordinance text to meet the needs of the company."[13] Obviously, it is easier, less expensive and more conducive to community good-will to be in compliance with existing zoning regulations than to try to obtain a variance. Although in the past many communities have very willingly changed zoning ordinances to accommodate desired employers, Tobin argues that increasingly "rezoning will become almost impossible, as well as tremendously costly, in terms of time and preparation of environmental impact statements."[14] Furthermore, consistent zoning can have a beneficial effect on industry by assisting the orderly development of attractive industrial districts (with the appropriate mix of other industries, auxiliary facilities and infrastructure and amenities), which both enhances current operations and protects resale value. A community which too readily changes ordinances to accommodate one manufacturer is likely to do so for others, possibly to everyone's long run detriment.

In addition to the longer run considerations of the development of orderly, efficient industrial districts with enhanced resale value, West indicates that the facility planner also "must evaluate the inherent costs to the company of a zoning ordinance's land/building ratios, set back requirements, landscaping requirements, parking requirements or other restrictions—all in terms of the company's particular processes, flows and policies."[15] He then proceeds to point out several problems that the most common existing zoning ordinances create for industrial sites. Among these is the extensive use of multiple zoning classifications for industry where lists of permitted or prohibited land uses are compiled for specific areas or sites. Unfortunately, such lists often lack clarity of definition leading to confusion and uncertainty, may be discriminatory and are slow to change. More progressive, and desirable, communities will recognize that technologies change over time, and that a plant's operating characteristics are more important than its classification by industry type.

Another problem with industrial zoning via the multiple classification method is the allied system of progressively inclusive districts. In this system "lower level" uses (e.g., industry) are excluded from "higher level" (e.g., residential) districts, but the reverse is not true. Thus, homes may be built in an industrial area which may diminish the industrial district's effective functioning and may in time lead to conflict. Under this system industry bears the restrictions of zoning but not its full protection. West suggests that a partial solution may be in single classification industrial zoning, with zones for the exclusive use of industry (such as in many industrial parks). Although there are also problems with this concept, West argues that explicit consideration of an alternatie system of industrial zoning would cause public officials to at least "*recognize* the specific and particular needs of industrial site locations and to *plan* for the industrial location in direct and equal relationship to other land uses in the community."[16]

The astute site selector will be alert to both the details of local zoning codes and to the community attitudes underlying them. He also will try to discern the compatibility of existing zoning ordinances with community master plans and community, county or state-wide land use plans. As pointed out in Chapter 6, the increasing concern for the environment, and evolving specific environmental regulations, are moving all governmental jurisdictions closer to comprehensive land use planning. Land use plans which specify types of occupancy and master plans which predict future land uses are likely to supersede traditional zoning at the macro-scale and to guide it explicitly at the micro-scale.

Tobin predicts that "site selection, purchase and construction will become more expensive in time and money, due to supply and demand and the difficulties of meeting stringent regulations." He advises site selectors to (1) option property with an all-inclusive clause covering the approval of all required permits in addition to the building permit, (2) know the master plans of states and regions in order to locate areas where land use allows industrial development, (3) match the proposed use with the area that will allow it in terms of environmental and land use requirements, and (4) spend more time in site review, involving corporate environmental law experts and other talents.[17]

Industrial Parks

Although an old concept, the growth of industrial parks in the United States is primarily a post-World War II phenomenon. Indeed, the growth of industrial parks has become so pervasive, and their attractiveness to industry so important, that extensive directories to their locations and characteristics are published.[18] And there is a professional organization, the National Assn. of Industrial and Office Parks (NAIOP) which sets goals and standards and provides useful information. But whether an industrial park is the correct environment for a specific plant is another question.

Hunker characterizes the industrial park as an area with a minimum size of 25 to 50 acres which "supports the orderly development and growth of a community by providing the necessary ingredients for the successful concentration of industry in the community. Through the provision of all physical services and with simplified zoning and other regulatory measures, the industrial park encourages industrial location in an area free of other land uses in the community ... The typical park today is characterized by three features; (1) a comprehensive plan for development of the park with enforceable restrictions that control land use, building types, building-to-land ratios, construction and even landscaping; (2) availability of all utilities, roads and services that meet the particular need and varied requirements of park residents; and (3) supervision and management that can enforce regulations and guarantee the maintenance of the esthetic and efficient environment."[19]

Why are manufacturers attracted to industrial parks? In theory, industrial parks should offer locating plants (1) significant external economies through the common provision of such factors as utilities, roads and nearby amenities, and (2) within park industrial linkages with suppliers and markets. The first appears to be the case in practice, especially for many small and medium sized plants. The second, however, is not supported by empirical research. A study in the United Kingdom, for example, indicates that linkages within industrial estates are rather weak and relatively unimportant to the firms concerned.[20]

A recent report stresses that while the original attractions of industrial parks (less expensive land, lower taxes and the nebulous back to nature lure) are still important, increasing governmental controls make them even more attractive at the present and for the foreseeable future. "An industrial park can offer a distinct advantage to industry because it has already obtained its environmental approvals and permits, its roads have been built, land uses have been authorized and utilities are in place. Industries locating in the parks are thus released from these burdens."[21]

One survey of industrial park tenants found that the major attractions were the park's package plan, established park standards, prepared sites and cost factors.[22] Another emphasized land costs, aesthetics, transportation (ease of highway access and rail service availability) and site readiness.[23] Yet another study found that out of state firms were more likely to locate in industrial parks than were locally managed firms.[24] This may suggest that whereas local firms have more knowledge of the territory and are better able to assess the merits of all available industrial sites, including the parks, the "out of towners" may be at a disadvantage and anxious both to avoid a major mistake and to minimize executive inconvenience. This last possibility is reinforced by the perhaps surprising observation that "most firms do not seek advice of impartial experts or persons who are familiar with a particular park."[25] Too bad.

While there may be many good reasons for a firm to locate in a planned industrial park, there are equally good reasons for another plant not be placed in such an environment. In the first place the deterrent may be that the available industrial parks are not set up to accommodate a specific type of plant. This is most often the case for "heavy" or "noxious" industries. The majority of existing industrial parks are relatively small and expressly designed for smaller "light" manufacturing operations and distribution facilities. Sydansk predicted an "acceleration in development of industrial clusters—multi-thousand-acre industrial communities such as Bayport, Texas;"[26] but at the least such developments catering to a larger range of manufacturing activities will be some time in coming and will not be available everywhere.

The usually tighter restrictions of industrial parks relative to other available areas may also deter some manufacturers. It may be decided that the aesthetic controls, and associated costs, that make a park attractive to many are simply not that important for a given plant. Also, because industrial parks are limited in number in any given area, they cannot offer the same variety of locations as available with non-park sites. This may be particularly important when a central location is desired but all available industrial park sites are suburban.

Finally, although generally they are more protected by virtue of their restrictive covenants and coordinated planning (most have shown they can police themselves), industrial parks can also develop problems. Traffic congestion can develop, park management may be faulty, and even the park development may not proceed as promised. As Pollina notes, "throughout the nation, there are many parks that have failed or fallen far short of expectations."[27] The developers' short-run problems may become the tenants' long-run problems.

In spite of the problems of some, most industrial parks are doing well, and their number continues to increase. One directory has seen its listings grow from 1,250 parks in 1965 to 4,000 in 1977. Also "though the trend in recent years was toward suburban parks, now both rural and highly urbanized areas are interested in competing for new industry with a wide variety of private, semi-private and government-owned industrial parks . . . (aided by) the federal allocation for economic development infrastructure building through the Commerce Department's Economic Development Administration, which allows small towns to compete without bankrupting themselves."[28] Thus, the trend toward industrial park locations continues. Perhaps as many as two-thirds of all new manufacturing plants are located in such comprehensively planned areas.

Research Aids

As noted, local site selection proceeds properly by first being explicit about the plant's requirements and the desired characteristics of a site, and by systematically compiling the requisite information with the aid of a checklist of factors tailored to the specific facility to be located. From whence cometh the good information and data?

The alert site selector can gather much information from readily available public documents before it becomes necessary to tip his hand to anyone in the local area. The state master plan, if such exists, can be obtained from the appropriate state agency. Useful topographic maps, which also include some cultural information, may be obtained from the United States Geological Survey. A bit of checking may also turn up relatively recent aerial photographic coverage.

A visit to the regional and community planning offices should allow the acquisition of a variety of useful maps, covering topics such as:

Land Uses (Existing)
Land Use Planning
Zoning
Highways and Traffic Flows
Railroads
Port Facilities
Water and Sewer Lines

At some point, either at the outset or after some preliminary data collection, it will be necessary to contact a variety of organizations and to talk to a number of competent individuals. Data collection is only part of this phase; equally important are the more subjective information and impressions. Although no good source should be ignored, experience indicates that useful help is more likely to be obtained from those with a professional interest in assisting industrial location. Among the normally useful organizations[29] are the:

State Industrial Development Commission
State Environmental Protection Agency
Electric Power Company
Railroads
Chamber of Commerce
Local Development Commission

Two other local sources can be of extreme usefulness. One is the good industrial realtor. Although an individual realtor will have vested interests in recommending specific sites, the true professional will be cognizant of the firm's special needs and will be willing and able to give a fairly comprehensive picture of all available industrial properties. Consult more than one realtor. Finally, do not overlook the wealth of good advice that can be obtained through candid discussions with manufacturers already located in the area.

Notes and References—Chapter 6

1. Yaseen, Leonard C. *Plant Location.* New York: American Research Council, 1960, p. 147.

2. Struyk, Raymond J., and James, Franklin J. *Intrametropolitan Industrial Location.* Lexington, Mass.: Lexington Books, D.C. Heath & Co., 1975, pp. 13-16.

3. "Checklist of Site Selection Factors;" *Site Selection Handbook,* Vol. XXIII, No. 1, Atlanta: Conway Publications, February, 1978.

4. *49 Things to Check Before You Locate and Build Your Plant.* Chicago: Continental Illinois National Bank and Trust Company of Chicago.

5. How DuPont Picks 'Em," *Industrial Development,* March/April, 1954. (In Conway, H.M., and Liston, L.L. (eds.), *Industrial Facilities Planning.* Atlanta: Conway Publications, 1976, pp. 123-126.)

6. Vaughn, Stuart H. "Engineering Aspects of Industrial Site Selection," *Industrial Development,* January/February, 1969. (In *Industrial Facilities Planning, op. cit.,* pp. 143-145.)

7. Burrus, Edward A. "AVCO's 53-Day Wonder," *Industrial Development,* March/April, 1967. (In *Industrial Facilities Planning, op. cit.,* pp. 271-274.)

8. See, for example, Collison, Koder M. *Community Survey.* Columbus, Ohio: Unlimited Consultant Services.

9. Sowers, George F. "Foundation Investations for Industrial Sites;" *Industrial Development,* September/October, 1956. (In *Industrial Facilities Planning, op. cit.,* pp. 263-266.)

10. Yaseen, Leonard C., *op. cit.,* p. 149.
11. Smith, David M. *Industrial Location.* New York: John Wiley and Sons, Inc., 1971, p. 53.
12. Sydansk, Raymond. "Site Selection Techniques-How Will They Change Over the Next Decade?," *American Industrial Properties Report,* October, 1976, p. 26.
13. West, James F., Jr. "Industrial Zoning: Evaluation of Multiple and Single Classifications," *AIDC Journal,* April, 1977, p. 59.
14. Tobin, John E. "Site Selection Techniques-How Will they Change Over the Next Decade?," *American Industrial Properties Report,* October, 1976.
15. West, James F., *op. cit.,* p. 59.
16. *Ibid.,* p. 79.
17. Tobin, John E., *op. cit.,* p. 24.
18. See, for example, *Office and Industrial Parks Index, Site Selection Handbook.* Vol. XXII, No. 4. (November, 1977). Atlanta: Conway Publications. In addition to over 4,000 listings, also included are maps showing park locations in 19 metropolitan areas and a "Uniform Outline for Deed Covenants and Performance Standards."
19. Hunker, Henry L. *Industrial Development.* Lexington, Mass.: Lexington Books© by Heath and Co. All rights reserved. pp. 179-180.
20. Bale, John R. "Toward A Geography of the Industrial Estate," *The Professional Geographer,* August, 1974, p. 295.
21. "More Firms Are Choosing Planned Parks Over Single Sites; SSHB List Pushes 4,000" *Site Selection Handbook,* Vol. XXII, No. 4 (November, 1977), p. 345.
22. Dick, Donald F. "Problems Attributed to Industrial Parks: A Survey of Tenants," *AIDC Journal,* January, 1969, pp. 1-11. (Noted in Hunker, *op. cit.,* p. 182.)
23. Pollina, Ronald R. "Industrial Parks: What Firms Look For," *AIDC Journal,* April, 1977, p. 55.
24. Rees, John. "Manufacturing Change, Internal Control and Government Spending in a Growth Region of the United States." Unpublished paper presented at the 24th North

American meetings of the Regional Science Assn., Philadelphia, Pa., November, 1977.

25. Pollina, Ronald R., *op. cit.,* p. 56.

26. Sydansk, Raymond, *op. cit.* p. 26.

27. Pollina, Ronald R. "Industrial Parks: Site Selection, Development and Promotion," *AIDC Journal,* July, 1977, p. 7.

28. "More Firms Arc Choosing Planned Parks Over Single Sites; SSHB List Pushes 4,000," *op. cit.,* p. 345.

29. Useful lists of names and addresses may be found in publications such as "Geographical Guide to Development Organizations," *Site Selection Handbook,* Vol. XXV, No. 2, 1980, and "1977 Office/Industrial Site Seekers' Directory," *American Industrial Properties Report,* 1977.

Part III Techniques
Of Analysis

VII
Comparative Costs and Revenues

VII
Comparative Costs and Revenues

The previous chapters have identified and discussed several of the major industrial location variables. It would be a very rare situation indeed where a single location was judged best on all the relevant criteria. Instead, the site selector is faced with the problem of balancing, for example, an area's relative advantages for marketing versus its relative disadvantages on labor. The complexities of evaluating the overall relative advantages of competing places are directly related to the number of variables measured and the number of locations considered. Procedures are necessary for assessing the total relative advantages of alternative locations. This chapter presents the methods most commonly utilized.

A. An Insoluble Problem

If it is assumed that the ultimate locational criterion should be maximum profit, and if the unrealistic assumption is made that all the key variables can be objectively measured, then the problem would seem to reduce to calulating spatially variable revenues and then subtracting costs. Unfortunately, even if these heroic assumptions are made the problem remains ultimately insoluble. Specific obstacles include the issues of future uncertainty, circular processes and the apparent intractability of the least cost and maximum revenue formulations.[1]

A prime theoretical and practical difficulty is that the factors are simultaneously interactive. Smith succinctly illustrates the dilemma when discussing the interrelationship between cost and revenue. "It would be quite possible to compute a market potential surface . . . and then to identify a total cost surface by working out for a sample of locations the total cost of producing and distributing the required quantity of output. However, such a procedure would imply that the level of sales attainable at a given location was unrelated to production costs, whereas in reality scale might affect average cost, cost might affect price, and price might influence sales and revenue . . . And to start with a total cost surface and then proceed to a demand or revenue surface is equally tortuous, since both average cost and total cost can be a function of volume of sales."[2]

B. Some Simplifications

Although there is no ultimate solution to the problem of simultaneous interaction, it is obvious that real world locations are chosen by more than random selection. In the final analysis, the process is judgmental, but relatively objective measurements are among the crucial inputs, Several procedural simplifications are common.

The type and size of the manufacturing plant to be established normally are taken as known quantities prior to the location search. They are determined by the firm's needs and are not allowed to vary according to location.

The problem of simultaneous interactions between costs and revenue is avoided by separately either minimizing the first or maximizing the second. Whereas retailing location models focus on sales, the least cost approach is the overwhelming favorite in industrial location. In the normal least cost model, markets are included only through the calculation of finished product shipping costs; market locations and potential sales volumes are taken as given, insensitive to the location of the manufacturing facility.

The primary focus on cost is as evident in theory as it is in practice. Smith presents an excellent conceptual discussion, plus some useful practical examples.[3] Isard likewise operates primarily in at least-cost framework; the detailed examinations of the petro-chemical industry via comparative costs techniques and Industrial Complex Analysis will repay careful study.[4] Russell exemplified the bias toward costs:

"Given good management, the profitability of a manufacturing plant is determined largely by the cost of accumulating all of the required materials and services from many places at one particular site, of converting these into products at that site, and finally of distributing the products from that site to all the places where they will be sold. Each of these costs will be different at alternative locations, and because the costs are interacting, their totality will also be different at the alternative locations. A change in any one of the costs has an impact on all the others. A special kind of geographic forecasting is required to predict the place at which the totality of the costs will be favorable during the whole time the plant is being built and its costs amortized, because the patterns of these costs change from time to time. There is a 'geography of industrial costs, detected by studying the locational system that controls its components.'[5]

Complexity also is reduced by including in the analysis only the most important of the almost infinite number of possible variables. The previous chapters have examined those most commonly considered. Of course, in a specific instance the selection of the relevant variables is uniquely conditioned by the firm's needs, operational procedures, competitive situation and its internal geography. Generally, if a factor is a very small contributor to the proposed plant's cost structure it can be dropped from the analysis. Conversely, even if a factor is a major cost component it is locationally unimportant if it does not exhibit place to place variation.

Finally, the practical approach is facilitated by spatial sequencing. The normal procedure is first to determine the region, then to conduct a detailed analysis of alternative areas within the acceptable region and then to select a site within the best of the relatively small areas. Of course, these steps are not mutually exclusive, and some interaction, especially between areas (e.g., cities) and sites is common. The primary focus in this chapter is on the selection of region and area (or city); the selection of specific building sites within designated small areas is discussed in Chapter 6.

Also, the relative importance of the variables may change with the scale of the search. Table 7-1, from a study of industrial location decision making in southeastern Ohio, provides one example.[6] Note that the rankings for many of the factors, according to the number of times mentioned by this sample of actual location decision makers, are relatively stable across the spatial scales. Labor productivity and labor rates are consistently high, executive convenience, dispersion tendencies, supplies accessibility and corporate communications tend to rank in the middle, and induced amenities and taxes are consistently ranked low. Some factors, however, significantly and consistently decrease or

National		Sub-national	
1. Labor productivity	(31)	Personal contacts	(34)
2. Market accessibility	(29)	Labor productivity	(30)
3. Labor rates	(25)	Market accessibility	(26)
4. Transport facilities	(22)	Labor rates	(23)
5. Dispersion tendencies	(14)	Dispersion tendencies	(21)
6. Facilities and utilities	(14)	Transport facilities	(20)
7. Supplies accessibility	(8)	Labor availability	(12)
8. Personal contacts	(8)	Supplies accessibility	(11)
9. Labor availability	(6)	Corporate communications	(7)
10. Executive convenience	(3)	Executive convenience	(5)
11. Corporate communications	(1)	Taxes	(4)
12. Local amenities	(0)	Local amenities	(3)
13. Induced amenities	(0)	Facilities and utilities	(2)
14. Taxes	(0)	Induced amenities	(0)
Totals	161		198

SOURCE: H.A. Stafford, "The Anatomy of the Location Decision: Content Analysis of *Decision Making*, (London: John Wiley & Sons, Ltd., 1974).

Table 7-1. Counts For Factors At Each Spatial Scale By Total Responses

Regional		Local	
Personal contacts	(71)	Personal contacts	(109)
Labor availability	(45)	Labor productivity	(46)
Labor rates	(38)	Local amenities	(36)
Labor productivity	(27)	Labor availability	(31)
Transport facilities	(23)	Dispersion tendencies	(22)
Local amenities	(22)	Facilities and utilities	(21)
Corporate communications	(16)	Executive convenience	(17)
Dispersion tendencies	(14)	Labor rates	(15)
Supplies accessibility	(14)	Transport facilities	(13)
Executive convenience	(13)	Supplies accessibility	(12)
Facilities and utilities	(11)	Corporate communications	(12)
Induced amenities	(7)	Induced amenities	(10)
Market accessibility	(4)	Market accessibility	(3)
Taxes	(3)	Taxes	(2)
	308		350

Case Studies," in F.E.I. Hamilton (ed.) *Spatial Perspectives on Industrial Organization and* increase in rank across the spatial scales. Market accessibility shifts downward with decreasing regional scale, while the local amenities and personal contacts factors shift upward. This suggests that for the firms in question, the "real" locational search—which requires area personal cooperation, contacts and information—gets started at the sub-national rather than the national scale, and continues at the regional and local levels. This tends to substantiate the hypothesis that the spatial search process is very quickly limited in scope, and marketing considerations are primarily important in determining the large region within which the primarily cost oriented search takes place. The fact that the sum of responses for all factors consistently increases as the scale becomes larger, indicating more effort at the more local scales where cost variations usually are most critical, helps explain the dominance in the industrial location literature of cost oriented analytic techniques.

C. The Comparative Costs Framework

Keeping in mind the inherent incompleteness of any practical approach, it is now possible to examine in some detail the most common technique for combining the relevant variables and comparing alternative plant locations. An examination of both the academic and applied industrial location literature clearly revels that the comparative costs technique, with the objecive of identifying the least cost point among reasonable alternatives, is preferred. All of the case studies included in *Industrial Facilities Planning*[7] (and summarized in Chapter 2) are focused on computing and comparing total costs.

Given the type and size and operating characteristics of the plant to be located, the comparative costs approach essentially consists of calculating the individual costs for each relevant variable—via the techniques discussed in Part II—and summing these for each reasonable alternate location being considered. Other things being equal, the potential location with the lowest total cost is the preferred manufacturing point.[8]

The elements of the typical comparative costs analysis can be illustrated by using hypothetical (but realistic) data on 25 cities for the location of an (imaginary) metal fabricating plant by the METFAB Co.[9] Previous to the actual location search it has been decided what the plant will manufacture and how it will be done. In this case the primary product is metal vessels to be sold to producers of heavy chemicals products (basic and agricultural chemicals). The plant is to be of medium size with a total employment of about 200 persons. The major production inputs are copper, steel and labor. Both materials inputs and outbound products will move by rail. It also has been previously determined, for a variety of reasons, that the factory must be located in a large city in the continental United States; thus, the 25 largest U.S. cities comprise the initial set of possible locations. (For the sake of simplification, it is assumed that the plant to be built is the firm's only manufacturing facility.)

From knowledge of the industry and the specifics of the proposed operation, management has determined that the key locational costs are (1) product shipping costs, (2) materials shipping costs, (3) labor cost and (4) taxes. A cost estimate must be made for each of these four factors.

Product shipping costs are compiled by figuring the amount of finished product from a potential location to be shipped to each market and multiplying the tonnages by the appropriate freight costs. The anticipated tonnages to be shipped are determined by measuring the market potential for each city, adjusted (in some way) to account for the locational advantages or disadvantages of competitors. Each of the 25 cities is considered, in turn, as a potential manufacturing site and cost of shipping the product to each of the other 24 is computed. Summing these gives product shpping costs for a city. The results are shown in the fourth column of the Total Costs, Table 7-2.

The materials transport costs similarily are computed for each city by multiplying the amount of steel to be shipped from the most economical supplier (in this case the closest) times the appropriate freight costs. The composite results are listed in the second column of Table 7-2. In this case, the transportation cost of the copper input is not computed since all the copper producers absorb transportation costs and sell at a uniform delivered cost regardless of location. (Only long distance transport costs are computed; intra-city transport costs are assumed essentially equal everywhere and are ignored, producing a zero materials transport cost for those cities with local steel suppliers.)

Taxes are estimated from examination of city and state schedules. It is realized that actual tax bills may be subject to negotiation, and also that there may be significant local variations within any metropolitan area, but some first approximations will at least give a sense of the relative variations between cities. These (hypothetical) guesses are in

Metropolitan Area	Taxes	Materials Transport Costs	Labor Costs	Product Shipping Costs	Total Costs
New York	$320,000	$120,000	$1,346,000	$1,830,900	$3,616,900
Chicago	130,000	0	1,361,000	1,715,900	3,206,900
Los Angeles	250,000	62,000	1,398,000	5,259,500	6,969,500
Philadelphia	275,000	0	1,308,000	1,719,300	3,302,300
Detroit	311,000	182,000	1,416,000	1,628,800	3,537,800
San Francisco	250,000	174,000	1,418,000	5,396,000	7,238,000
Boston	175,000	200,000	1,241,000	2,281,100	3,897,100
Pittsburgh	125,000	0	1,325,000	1,496,800	2,946,800
St. Louis	140,000	182,000	1,320,000	1,695,500	3,337,500
Washington, D.C.	160,000	136,000	1,276,000	1,680,500	3,252,500
Cleveland	122,000	132,000	1,301,000	1,534,400	3,089,400
Baltimore	264,000	124,000	1,304,000	1,642,900	3,334,900
Minneapolis	180,000	212,000	1,296,000	2,472,600	4,160,600
Buffalo	118,000	170,000	1,309,000	1,724,300	3,321,300
Houston	100,000	300,000	1,299,000	2,848,600	4,547,600
Milwaukee	180,300	114,000	1,339,000	1,872,300	3,505,300
Seattle	200,000	530,000	1,335,000	5,457,900	7,522,900
Dallas	150,000	284,000	1,179,000	2,730,600	4,343,600
Cincinnati	125,000	188,000	1,295,000	1,496,100	3,104,100
Kansas City	135,000	222,000	1,286,000	2,179,100	3,822,100
San Diego	200,000	82,000	1,361,000	5,219,600	6,862,600
Atlanta	130,000	148,000	1,182,000	1,999,200	3,459,200
Denver	150,000	366,000	1,295,000	3,231,300	5,042,300
Miami	120,000	314,000	1,189,000	3,311,700	4,934,700
New Orleans	130,000	206,000	1,224,000	2,430,300	3,990,300

SOURCE: *Manufacturing and Agriculture Unit. High School Geography Project,* 1966.

Table 7-2. Total Costs (Hypothetical Example)

the first column of Table 7-2. Including these with the other variable costs provides a clue as to whether the tax issue is of sufficient magnitude to warrant detailed site level examination.

The previously decided type and scale of operation determines the number and composition of the labor force to be employed (e.g., 70 welders, 40 metal workers, 30 machinists, 20 engineers, 20 draftsmen, 2 secretaries, etc.). From a variety of sources (such as those described in Section A of Chapter 4) the average wage and fringe payments are obtained for each job classification. Multiplying the number to be employed in each category by the appropriate average labor cost, and summing, produces the total labor costs of column three in Table 7-2.

An examination of Table 7-2, "Total Costs," reveals considerable variation in the general magnitudes of the dollar figures among the four key factors, as well as variations for each factor among the cities. Of the individual factors, product shipping costs shows the largest magnitudes and a dollar variation of $3,961,800 between the least expensive city (Cincinnati) and the most expensive (Seattle). Although also of large magnitude, total labor costs show relatively little variation among cities (the difference between the highest cost city, San Francisco, and the lowest cost city, Dallas, is $239,000).

The high degree of variability among cities on materials transport costs is partly mitigated by the relatively small magnitudes of the dollar figures. The spread between highest to lowest is $530,000, a range intermediate between those for product shipping costs and labor costs. Taxes, with both relatively small magnitudes and variability, show a gross range of only $220,000.

The comparative total cost figures in column five of Table 7-2 probably will allow the site selector to eliminate from further consideration the very high cost cities (e.g., Los Angeles, San Francisco, Houston, Seattle, Dallas, San Diego, Denver, Miami, etc.). Very good non-cost arguments would have to be put forward to compensate for the cost penalty which would be incurred by locating in any one of them. Conversely, the least cost cities (e.g., Chicago, Pittsburgh, Cleveland, Cincinnati, etc.) would be prime candidates for more detailed examination.

Since the determining locational factor is the cost of shipping the finished product to market, this would be the variable to focus on if further refinement at the national scale is deemed necessary. This may not be true, however, at the regional or local scale. For example, for the four lowest cost cities variations in materials transport costs are almost as important as variations in product shipping costs. As the scale of investigation changes, so too will the relative importance of the locational variables.

D. The Least Cost, Weighted Criteria Approach

The site selection study sequenced utilized by The Gates Rubber Co.[10] provides a useful industry-developed example of the commonly employed extension of the comparative costs framework, the Least Cost/Weighted Criteria approach which attempts to combine both quantitative and qualitative factors. The Gates Site Selection group becomes active *after* management has decided to locate a new facility and has outlined the criteria to be met. The selection group is then engaged in a spatially sequential search for the best (lowest cost) combination of labor, transportation, taxes and utilities factors, but with due consideration for other less tangible influences.

The specification of the acceptable region is dependent upon comparative transportation (freight) costs on materials acquisition and product shipping for a number of likely cities. (The prior selection of cities to be included is not discussed; presumably, these are intuitively chosen based on previous company experience.) The calculation of product shipping costs proceeds by taking existing market points and volumes as given, figuring the "center of the market," and then computing the cost of reaching the "center of the market" for a given volume of product from each of the possible plant locations. The "Grid System Location Procedure" for determining the center of the market is a relatively simple technique, apparently the same as that advocated by Yaseen.[11] (With the number crunching power of modern computers, it would be feasible and more precise to bypass the "center of the market" routine, and directly compute the shipping costs to all markets from each city under consideration.)

The freight costs on incoming supplies are computed in the same manner, utilizing the grid-determined "center of supply." The incoming and outgoing freight costs can then be compared for each city. In the Gates situation, market access is (somehow) deemed more important than supplies access, and thus outbound freight costs are more heavily weighed. Generally, Gates favors cities close to the "center of market" point.

After identifying, on the basis of transportation costs, access and population, a small set of most likely cities, more detailed data are collected. Including the transportation figures, information is gathered on 43 separate criteria under six major headings: Transportation, Labor, Taxes, Site, Utilities and Services. Where estimated annual operating costs can be determined, the dollar amounts are entered for each criterion. These figures can then be displayed for each of the alternative locations and annual operating costs (so far as determined) compared.

For each criterion where dollar estimaters are either unavailable or inappropriate, the city should be rated according to some scale (e.g., 5 = Excellent, 4 = Above Average, 3 = Average, 2 = Substandard, 1 = Poor). How Gates determines a given rating is not explained, but presumably reliance is on experience to make judgments according to some absolute scales and relative to the alternative prospective locations.

After simplifying the problem by selecting a relatively few cities for detailed analysis (and assuming that the best location has not been left out), then gathering detailed information and measuring each criterion either objectively or subjectively (as appropriate or feasible), the analyst is faced with one set of qualified data and another of qualitative information. How may the quantiative and the qualitative be merged to provide final answers? Also, in developing the final composite index for each city how may the criteria be assessed according to their relative importance in the location decision? Gates resorts to a "weighted average point system" for scaling criteria and comparing dollar cost data with intangible factors.

The Gates article illustrates the weighting process by showing the variable number of points assigned the 43 criteria. The weights reflect the relative importance of each variable in determining locational choice. The previously determined dollar figures are converted to the same rating scale (5 = Excellent through 1 = Poor) used for the "nonquantifiable" criteria. Now that all the variables are rated on a common five point scale they may be compared and combined. Multiplying each rating by the criterion's weight and summing these produces a composite total point count for each city. The city with the highest point count is the best choice.

The weighting of the criteria obviously is a key ingredient in the Gates process. For example, transportation is assigned 50 percent of the total possible 10,000 points (that is, a rating of five times the specific weight of 1,000 equals 5,000 points). Within the transportation category, truck-in is assigned 80 percent, or 4,000 points, and truck-out is assigned 70 percent of these 4,000. Unfortunately, how these variable point counts are assigned is not explained. That they are dependent on Gates' experience and the specific situation under consideration is suggested by the note that "the factors can be modified, rearranged and weighted differently for various types of facilities."[12] The necessity of tailoring the weights to the problem is frequently expressed, but precise procedures are doing so are not given.

When discussing RCA's approach, Burns states that:

"Depending upon the type of product, the size of operation, and the purpose (to increase productive capacity, to handle a new product, to serve a particular market, to replace an inefficient operation, or a combination of these), we weight certain factors more heavily than others in our search for plant site."[13]

Similarly General Electric's Gates suggests that:

". . . you can take the criteria you have developed and apply weights to it. You can decide what criteria are important to your business. The degree of sophistication is up to you; you can use a ten (10) point, 100 point, or 1000 point system. The numbers aren't imporant—what is important is that you collect and formalize data at every step and that you make the decision as to what is important for your business. For instance, if you have a highly mechanized or automated operation, a large labor supply isn't as important as good repair shops and a stable, reliable power supply."[14]

The assessment of ratings and the assignment of weights are tricky procedures. They rely heavily on the expertise and wisdom of managers and site selectors. There is no measure of rightness other than the imperfect test of experience.

E. The Revenue (Demand) Factor

A simple definition of profit is revenues minus costs. The typical comparative costs model calculates only part of the equation; it assumes revenues are insensitive to location. If a firm's objective is to maximize profit (or maximize sales) then the strict least cost formulation is incomplete.

The least-cost solution *does* incorporate the marketing factor by including outbound freight costs and can be extended to include direct selling costs. If the inclusion of these marketing costs produces total costs which are in turn directly related to selling price, which then determines sales volumes, then there is no problem. But what if sales are also dependent on servicing time? What if sales are a function of the amount of personal contact between producer and customer, and the frequency of contact decreases with distance (or access)? What if customers buy partly on the basis of familiarity and regional loyalty (including political pressures)? If the distance component of the finished product shipping charges also adequately expresses these relationships, then again there is no problem with the standard least-cost formulation. In reality, however, this is not the normal situation. In reality, proximity gives a competitive edge over and above costs.

How can the total issue of proximity to markets be included in the locational calculus? As noted in Section A, the problem is insoluble in an absolute sense. In practice there are some appropriate adjustments.

One possibility is to weight the measurable outbound shipping costs more heavily than the simple expensive calculations warrant. To the extent that the relative differences in shipping costs also express the other distance-related sales influences, such an adjustment may be adequate. Industrial location case studies reveal that such adjustments are common, especially when using the weighted criteria approach. In the above noted Gates Rubber Co. procedure, for example, the comprehensive importance of market access is revealed by the truck transport 7:3 weighting ratio of outbound shipping costs versus inbound freight costs.

How may a firm determine if market proximity is not adequately measured by finished product shipping costs? If it is not, how may the appropriate weights be determined? There are no precise, or even easy, answers. Possible clues may be provided by taking data for an existing plant and comparing for major markets the relationship between sales and average shipping costs versus the relationship between sales and some other measure of access, such as distance alone or travel time. If data are adequate, these may be compared via simple correlation and partial regression techniques. Keep in mind that the total explanation in sales is acknowledged to be a function of many more variables than the proximity measures; here the emphasis is only on their relative predictive power. It also may be useful to plot the relationships on cross section paper, producing two graphs which may be compared for relative dispersion. Comparing the slopes may also be instructive; for example, it may be discovered that the proportionately decreasing influence on shipping costs as distance increases (due to long haul economies) does not explain the diminution in distant sales as well as the disporportionately large influence of great distances on the lesser frequency of potential buyer-seller contacts.

These are crude devices. So are the other procedures sometimes advocated for more fully accounting for the demand factor, such as the market potential model and market-area analysis.[15] There is enormous scope and need for the sound judgment of experienced management. In reality, the location of the market is usually the most important of all the variables (see Chapter 4). The common solution to the difficulties of combining the cost and demand factors is to split the problem. The distribution of the market delimits the large search region ("Where in the Northeast shall we put our plant to serve that market?" "Where in the United Kingdom shall we locate to serve the British market?"). Then the search concentrates on finding the least cost location ("Does New York offer cost advantages over Boston?" "Are the labor costs in mid-Wales enough lower to compensate for added transport expenditures?"). The most often expressed general justification for a new plant is not costs, or profits, or rate of return, but rather need for additional productive capacity and marketing opportunities.[16] The repeated emphasis on the geography of industrial *costs* is thus misleading. Most commonly, the costs are determinate only within the context of the market region. Dealing first with marketing considerations and then determining on the basis of costs the best location within the broad market area is not an ideal solution, but it often has practical advantages.

F. Other Complications

Even if the costs and revenue factors could be simultaneously assessed, all problems would not be solved. The size of plant to be located has been taken as given. How is this decided? The optimum size of plant is in part a function of its location, which is a function of the size of plant. The Linear Programming techniques discussed in Chapter 8 are of some assistance in addressing this conundrum. The procedures so far discussed are concerned with the location of one plant; the solution to the two plant problem (e.g., one now, another in the near future but included in current planning) is different. How does the site selector compensate for possible future changes in the locations of markets, materials and competitors? These relate to the discussion in

Chapter 1 of the uncertain future and forecasting; in practice such possible changes are ignored. Finally. how is it decided if an investment is financially sound? What if the returns vary over time? These questions are addressed in Chapter 9.

Notes and References—Chapter 7

1. Stafford, Howard A. "Industrial Location Decision Model," *Proceedings, Association of American Geographers,* 1969, pp. 141-145.

2. Smith, David M. *Industrial Location.* New York: John Wiley and Sons, Inc., 1971, p. 328.

3. *Ibid.*

4. See Isard, Walter. *Methods of Regional Analysis: An Introduction to Regional Science.* Cambridge, Mass.: The M.I.T. Press, 1960.

5. Russell, Joseph A. "Modern Geography: Foundation of Corporate Strategy," *The Professional Geographer,* Vol. XXIX, No. 2 May, 1977, p. 203.

6. Stafford, Howard A. "The Anatomy of the Location Decision: Content Analysis of Case Studies." Reproduced with permission from *Spatial Perspectives on Industrial Organization and Decision Making,* by F.E. Ian Hamilton (ed.), p. 176. Copyright© 1974, by John Wiley and Sons, Ltd., London.

7. Conway, H.M., and Liston, L.L., *Industrial Facilities Planning.* Atlanta. Conway Publications, 1976.

8. Excellent examples of the "anatomy of comparative costs frameworks" are provided by Smith, David M., *op. cit.,* especially pp. 320-326 and pp. 361-387.

9. This illustration is taken from Stafford, Howard A., *Manufacturing and Agriculture Unit,* High School Geography Project of the Assn. of American Geographers, Washington, D.C., 1966. (Subsequently published as part of *Geography in an Urban Age.* Toronto: Macmillan, 1970.)

10. Gabe, Vernon. "One Approach to Facility Search, Selection and Acquisition: The Site Selection Study Sequence," *Industrial Development*, July/August, 1974. (In *Industrial Facilities Planning, op. cit.,* pp. 146-148.)

11. Yaseen, Leonard C. *Plant Location.* New York: American Research Council, New York, 1960, pp. 19-21.

12. Gabe, Vernon, *op. cit.,* p. 146.

13. Burns, John L. "RCA Advocates Systematic Approach," *Industrial Development*, November, 1961. (In *Industrial Facilities Planning, op. cit.,* p. 131.)

14. Gates, Elmer D. "Location Analysis and Site Selection," *Industrial Development*, May, 1962. (In *Industrial Facilities Planning, op. cit.,* p. 131.)

15. Smith, David M., *op. cit.,* p. 388.

16. Tugendhat, Christopher. *The Multinationals.* London: Eyre and Spottiswoode, London, 1971, p. 167.

VIII Linear Programming/ Operations Research

VIII
Linear Programming/Operations Research

The overly broad term "Operations Research" refers to the processes of logical model building and application of mathematics to aid in decision-making. It is an applied field with special appeal to management. Indeed, rather than the commonly accepted, but perhaps misleading, appellation "O.R.," some prefer to label the field as "Management Sciences" or "Decision Analysis." Since its inception in the 1940's, the body of applications and techniques falling under the rubic "operations research" has greatly expanded. Wagner's standard text and reference volume alone runs to over 1,000 pages and contains more than 1,000 exercises.[1] The various techniques include Linear Programming, Network Analysis, Dynamic Programming, Integer Programming, Non-Linear Programming, Unbounded Horizon Models, Stochastic Models, Waiting Line Models, Markov Chains, Game Theory and Computer Simulation. These may be applied to problems such as inventory control and scheduling, machine scheduling, purchasing policy and assignments of people and things.

Operations research also includes techniques which are useful in solving problems of special concern to facility planners and site selectors. Of particular interest are those which help determine the optimum size of a plant, the optimal product mix within a plant and the best location for the plant. These three problems, of course, are interdependent, which condition greatly complicates industrial location analysis. The optimum size of a plant influences the number of plants and thus locational strategies. This is the tension between economies of scale and the friction of distance. Likewise, product mix influences the optimum location, and the location of the plant influences the optimum product mix. Like the difficulty in Chapter 7 of integrating minimum costs and maximum demand, these simultaneously interacting forces render the problems ultimately insolvable. Operations research techniques, however, can offer some decision making aids and provide "state of the art" solutions through partial integration and through successive iterations. A full discussion of the potentially useful techniques is far beyond the scope of this chapter. Rather, the product-mix issue is treated separately, and the location analysis focuses on cost, with the optimum size of plant issue only mentioned.

Even restricting the discussion to locational analysis and focusing on the most popular technique, Linear Programming, does not solve the exposition problem. A complete discussion would require a very large volume of its own. Rather, the approach taken here is a very simple introduction to provide site selectors with a "feel" for the model building process and the elements of the analysis so that insightful questions may be posed and to aid in the interpretation of the results of "canned" computer programs. For those already familiar with the basics, and for those who wish to make maximum use of these technical aids, reference to the vast operations research and Linear Programming literature is highly recommended.

Although it is unlikely that the experienced site selector has totally avoided exposure to the decision-aiding methods of operations research, the uninitiated may wish to inquire before proceeding whether such techniques are indeed utilized in "real-world" practice. The very practically oriented *Industrial Development*[2] articles reprinted in *Industrial Facilities Planning*[3] provide a clue. The 22 case studies synthesized in Chapter 2 of this volume contain under "techniques of analysis" three references to Linear Programming, one to systems analysis, and three references to modeling and simulation. The lack of specific mention does not necessarily indicate that O.R. techniques were not used in other cases. These figures also are likely to be conservative in terms of present practice because the majority of the case studies reflect procedures of over 15 years ago; only one case carries a 1970's date.

Additionally, three articles deal primarily with the application of operations research techniques. In his 1965 article Jeske outlines "Linear Programming as an Aid in the Solution of Plant Location Problems."[4] The 1959 article by Johnson provides an actual data presentationof plant site selection via Linear Programming and also touches on the product-mix problem.[5] Wortham's 1962 "New Planning Tools" article discusses and illustrates Simulation, Linear Programming, Critical Path Scheduling and Subjective Probabilities.[6] There is evidence that the methods of operations research, and especially the linear optimization models, have found a place in the analytical processes of locating factories. There also is the suspicion that they are not utilized as often as they should be.

A. Product-Mix Selection

Plant site selection is simplified (but not optimized) if the mix and magnitudes of the products to be produced are determined exogenously[1] and prior to the location search. Alternatively, the product-mix may be adjusted after the location is chosen, as Johnson suggests.[7] Beginning with the product-mix issue in this discussion is not meant to infer anything about the merits of either the before or after sequence. Rather, product-mix is first to aid in exposition. The variable product-mix illustrations used here are very, very simple and can be solved graphically. The graphic solution should help elucidate the basic structure of the linear optimization (Linear Programming) approach. More complex problems cannot be solved graphically, but the principles remain the same. Linear Programming always is concerned with solving simultaneous linear equations.

Consider a hypothetical manufacturer who produces in the same factory two kinds of shirts, full button-down-the-front dress shirts (dress) and pull-over sport shirts (sport).[8] There are three separate fabricating processes, (1) Cutting, (2) Sewing and (3) Packaging. The time required per shirt for each operation varies with the type of shirt, as follows:

	Cutting	Sewing	Packaging
DRESS	6 minutes	24 minutes	10 minutes
SPORT	8 minutes	20 minutes	4 minutes

Assume that the labor force cannot be altered in the short run. There are two Cutting workers, six Sewers and two Packagers. Each worker can make either dress or sport shirts, but cannot switch jobs.

If the profit per dress shirt is 75 cents and the profit per sport shirt is 50 cents, determine how many of each the manufacturer should schedule so to achieve maximum profit for an eight-hour production day (all other things being equal).

Let x = the number of dress shirts to be made.
   y = the number of sport shirts to be made.

Then, set up the constraints on production:

$x \geq 0$ since negative production
$y \geq 0$ is impossible)

The total cutting time for producing x dress and y sport shirts is 6x + 8y. The total worker time available for cutting is two workers for eight hours each = 16 hours or 960 minutes. Therefore, the cutting time constraint is:

$$6x + 8y \leq 960$$

Similarly, the sewing time constraint is:

$$24x + 20y \leq 2880$$

and the packaging time constraint is:

$$10x + 4y \leq 960$$

The profit function is written:

$$P = 75x + 50y$$

The problem now is to determine the production mix of dress and sport shirts that will produce profits, given the above constraints.

First, graph the three production constraint equations, Cutting (CC'), Sewing (SS'), Packaging (PP'), as shown on Figure 8-1. Since both x and y must be positive amounts (or zero) the feasible region for combinations of dress and sport shirts must lie in the first quadrant. The outer bound of the feasible region is determined by the inward most segments of each constraint equation. Thus, the feasible region is that bounded by the origin and C' GHP.

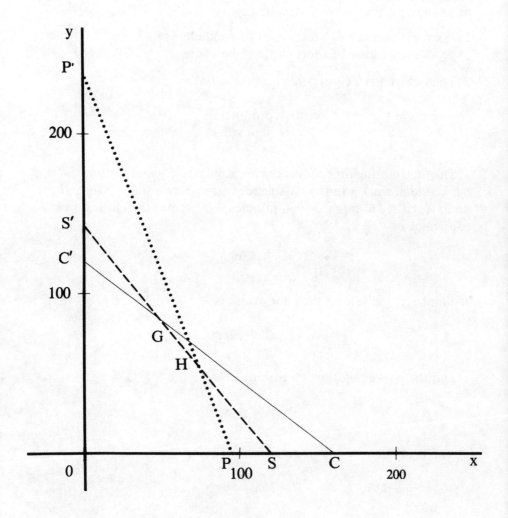

Figure 8-1. Production Constraints.

Next plot the profit function, P = 75x + 50y. The various profit levels yield a family of parallel straight lines, each with slope of -2/3, as shown on Figure 8-2.

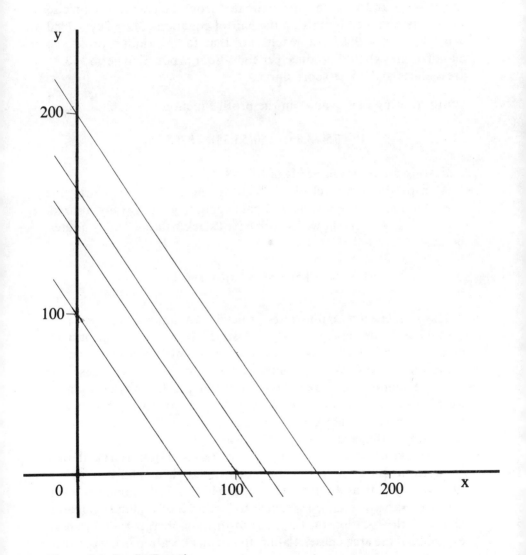

Figure 8-2. Profit Function.

Now superimpose Figure 8-2 on Figure 8-1 as shown in Figure 8-3. The outermost point of the feasible region which just touches, but is not intersected by, one of the family of profit lines, indicates the number of dress (x) and sport (y) shirts which should be produced to provide maximum profit. In this example the maximum profit combination is given by the coordinates of point H, which is the intersection of the sewing and packaging constraint equations. The values for x and y can be approximated from the graph. The precise values are obtained by solving the pair of equations $24x + 20y = 2880$ and $10x + 4y = 960$. The results are that for maximum profit the manufacturer should produce per eight-hour production period 73.85 dress shirts and 55.38 sport shirts.

Substituting these values in the profit function:

$$P = 75(73.85) + 50(55.38) = 8307.75,$$

indicating a maximum profit of $83.08.

At a production level of 73.85 dress and 55.58 sport shirts, the available time of the sewing and packaging workers is fully utilized. The cutting workers, however, will have "slack" time of 73.86 minutes, because

$$[6(73.85) + 8(55.38)] = 886.14.$$

This simple exercise illustrates principles common to all linear programming. It also may be used to illustrate the previously mentioned mututal interdependences between product-mix, optimum size of plant and the friction of distance in plant location. In this case, the optimum amount and mix of production is dependent on the availability of labor, which is an area attribute. If the area was chosen with product amount and mix given prior to the search, then it is probable, for example, that access to materials was part of the location calculus. For the sake of illustration, suppose the dress and sport shirt materials come from quite different source areas, and their relative access is locationally critical. In order to assess the impact of supplies access it was necessary to assume a specific production level and mix. But after choosing the location on the basis of this factor, it is found that an attribute of the area chosen (labor) forces an alteration in the product-mix. This might mean that the original location choice is no longer

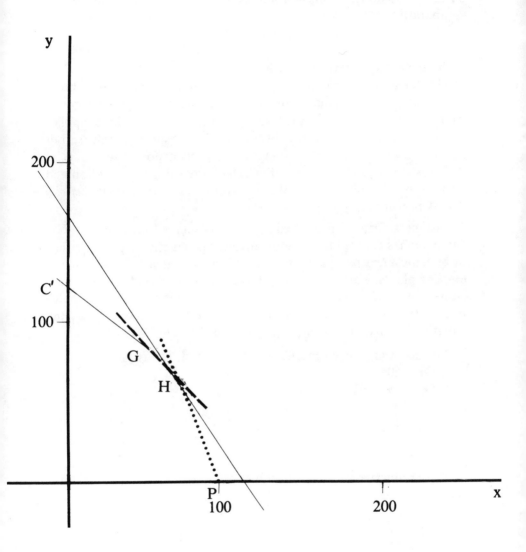

Figure 8-3. Maximum Profit Combination.

optimal; and so the analyst would be led into a series of narrowing, comparative interations.

B. The Transportation Problem

The linear programming algorithm (a set of repetitive computational rules) most popular in plant location analysis is the "transportation problem." Actually, the "transportation problem" label applies to any matrix of interactions, not necessarily transportation per se, but for the site selector an example using transportation costs is appropriate. The algorithm is illustrated here using the situation and approach of Johnson in the previously mentioned *Industrial Development* article.[1]

Assume a firm with two existing plants serves four markets. The company has decided that it must increase productive capacity, either by building a new plant and/or by increasing the capacity at either of the existing plants. Three alternative locations for a new plant have been (somehow) identified. The only variable to be considered in the solution is the cost of transporting the product to market. Thus, the situation as given is set out in Figure 8-4.

The demand at each market (or destination, Dj) is given as:
$$D_1 = 20$$
$$D_2 = 25$$
$$D_3 = 40$$
$$D_4 = 10$$

The productive capacity at each existing or proposed plant is given as:
$$P_1 = 25$$
$$P_2 = 30$$
$$P'_1 = 50$$
$$P'_2 = 50$$
$$P'_3 = 50$$

Making the simplifying assumption that only one construction project will be undertaken, the problem then is to decide, based solely on marketing transportation costs, whether the additional capacity (50 units) should be added to one of the existing plants (P_1 or P_2) or put in

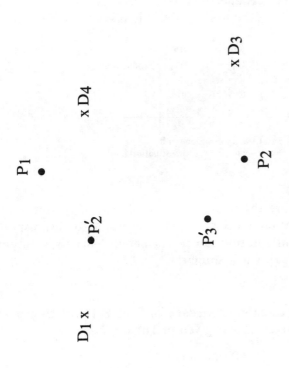

Figure 8-4. Transportation Costs.

a new plant at one of the previously determined alternative locations (P_1', P_2', or P_3'). The problem may be solved by using the transportation problem algorithm on each possible combination of plant sites and comparing the results to determine the least cost configuration. This process may be illustrated by computing, for example, the allocation of products to markets and the total transportation costs of the P_1, P_2, P_3' configuration. The basic problem is as set out in Table 8-1.

Destinations:

Origins:		D_1	D_2	D_3	D_4	Production:
	P_1	C_{11}	C_{12}	C_{13}	C_{14}	P_1
	P_2	C_{21}	C_{22}	C_{23}	C_{24}	P_2
	P_3'	C_{31}	C_{32}	C_{33}	C_{34}	P_3
Demand		d_1	d_2	d_3	d_4	

where c_{ij} = the cost of transporting one unit
of product from origin i to destination j.

Table 8-1

To be determined are the unknown optimal flows (f_{ij}) from each origin to each destination. Once these are known, the total transport costs for this plant configuration can be calculated. Thus, the solution which minimizes $\sum_1^n \sum_j^m f_{ij} C_{ij}$ is sought.

Assume that in this case the actual data for Table 8-1 (with transport costs in the matrix boxes) are as given in Table 8-2.

Destinations:

	D_1	D_2	D_3	D_4	D_5	P_i
Origins: P_1	20	50	30	10	0	25
P_2	35	45	15	25	0	30
P_3'	30	25	20	20	0	50
d_j	20	25	40	10	10	

Table 8-2

Note that a fifth, imaginary, destination (D_5) has been added to the matrix. The addition of this "slack" (or "dummy" or "dump") variable is necessary in this case because the total proposed productive capacity (105) exceeds the amount currently demanded (95).

The solution proceeds by a series of iterations in which an initial trial allocation is made, which is then assessed to determine whether total costs may be lowered by a different allocation. If so, a new allocation is made and it is assessed. This process continues until no further reductions in total transport costs are possible by further reallocation.

Of course, the solution could be achieved by trial and error, but in any real problem the number of possible combinations is too large to make such an approach practical. An efficient search procedure is provided by the transportation problem algorithm. For ease of exposition, the so-called "northwest corner" technique is here illustrated.[10]

The first iteration starts by taking $cell_{11}$ (the "northwest corner"). Compare the values of p_1 and d_1 and take the lesser value and enter as the unknown f_{11}

	D_1	D_2	D_3	D_4	D_5	p_i
P_1	20					25
P_2						30
P_3						50
d_j	20	25	40	10	10	

Since all of the demand at D_1 is immediately satisfied by P_1, enter zeros for P_2 (f_{21}) and P_3 (f_{31}). Then determine where the excess capacity of P_1 (25 - 20 = 5) should be shipped. Allocate five units to D_2 (f_{12}). All of the production of P_1 is now allocated, so zeroes are entered for D_3 (f_{13}), D_4 (f_{14}), and $D5$ (f_{15}).

	D_1	D_2	D_3	D_4	D_5	
P_1	20	5	0	0	0	25
P_2	0					30
P_3'	0					50
	20	25	40	10	10	

Now, allocate the capacity available at P_2 to D_2 (f_{22}), again using the "lesser" criterion, i.e., $f_{22} = 25$. However, in this case D_2 has already been allocated five from P_1, so the entry must be 20 units. Then allocate the remaining capacity of P_2 to D_3 (f_{23}), and a zero in f_{32} because the demand at D_2 is now satisfied.

	D_1	D_2	D_3	D_4	D_5	
P_1	20	5	0	0	0	25
P_2	0	20	10	0	0	30
P'_3	0	0				50
	20	25	40	10	10	

Similarly, allocate the production of $P'3$. The resultant first allocation is then:

	D_1	D_2	D_3	D_4	D_5	Production:
P_1	20	5	0	0	0	25
P_2	0	20	10	0	0	30
P'_3	0	0	30	10	10	50
Demand	20	25	40	10	10	

Table 8-3 First Allocation

The total transportation costs can now be computed for this allocation by multiplying the flow (amount, f_{ij}) in each cell by its transport costs (C_{ij} from Table 8-2) and adding. For this allocation the total transportation costs are:
$\Sigma\Sigma$ f_{ij} c_{ij} = 20(20) + 5(50) + 20(45) + 10(15)+ 30(20) + 10(20) + 10(0) = 2500.

Is this the optimal allocation? A device known as "shadow prices" is used as the first step in checking the optimality of the allocation. A shadow price, U_i, is computed for each row, and a shadow price, V_j, is computed for each column. These are computed with reference to the original cost matrix, C_{ij} (Table 8-2), according to the formula $V_j - U = C_{ij}$.

The row (U_1) and column (V_j) shadow prices are figured only from the filled in (non-zero) cells of the first allocation. These cells are marked by asterisks in Table 8-4.

	D_1	D_2	D_3	D_4	D_5	U_i
P_1	*	*				0
P_2		*	*			5
P'_3			*	*	*	0
V_j	20	50	20	20	0	

————Shadow Prices————

Table 8-4. Shadow Prices, First Allocation

Since only the relative values are important, the computation may be started by inserting any arbitary number for one of the U_i's. It is usually convenient to assign $U_1 = 0$. Then, $V_1 = 20$ because:

$$V_1 - U_1 = C_{11}$$
$$V_1 - 0 = 20 \text{ (from the cost matrix of}$$
$$\text{Table 8-2)}$$
$$V_1 = 20$$

Likewise,

$$V_2 - U_1 = C_{12}$$
$$V_2 - 0 = 50$$
$$V_2 = 50$$

And then,

$$V_2 - U_2 = C_{22}$$
$$50 - U_2 = 45$$
$$- U_2 = -5$$
$$U_2 = 5$$

and so on until all the U_i and V_j values are filled in, as shown on Table 8-4.

Now attention is turned to the *unfilled* (zero) cells of the first allocation. "Shadow Costs" or "opportunity costs" $(\overline{C}_{ij})$ are computed for each of the *unfilled* cells according to formula

$$V_j - U_i = \overline{C}_{ij}. \text{ Thus,}$$
$$V_1 - U_2 = \overline{C}_{21}$$
$$20 - 5 = \overline{C}_{21}$$
$$15 = \overline{C}_{21}$$
$$V_1 - U_3 = \overline{C}_{31}$$
$$20 - 0 = \overline{C}_{31}$$
$$20 = \overline{C}_{31}$$

and so on until the unfilled cells of the first allocation are filled in with $\overline{C}_{ij}$ values, as shown in Table 8-5.

	D_1	D_2	D_3	D_4	D_5	U_i
P_1	*	*	20	20✓	0	0
P_2	15	*	*	15	-5	5
P_3	20	50✓	*	*	*	0
v_j	20	50	20	20	0	

Table 8-5. Opportunity Costs, First Allocation

Now, search for all those cells in which the "opportunity costs" exceed the transport costs ($\overline{C}_{ij} > C_{ij}$). Comparing the original cost matrix (Table 8-2) with the opportunity costs of the first allocation (Table 8-5) reveals two unfilled cells in which $\overline{C}_{ij} > C_{ij}$, cell 32 and cell 14, which are checked in Table 8-5.

If there are no cells in which $\overline{C}_{ij} > C_{ij}$, then the allocation is optimal. However, if the opportunity costs of not filling a cell exceeds the cost of filling it ($\overline{C}_{ij} > C_{ij}$) then the allocation can be improved. Thus, in this case a second allocation is in order.

The greatest improvement can be made by reallocating some product to the cell which has the largest difference between $\overline{C}_{ij}$ and C_{ij}. Since $\overline{C}_{32}-C_{32} = 25$ and $\overline{C}_{14}-C_{14} = 10$, the second allocation begins by making an allocation to cell 32. Of course, a reallocation requires some adjustments in other allocations so as not to violate the program constraints; that is, the supply (row) and demand (column) totals must be maintained.

A condition of the reallocation is that only one previously filled cell can be emptied, and only one previously unoccupied (zero) cell can be filled. The process is a series of additions and subtractions which successively alternate between vertical and horizontal transfers; diagonal transfers can never be made.

Start the second allocation by marking the previously unoccupied cell designed to receive an allocation (cell 32) with a plus (+). then mark with a minus (-) the closest row and column cells which might give up some product to balance the row and column totals, as shown on Table 8-6 (for ease of reference, the first allocations are noted within parentheses in each cell).

	D_1	D_2	D_3	D_4	D_5	Production
	(20)	(5)				
P_1	20	5				25
		(20)	(10)			
P_2		(-)	30			30
P_3'		(+)20	(-)10	10	10	50
Demand 20		25	40	10	10	

Table 8-6. Second Allocation

Transfer as much as possible. In this case, transfer 20 units from cell$_{22}$ to cell$_{32}$. Immediately, one cell has been emptied and one new cell filled, reaching the limit. From now on, all transfers must be between occupied cells. With the cell$_{22}$ to cell$_{32}$ transfer, the column total remains correct, but the third row total has 20 units too many and the second row is 20 units short. Therefore, subtract 20 units from cell $_{33}$ and transfer them to cell$_{23}$. Now all constraints are satisfied and the second allocation complete. But is it optimal? Finding out calls for another sequence as before, first computing "shadow prices," $V_j-U_i =$ C_{ij} (Table 8-7).

	D_1	D_2	D_3	D_4	D_5		U_i
P_1	*	*	45✓	45✓	25✓		0
P_2	-10	20	*	15	-5		30
P_3'	-5	*	*	*	*		25
v_j	20	50	45	45	25		

———————————————— Shadow Prices ————————————————

Table 8-7. Shadow Prices, Second Allocation-Opportunity Costs, Second Allocation

and then computing "opportunity costs" ($\overline{C}_{ij} = V_j-U_i$) for the unoccupied cells of Table 8-7.

Now, compare the opportunity costs of the second allocation with the original cost matrix and note each cell in which $\overline{C}_{ij} > C_{ij}$ (checked in Table 8-7). The value $\overline{C}_{ij}-C_{ij}$ is 15 for cell$_{13}$, 35 for cell$_{14}$ and 25 for cell$_{15}$. The third allocation starts by assigning some units to currently unoccupied cell$_{14}$.

And so the process continues through a series of iterations. The stopping point is reached when an allocation has *no* opportunity costs greater than the transport costs ($C_{ij} > C_{ji}$). Then no further improvements can be made. The allocation is optimal. In this case, the third allocation (Table 8-8) is the best (optimal) allocation. (Some other allocations may be as good but none better; try some).

	D_1	D_2	D_3	D_4	D_5	Production
P_1	20			5		25
P_2			30			30
P_3'		25	10	5	10	50
Demand	20	25	40	10	10	

Table 8-8. Third Allocation

The total transportation costs for each of the three allocations are:

First: $\quad \sum_i \sum_j f_{ij} C_{ij} = 2500$

Second: $\quad \sum_i \sum_j f_{ij} C_{ij} = 2000$

Third: $\quad \sum_i \sum_j f_{ij} C_{ij} = 15(20) + 10(10) +$
$$30(15) + 5(30) +$$
$$25(25) + 10(20) +$$
$$10(0) = 1825$$

Figure 8-5 utilizes the situation "map" of Figure 8-4 to display the results of this linear programming transportation problem. The magnitudes and directions of product flows from plants to destinations appear quite reasonable. Indeed, they appear so commonsensical that one might conclude that the allocation could have been made more easily by simple inspection. But remember that a simple situation has been used to illustrate the procedure, so as to give insights into the technique. Real problems are normally more complex. For example, Johnson[11] works the problem with actual transport cost data for two existing plant sites, three proposed new plant sites and 41 destinations. Furthermore, keep in mind that once the basic principles are understood, the simple transportation problem can be easily programmed for the modern high-speed computer. Once set up, solutions are almost always obtained more easily and quickly via computer and are more fool-proof than the inspection, trial-and-error routine.

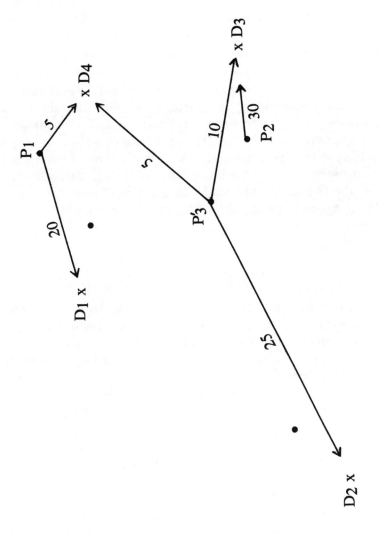

Figure 8-5. Results of Linear Programming Transportation Problem.

Returning to the problem set out in the beginning of this section, it is still necessary to decide which of the alternate sites is best for the location of the additional capacity, according to transportation cost (P_1, P_2, P'_1, P'_2 or P'_3). This may be decided by assigning the additional 50 units of production to each of the other possible sites and solving the transportation problem (optimal allocation) for each. Comparison of the total product distribution costs ($\sum_i^n \sum_j^m f_{ij} C_{ij}$) for each of the five alternatives will indicate which is best (least cost).

So far attention has been on product distribution costs. What if the transportation costs for supplies are also important? No difficulty. Just run the linear programming transportation problem for each alternative plant site, using the plants as destinations and the suppliers as origins. Then compare the five transportation cost totals. Then, the optimal input transport costs can be added to the optimal output transport costs to produce a grand total of transportation costs for each of the five alternative sites. (In practice, the process may be simplified by combining all of the operations in one computer program.)

C. Some Extensions

As noted at the outset, the purpose of this chapter is to provide an introductory sense of operations research techniques, and especially linear programming as applied to plant location problems. It is far beyond the scope of this chapter to discuss in any detail the intricacies, potential difficulties and numerous more complex variations. Rather, the purpose is to remove some of the aura of mystery surrounding what are often rather simple procedures. At least some rudimentary knowledge is necessary to know both what the techniques can and cannot do, to ask appropriate questions, to select useful decision-making aids, to secure adequate specialized assistance when needed and to analyze and integrate results properly.

Before leaving the topic entirely, however, a brief mention of some of the extensions may be useful, both to give an indication of the richness and potentials of the techniques and as an initial guide to further study.

Johnson, [12] for example, briefly discusses the complications arising when no specific alternative sites have been identified a priori by management but only a general area (e.g., the "East Coast") has been nominated. His suggested solution is to assume that freight rates vary directly with distance and then to search for the weighted central point in terms of transportation costs. Then, recognizing that the total plant location problem involves many considerations other than transport cost minimization, transport cost penalties are calculated for a series of distance bands outward from the calculated central point. This is an aid to management in deciding if a location at some place other than the central point provides sufficient attractions to compensate for the additional transportation expenditures.

A particularly useful extension of the basic transportation problem algorithm is to incorporate both production costs and transportation costs. As Scott explains, "producers at different locations will usually have different unit production costs, and these differences will be apparent in delivered commodity prices. Thus consumers may buy from a relatively distant producer providing that the additional transport cost incurred is offset by a concomitantly lower production cost. For this reason it is often desirable to minimize over a joint function of production costs and transport costs."[13] The objective function for this joint cost structure may be written as:

$$z = \sum_i^n \sum_j^m (C_i + t_{ij}) x_{ij}$$

where:
n = number of sources
m = number of destinations
x_{ij} = number of units shipped from i to j
C_i = unit production cost at source i
t_{ij} = unit cost of transportation from i to j

This production cost and transport cost problem can be solved as a basic transportation problem by treating the sum $C_i + t_{ij}$ as an ordinary transport cost. This also, incidentally, points up the fact that the linear programming "transportation problem" is not limited to minimizing only transport costs, but rather is an general algorithm which can be used on any problem which fits the basic format.

Wagner presents a similar, but extended, situation in an Integer Programming format. "Suppose that Plant Site i represents a potential location. Assume the plant will have capacity S_i and incur a fixed overhead cost $F_i > 0$, independent of the amount it produces. There are m possible sites for these new plants, but the overhead expenses are so significant that it is too costly to open plants on all the sites. Let $C_{ij} \geq 0$ be manufacturing and transportation expenses for shipping an item from Plant Site i to Marketing Area j. Assume, in addition, that there is a set-up cost $F_{ij} \geq 0$ associated with maintaining a shipping route from Plant Site i to Marketing Area j; this amount Fij is independent of the magnitude of $x_{ij} > 0$, but is not incurred when $x_{ij} = 0$."[14]

Thus,

$$Y_i = \begin{cases} 1 \text{ if Plant Site is selected} \\ \qquad\qquad \text{for } i = 1, 2, \dots m \\ 0 \text{ otherwise} \end{cases}$$

and

$$Z_{ij} = \begin{cases} 1 \text{ if route from Plant Site i to} \\ \text{Area j is used for all i and j} \\ 0 \text{ otherwise} \end{cases}$$

and the objective function is

$$\text{Minimize} \left[\sum_{i=1}^{m} F_i Y_i + \sum_{i=1}^{m} \sum_{j=1}^{n} C_{ij} X_{ij} + \sum_{i=1}^{m} \sum_{j=1}^{n} F_{ij} Z_{ij} \right]$$

with a set of appropriate constraints.

A key feature of this model is that a plant site is either open (selected) or closed (not selected), and a shipping route is likewise either open or closed. It is not possible to have a fractional plant site or shipping route; they either exist or they do not. Hence, the model was cast in the Integer Programming format, a more difficult variation of Linear Programming.

As a final illustration from the many which could be chosen, consider the situation when it is desirable to account explicitly for economies of scale. So far, the illustrations have dealt with linear relationships, but economies of scale, for example, often introduce significant nonlinearities. In practice, since any model only approximates reality, comparative linear approximations for inherently nonlinear situations are often sufficient for decision making. However, there are situations which require nonlinear programming. Thus, as Wagner notes, "the preponderance of mathematical programming applications to real managerial decision-making situations employ linear approximations rather than explicit nonlinear formulations. But the importance of nonlinear programming applications is growing. This is due to the rapidly increasing sophistication of managers and operations researchers in implementing decision-oriented mathematical models, as well as to the growing availability of computer routines capable of solving large-scale non-linear problems."[15]

The preceding example touched on the general issue of the tension between economies of scale and the friction of distance. The efficient size of plant was assumed sufficiently large to preclude factories at all the possible sites; the larger the efficient size of plant, the fewer plant sites selected. However, it was assumed that a plant had a fixed overhead independent of the amount produced. A more realistic situation is when production costs increase (or decrease) at a decreasing (or increasing) rate with changes in the volume of production.

Osleeb and Cromley present an interesting model which "incorporates the assumptions of nonlinear production functions, that is, economies and diseconomies of scale, and a uniform delivered price."[16] Their location-production-allocation model is formulated as:

$$\min TC = \sum_{i=1}^{m} P_i (Y_i) + \sum_{j=1}^{m} \sum_{i=1}^{m} T_{ij} X_{ij}$$

where

$$Y_i = \sum_{j}^{m} X_{ij} , \quad (i = 1, \ldots, m),$$

subject to

$$\sum_{i}^{m} X_{ij} = D_j, \quad (j = 1, \ldots, m),$$

and

T_{ij} = per unit transportation costs from i to j or j to i.
X_{ij} = flow of a given product from source i to market j.
D_j = demand level of market j.
Y_i = output level of plant i.
$P(Y_i)$ = cost curve for plant i.

Osleeb and Cromley provide a heuristic solution technique by which "given the per unit transportation costs and the production schedule for each potential plant, the optimal locations, output levels, and allocation among plants can be found."[17] The heuristic was programmed for the computer. Third-degree polynomials were incorporated to simulate the nonlinear production functions at each plant. The results of trial runs using production functions with (1) high diseconomies of scale, (2) economies and diseconomies of scale being equal, and (3) high economies of scale were compared. As expected, the greater the economies of scale, other things being equal, the fewer the number of plants located.

There is little doubt that Operations Research techniques include useful site selection aids. The up-to-date location analyst should grasp the essence of elementary linear programming. Such has been the primary purpose of this chapter. It also is apparent that linear programming (plus integer, dynamic and non-linear programming) in particular, and Operations Research in general, are dynamic, continually producing research and decision-making aids of increasing power. The site selector at least should be aware of the existence of appropriate, potentially useful techniques; the more ambitious will continue to study and experiment. And all the while, it will be kept in mind that all models are abstractions from reality. That is both their strength and their weakness.

Notes and References—Chapter 8

1. Wagner, H. M *Principles of Operations Research,* Prentice-Hall, 1975.

2. *Industrial Development,* Atlanta: Conway Publications.

3. Conway, H.M., and Liston, L.L. *Industrial Facilities Planning.* Atlanta: Conway Publications, 1976.

4. Jeske, J.W. "Linear Programming as an Aid in the Solution of Plant Location Problems;" *Industrial Development, op. cit.,* January, 1965. (Reprinted in Conway, H.M., and Liston, L.L., *op. cit.,* pp. 78-79.)

5. Johnson, R.E "Science and Site Selection," *Industrial Development, op. cit.,* July, 1959. (First published in *The Engineering Economist,* Fall, 1958, pp. 1-16. Reprinted in Conway, H.M., Liston, L.L., *op. cit.,* pp. 40-43.)

6. Wortham, R.A. "New Planning Tools," *Industrial Development, op. cit.,* April, 1962, (Reprinted in Conway, H.M., and Liston, L.L., *op. cit.,* pp. 40-43.)

7. Johnson, R.E., *op. cit.,* p. 68.

8. This illustration is adapted from Glicksman, Abraham M. *Linear Programming and the Theory of Games.* John Wiley and Sons, Inc., 1963, pp. 10-13.

9. Johnson, R.E., *op. cit.,* p. 68.

10. The "northwest corner" format and symbolization are drawn primarily from A. Hay, *Linear Programming: Elemen-*

tary Geographical Applications of the Transportation Problem (London: CATMOG 11, Institute of British Geographers, London, 1977), and A.J. Scott, *An Introduction to Spatial Allocation Analysis,* Resource Paper No. 9 (Washington: Commission of College Geography, Assn. of American Geographers, 1971). It should be noted that the most widely used solution to linear programming problems is via the SIMPLEX algorithm. See, for example, Wagner, H.M., *op. cit.,* pp. 91-125, or Glicksman, A.M., *Linear Programming and the Theory of Games, Ibid.,* pp. 58-83.

11. Johnson, R.E., *op. cit.*

12. *Ibid.*

13. Scott, A.J., *op. cit.,* p. 13.

14. Wagner, H.M., *op. cit.,* p. 478.

15. *Ibid.,* p. 527.

16. Osleeb, J.P., and Cromley, R.G. "The Location-Production-Allocation Problem with Nonlinear Production Costs," *Geographical Analysis,* April, 1977, p. 142.

17. *Ibid.,* p. 155.

IX A Capital Budgeting Framework

IX
A Capital Budgeting Framework

Based on projected variations among locations in costs and revenues (either assuming constant scale of operation in the various locations, or adjusted for expected locational variations in economies of scale) it usually is possible to identify a few (three to five) most likely (profitable) production points. This is consistent with general search/decision making behavior. "Search behavior is stimulated when a problem area is recognized. At the first stage, however, only rough expectational data are used to screen obviously inappropriate actions. In general the early search is stopped after a few suitable alternatives are generated. These alternatives are then considered in greater detail. In most cases studied, a rather firm commitment to an action was taken before the search for information proceeded very far."[1]

For the relatively few areas subjected to more detailed examination, typical industrial location analysis utilizes expected costs and income figures for a specific point in time, with the location showing the greatest spread between total costs and revenues deemed the most desirable. The preceding chapters have discussed the most important variables and illustrated commonly utilized techniques. Even ignoring the important non-quantifiable factors excluded, such an analysis typically has three deficiencies. (1) Although a major capital investment, the results of the locational analysis are not cast in a capital budgeting format compatible with the normal investment analyses done by a firm, and thus are less readily comprehended and compared by management. (2) The simple existence of *some* net profit does not necessarily indicate sufficient profit to warrant the investment (a screening problem). (3) Simple comparisons of total profit (revenues-costs) over the expected life of the project may lead to erroneous conclusions if the cash inflows and outflows vary over time among the locations considered.

Beginning wth the third deficiency, the difficulty of comparing projects in terms of profit (costs-revenues) when projected cash flows show temporal variations (even assuming the projections are of equal accuracy) arises because the value of a promised future dollar is less than the value of a current dollar. Even assuming away the effects of inflation (which further compounds the problem), the simple fact is that $100 today is worth more than $100 in one year's time, since today's amount can be invested and earn interest for a year. Thus, accurate analysis of new investment projects demand that later cash flows be discounted more heavily than early cash flows to permit correct comparisons. The set of capital budgeting techniques which compensates for temporal variations in cash flows is known as "Discounted Cash Flow."[2]

These same Discounted Cash Flow (D.C.F.) techniques may be used to calculate the varying rates of return on investments, thus addressing the second above noted deficiency. The D.C.F. methods here advocated for locational analysis are those favored by financial experts for all types of investment analysis, and are becoming increasingly popular with corporate management. C.D.F. techniques also, then, address deficiency one.

That the capital budgeting techniques are underutilized in industrial location studies is confirmed by the almost total lack of mention of such procedures in the theoretical literature. The fact that only three of the 100 articles in *Industrial Facilities Planning*[3] deals extensively with capital budgeting suggests that the same underemphasis occurs in practice. On the other hand, the three strongly pro-capital budgeting articles, plus other scattered references, confirm that this is not an unimportant topic. Blyth in 1961 made a strong case for presenting a project's economic justification in terms of return on the money invested and the period of time required for recovery of the invested money. Although mainly concerned with payback, at the end of his article Blyth mentioned the superiority of discounting procedures.[4]

Nieman (1972) presents the argument for making project judgments based on several screens, and in the process puts a variety of techniques in perspective. His six general ratio screens and "rule of thumb" passage quantities, modifiable due to particular industry environment, cost of money, type of market or exterior influences, are worth noting:

"1. Each entity should be expected to yield 20 percent Return on Gross Assets per year both with and without proposed additions. This ratio measures the productivity of the acquisition cost of assets.

2. Cash Payback measures, in time, the return of invested cash by the productivity of the investment itself. Payback will probably be no shorter than two years nor ever longer than five years. A four-year payback indicates a marginal project and would require more thorough analysis.

3. Return on Investment, incremental to the particular investment requested, is another measurement of productivity. A return of over 15 percent is considered successful passage.

4. A reciprocal of item three measures productivity of capital from sources outside the division such as long term debt and equity. Return on Capital Utilized should be in excess of 20 percent per year on the incremental investment.

5. Financial Risk, as defined before, should be not more than 25 percent of asset acquisition cost. The assets include Accounts Receivable, Inventories, Land, Buildings and Machinery and Equipment.

6. Discounted Cash Flow - Rate of Return measures the rate of return applied to the unrecovered portion of the investment rather than the initial investment itself. This rate should be no less than 15 percent per year. Another rule that can be employed here is double the cost of money rate (if money currently costs eight percent then the return should be more than 16 percent).

It must be clearly understood, regarding application of the above ratio screens, that the screens can be altered, depending upon the investment strategy. If the division is forced into investing in capital in order to maintain its competitive position in the marketplace, then the screens should be logically expanded to allow passage. If, however, the opportunity is strategic or offensive, then the screens might be contracted so as to minimize risk."[5]

Hawkins states the three things necessary for making correct capital budgeting decisions as (1) estimates of net capital outlays required and future cash earnings promised by each proposed project (he assumes these given by the firm's marketing, engineering and accounting departments), (2) estimates of availability and cost of capital (assumed given), and (3) correct standards to select project. He illustrates the inadequacies of the popular pay-back method, and provides very useful discussions and examples of measuring cash flows, utilizing discounting techniques and determining the cost of capital.[6]

It is probable that the practice of presenting industrial location alternatives if formal capital budgeting formats will increase. Furthermore, discounting techniques will be increasingly utilized, in line with their general acceptance in the business community. A recent survey of the capital expenditure decision-making process of large corporations by Petty, Scott and Bird revealed that the preferred discounting techniques are now used by over half of the firms, and the theoretically incorrect pay-back criteria has dropped in popularity. Regarding methodologies for evaluating risk, payback is still preferred, but risk adjusted discount rates are now second in use and gaining popularity.[7]

There are several procedures for discounting the future. "The two chief methods of bringing the interest factor into the calculations employ Discounted Cash Flow (DCF) techniques and are the Net Present Value (NPV) and Adjusted (or Internal) Rate of Return (IRR). These are really different ways of expressing the same arithmetical results and both will result in the same decision - whether or not to invest in one particular project as against some alternative."[8]

Anthony summarizes the steps involved in using the present value method as follows:

"1. Select a required earnings rate. Presumably, once selected, this rate will be used for all proposals in the same risk category.

2. Estimate the differential cash inflows, or 'earnings,' for each year or sequence of years including:

a) The cash earnings, neglecting depreciation, after taxes, for each year of the economic life.

b) The depreciation tax shield.

c) Residual values at the end of the economic life, consisting of disposal value of equipment plus working capital that is to be released.

3. Estimate the cash outflows other than the invesment itself, if there are any, for the year in which they occur.

4. Find the net present value of all future inflows and outflows by discounting them at the required earnings rate.

5. Find the net investment, which includes the additional outlays made at 'the present time,' less the proceeds from disposal of existing equipment (adjusted for tax consequences), plus the present value of investment outlays made at some time other than the present. Use a low discount rate if these future outlays are quite certain to be made.

6. If the present value of the cash flows exceeds the amount of the net investment, decide that the proposal is acceptable, insofar as the monetary factors are concerned. This comparison is often made by treating the net investment as a cash outflow in year 0; i.e., with a present value of 1.000. When this is done, adding the numbers algebraically gives the result directly. A positive sum indicates an acceptable proposal; a negative sum, an unfavorable one.

Taking into account the nonmonetary factors, reach a final decision. (This part of the process is at least as important as all the other parts put together, but there is no way of generalizing about it ...)"[9]

Of course, knowing what to do does not necessarily indicate how to do it. Capital budgeting is simply a tool to assist in decision-making and requires both the application of proper procedures and sound executive judgment. The generation of reasonable data and selection of appropriate criteria rely heavily on management perceptions. For example, the specification of the required earnings rate (for the NPV technique) relates to the risk factor; risk is a function of the uncertain future. Although the "opportunity cost principle" may be the rationale for advocating the weighted average cost of finance as the proper discount rate,[10] in practice the determination is usually more subjective. Petty, Scott and Bird report the relative use of five methods of determining minimum return standards: Cost of a Specific Source of Funds = 17 percent; Weighted Cost of Sources of Funds = 30 percent; Firm's Historical Rate of Return = 11 percent; Industry Historical Rate of Return = 2 percent; Management Determined Target Rate of Return = 40 percent.[11] The management forecasts and criteria are imbedded in the broader issue of how decision makers deal with uncertainty; thus we are referred back to some of the considerations of Chapter 2. The more mechanical aspects of industrial location analysis in a capital budgeting framework are illustrated in the two following examples.

A. Net Present Value: A Simple Example:

A simple Net Present Value example expressed in a locational context[12] can be used to illustrate the problem and the solution (using hypothetical data and making all the necessary assumptions). Take as given that for a project in any reasonable location the *immediate* cash outlay is $11,000,000. The projected *net* cash flows for this project (e.g., a new manufacturing plant) in three different possible (reasonable) locations are:

NET CASH FLOWS ($1,000)			
Year	Atlanta	Chicago	Cincinnati
1	1,000	2,000	3,000
2	2,000	3,000	4,000
3	3,000	5,000	3,500
4	4,000	3,000	2,500
5	5,500	2,000	2,000
TOTAL	15,500	15,000	15,000

At first glance, Atlanta appears to produce the greatest profit over the five year life of the project. Is this still true when the interest factor is taken into account? After taking the interest factor into account, do *any* of the projects produce enough profit to make the investment worthwhile?

Assume, for simplicity, that management demands a minimum 10 percent rate of return on its investment. From a table of compound interest we obtain:

PRESENT VALUE OF $1	
Due at end of year	Rate of Interest 10%
1	0.909
2	0.826
3	0.751
4	0.683
5	0.621
10	0.386
	(and so on)

Applying these compound interest rates to our project in the three locations we calculate:

Year	10% Factors	Atlanta		Chicago		Cincinnati	
		Cash Flows	NPV's	Cash Flows	NPV's	Cash Flows	NPV's
1	0.909	1,000	909	2,000	1,818	3,000	2,727
2	0.826	2,000	1,652	3,000	2,478	4,000	3,304
3	0.751	3,000	2,253	5,000	3,755	3,500	2,629
4	0.683	4,000	2,732	3,000	2,049	2,500	1,708
5	0.621	5,500	3,415	2,000	1,242	2,000	1,242
TOTAL		15,500	10,961	15,000	11,342	15,000	11,610

From this analysis, it is clear that Atlanta, although it shows the greatest absolute profit is *not feasible*. At the demanded 10 percent rate of return, the discounted net cash flows have a Net Present Value below the initial $11,000,000 investment.

Both Chicago and Cincinnati are viable locations, but Cincinnati is the best, by virtue of having greater cash flows earlier. Cincinnati's total advantage over Chicago is $11,610,000 - $11,342,000 = $268,000. The rate of return for Cincinnati obviously is over 10 percent; the actual rate of return for Cincinnati is 12.33 percent (calculations not shown). Note that the present values can be compared directly in this case because the investments are of the same size. When the present value method is used with investments of unequal sizes, a "profitability index" must be calculated to determine preferences. The profitability index is simply the present value earnings divided by the amount of investment. The preference rule is the higher the index number, the better the project.[13]

B. More Complex and Realistic Examples.

This second group of examples, utilizing the "Internal Rate of Return" (IRR) procedure, illustrates more fully (1) how the requisite cash flows are built up from projections on individual costs and earnings factors, (2) how two different potential locations are compared, and (3) how the result changes as costs and earnings are temporally variable.[14]

The first set calculates, for a 10 year period, the discounted rate of return on investment for "City A." The data are hypothetical but realistic. A key assumption in this first set is that sales volumes and production costs remain constant from year to year.

The first step in obtaining rate of return is calculating net profit. Net profit is derived from subtracting total costs from net sales. In this example the fabricator produces 500 items, each with a selling price of $15,750. Multiplying 500 times $15,750 produces a yearly sales volume of $7,875,000.

Total operating costs are derived by accounting for the following: material costs (copper, steel and other); direct labor (includes total wage cost minus clerks); assembly costs; product shipping; utilities and taxes; clerical; supply expense; lift truck rental; overtime expenses; and fringe benefits. Also calculated is depreciation, which is the allocation of the original costs of plant, property and equipment to the particular periods that benefit from the utilization of assets.[15] In order to obtain overtime expenses, the total labor costs are multiplied by 15 percent. These labor costs include: direct labor, indirect labor, repairs and clerical. Fringe benefits are equal to 8.5 percent of the total labor costs.

Gross profit is derived by subtracting total operating costs from net sales. Selling and administrative costs are set at 7 percent of net sales. Subtracting selling and administrative cost from gross profit produces net profit.

Capital requirements are listed by type of investment. A schedule of capital investments is formulated and the end product is an annual total. All of the capital requirements except for land have an estimated life of 20 years. Using straight line depreciation, the annual depreciation for capital investments is calculated.

Book value is determined for each year by subtracting annual depreciation from the original cost of capital investments. These also include inventory and receivables. Inventories consist of merchandise, finished products of manufacturers, goods in the process of being manufactured and raw materials. Receivables are the sum of all amounts owed the business by its customers.

The capital investments are listed by the year of investment. In the cash flow table, profits and depreciation are listed for each year of the period under consideration. In the last year of the period, cash flow includes not only profit and depreciation but also inventory and receivables. The book value of capital investments are also included in this calculation.

In the cash flow discounted to present table, cash flow out is the annual total of capital investments and cash flows. Cash flow-in is equal to the annual total of profit and depreciation plus the value of assets in the last year. "Cash flow out and in is multiplied by the incremental receipts of each year by the present value of $1 for the number of time periods from the present to that particular year, using a trial rate . . . The products in the aforementioned step represent the present value of each annual receipt. When added together they should equal the incremental investment. If the total is greater than the incremental investment, the trial interest rate is too low, and a higher rate should be tried. If the sum of the present values is less than the incremental investment, the trial rate is too high. The trial process should be repeated until the correct interest rate can be approximated to the nearest whole per cent."[16] The Cash Flow Discounted To Present Table is used to determine the return on the investment.

City A

Net Sales	$ 7,875,000
Material Costs	
Copper	500,000
Steel	2,000,000
Other	250,000
Direct Labor	1,187,000
Burden Accounts	
Indirect Labor	70,000
Supplies Expense	180,000
Repairs	60,000
Assembly Costs	188,000
Product Shipping	1,496,100
Other Controllable	
Overtime Expenses	121,125
Lift Truck Rental	13,560
Fixed Expenses	
Clerks	108,000
Property Taxes	125,000
Depreciation	66,000
Fringe Benefits	213,750
Utilities	55,000
Total Operating Costs	6,633,535
Gross Profit	1,241,465
Selling and Administrative Costs	551,250
Net Profit	**690,215**

City A

Capital Requirements

Land	$ 35,000
Building and Site	850,000
Equipment and Installation	470,000
Additional Equipment	155,000
Total	**$ 1,510,000**

City A

Capital Investments

Year of	Investment	Amount	Annual Total
0	Land	$ 35,000	
0	Building Installed	850,000	
0	Plant Equipment Installed	470,000	1,355,000
1	Additional Equipment	110,000	110,000
2	Additional Equipment	45,000	45,000

City A

Capital Depreciation

Capital	Amount	Estimated Life	Annual Depreciation
Land	$ 35,000	Indefinite	0
Building	850,000	20 years	42,500
Plant Equipment	470,000	20 years	23,500
Additional Equipment (First Year)	110,000	20 years	5,500
Additional Equipment (Second Year)	45,000	20 years	2,250

City A

Book Value

Year	Annual Depreciation	Capital Investment	Book Value
0	$ 0	$ 1,355,000	$ 1,355,000
1	66,000	110,000	1,399,000
2	71,500	45,000	1,372,500
3	73,750	0	1,298,750
4	73,750	0	1,225,000
5	73,750	0	1,151,250
6	73,750	0	1,077,500
7	73,750	0	1,003,750
8	73,750	0	930,000
9	73,750	0	856,250
10	73,750	0	782,500

City A
Investment and Cash Flow

Year	Investment	Amounts	Annual Totals
0	Land	$ 35,000	
	Building	850,000	
	Plant Equipment	470,000	$ 1,355,000
1	Additional Equipment	110,000	
	Inventory	1,000,000	
	Receivables	1,000,000	2,110,000
2	Additional Equipment	45,000	45,000

City A

Year	Cash Flow	Amount	Annual Total
1	Profit and Depreciation	$ 756,215	$ 711,215
	Start Up	45,000	
2	Profit and Depreciation	761,715	761,715
3	Profit and Depreciation	763,965	763,965
4	Profit and Depreciation	763,965	763,965
5	Profit and Depreciation	763,965	763,965
6	Profit and Depreciation	763,965	763,965
7	Profit and Depreciation	763,965	763,965
8	Profit and Depreciation	763,965	763,965
9	Profit and Depreciation	763,965	763,965
10	Inventory	1,000,000	
	Receivables	1,000,000	
	Book Value of Equipment	782,500	
	Building and Land		
	Profit and Depreciation	763,965	3,546,465

City A

Cash Flow Discounted to Present

Year	Cash Flow Out	Cash Flow In	Net
0	$ 1,355,000	$	$ (1,355,000)
1	2,110,000	711,215	(1,398,785)
2	45,000	761,715	716,715
3		763,965	763,965
4		763,965	763,965
5		763,965	763,965
6		763,965	763,965
7		763,965	763,965
8		763,965	763,965
9		763,965	763,965
10		3,546,465	3,546,465

Return on Investment **24.0%**

The second set performs the same analysis for another potential location, "City B." The basic difference is that operating costs are higher than in City A. It is assumed that the sales volumes and materials costs are the same at each location. Although unrealistic, the assumption simplified the computations; to obtain more realism, sales and material costs can be allowed to vary according to location, utilizing the same type of analysis as illustrated. Common sense indicates that if only operating costs are allowed to vary, and all other things are equal, then the lower cost city is the preferred location. However, if sales volumes also vary by location of the plant, then the conclusion is not obvious.

Both sets one and two illustrate some of the requisite data and the procedures in calculating the discounted rate of return. Of equal importance, they provide an example of the use of discounting procedures in providing criteria for both screening and preference problems. If the externally determined acceptable rate of return is no higher than 13.8 percent, then both cities are viable, but City A is preferable. To be selected over City A, City B would have to show extraordinary strengths among the unmeasured and "intangible" factors. If the required rate is over 13.8 percent, but no larger than 24.0 percent, then only City A can even be considered. If the acceptable rate of return is over 24 percent then neither city is a viable alternative.

Method of Determing the Rate of Return on Locating the investment in City A by Use of the Present Value Table

24%

Cash Flow Out

Year	Present Value of a Dollar	Cash Flow Out	Cash Flow Discounted to Present
0		1,355,000	1,355,000
1	.808	2,110,000	1,700,660
2	.650	45,000	29,250
3	.524		
4	.423		
5	.341		
6	.275		
7	.222		
8	.179		
9	.144		
10	.116		

Total 3,084,910

25%

Cash Flow Out

Year	Present Value of a Dollar	Cash Flow Out	Cash Flow Discounted to Present
0		1,355,000	1,355,000
1	.800	2,110,000	1,688,000
2	.640	45,000	28,800
3	.512		
4	.410		
5	.328		
6	.262		
7	.210		
8	.168		
9	.134		
10	.107		

Total 3,071,800

$$\text{Rate of Return} = 24\% + \frac{\text{Cash Flow in 24\% - Cash Flow Out 24\%}}{\text{Cash Flow In 24\% - Cash Flow In 25\%}}$$

$$= 24\% + \frac{3,090,182 - 3,084,910}{3,090,182 - 2,982,208} = 24.04\%$$

Present Value of a Dollar	Cash Flow In Cash Flow In	Cash Flow Discounted to Present
.806	711,215	573,239
.650	761,715	495,115
.524	763,965	400,318
.423	763,965	323,157
.341	763,965	260,512
.275	763,965	210,090
.222	763,965	169,600
.179	763,965	136,750
.144	763,965	110,011
.116	3,546,465	411,390
		Total 3,090,182

Present Value of a Dollar	Cash Flow In Cash Flow In	Cash Flow Discounted to Present
.800	711,215	568,972
.640	761,715	487,498
.512	763,965	391,150
.410	763,965	313,226
.328	763,965	250,581
.262	763,965	200,159
.210	763,965	160,433
.168	763,965	128,346
.134	763,965	102,371
.107	3,546,465	379,472
		Total 2,982,208

City B

Net Sales	$ 7,875,000
Material Costs	
Copper	500,000
Steel	2,000,000
Other	250,000
Direct Labor	1,072,000
Burden Accounts	
Indirect Labor	60,000
Supplies Expense	200,000
Repairs	50,000
Assembly Costs	148,000
Product Shipping	1,999,200
Other Controllable	
Overtime Expenses	109,820
Lift Truck Rental	13,560
Fixed Expenses	
Clerks	110,000
Property Taxes	130,000
Depreciation	62,500
Fringe Benefits	193,800
Utilities	55,000
Total Operating Costs	6,953,880
Gross Profit	921,120
Selling and Administration Costs	551,250
Net Profit	369,870

City B

Capital Requirements

Land	$ 30,000
Building and Site	800,000
Equipment and Installation	450,000
Additional Equipment	140,000
Total	**1,420,000**

City B

Capital Investments

Year of	Investment	Amount	Annual Total
0	Land	$ 30,000	
0	Building Installed	800,000	
0	Plant Equipment Installed	450,000	$ 1,280,000
1	Additional Equipment	100,000	100,000
2	Additional Equipment	40,000	40,000

City B

Capital Depreciation

Capital	Amount	Estimated Life	Annual Depreciation
Land	$ 30,000	Indefinite	0
Building	800,000	20 years	$ 40,000
Plant Equipment	450,000	20 years	22,500
Additional Equipment (First Year)	100,000	20 years	5,000
Additional Equipment	40,000	20 years	2,000

City B

Book Value

Year	Annual Depreciation	Capital Investment	Book Value
0	0	$ 1,280,000	$ 1,280,000
1	$ 62,500	100,000	1,317,500
2	67,500	40,000	1,290,000
3	69,500	0	1,220,500
4	69,500	0	1,151,000
5	69,500	0	1,081,500
6	69,500	0	1,012,000
7	69,500	0	942,500
8	69,500	0	873,000
9	69,500	0	803,500
10	69,500	0	734,000

Investment and Cash Flow

Year	Investment	Amounts	Annual Totals
0	Land	$ 30,000	
	Building	800,000	
	Plant Equipment	450,000	$ 1,280,000
1	Additional Equipment	100,000	
	Inventory	750,000	
	Receivables	1,000,000	1,850,000
2	Additional Equipment	40,000	40,000

City B

Year	Cash Flow	Amount	Annual Total
1	Profit and Depreciation	$ 432,370	$ 392,370
	Start Up	40,000	
2	Profit and Depreciation	437,370	437,370
3	Profit and Depreciation	439,370	439,370
4	Profit and Depreciation	439,370	439,370
5	Profit and Depreciation	439,370	439,370
6	Profit and Depreciation	439,370	439,370
7	Profit and Depreciation	439,370	439,370
8	Profit and Depreciation	439,370	439,370
9	Profit and Depreciation	439,370	439,370
10	Inventory	750,000	
	Receivables	1,000,000	
	Book Value of Equipment	734,000	
	Building and Land		
	Profit & Depreciation	$ 439,370	$ 2,923,370

Cash Flow Discounted to Present

Year	Cash Flow Out	Cash Flow In	Net
0	$ 1,280,000		$ (1,280,000)
1	1,850,000		(1,457,630)
2	40,000	$ 392,370	397,370
3		437,370	439,370
4		439,370	439,370
5		439,370	439,370
6		439,370	439,370
7		439,370	439,370
8		439,370	439,370
9		439,370	439,370
10		2,923,370	2,923,370

Return on Investment 13.8%

Set 3 performs the same type of analysis for the 10-year period, again for City B, but this case projects that *sales and costs both vary over time.* The key projection is that sales volumes will increase yearly (perhaps by increasing the firms market share, or through higher industry-wide demand). For the most part, increasing costs are a function of higher sales and consequent increases in production.

Comparing the constant sales volume model of Set 2 with the increasing sales model of Set 3 is instructive. (The details are shown only for years one, two, three and 10; however, the results of similar calculations for years four through nine are shown in the summary tables.) Whereas in the constant model the profits are much higher in the early years, so too are the outward cash flows. In the temporally variable sales model a positive discounted net cash flow is not reached until the fifth year; this situation is attained by the second year in the constant model. However, the discounted net cash flows are considerably higher in the later years in the variable model, producing a much higher rate of return on investment (24.3 percent vs. 13.8 percent). The growth pattern and the time span of the analysis clearly are critical.

City B

Year One

Net Sales	$ 1,220,625
Material Costs	
Copper	77,500
Steel	310,000
Other	38,750
Direct Labor	166,500
Burden Accounts	
Indirect Labor	9,300
Supplies Expense	31,000
Repairs	7,750
Assembly Costs	22,940
Product Shipping	212,100
Other Controllable	
Overtime Expenses	17,004
Lift Truck Rental	2,102
Fixed Expenses	
Clerks	16,500
Property Tax	70,460
Depreciation	35,000
Fringe Benefits	30,008
Utilities	8,525
Total Operating Costs	1,055,439
Gross Profit	165,186
Selling and Administration Costs	85,444
Net Profit	79,742

City B

Year Two

Net Sales	$ 1,281,656
Material Costs	
Copper	81,375
Steel	323,950
Other	40,300
Direct Labor	175,659
Burden Accounts	
Indirect Labor	9,812
Supplies Expense	32,473
Repairs	8,138
Assembly Costs	23,870
Product Shipping	220,584
Other Controllable	
Overtime Expenses	17,937
Lift Truck Rental	2,186
Fixed Expenses	
Clerks	17,409
Property Tax	100,870
Depreciation	37,000
Fringe Benefits	31,653
Utilities	9,037
Total Operating Costs	1,132,253
Gross Profit	149,403
Selling and Administration Costs	89,716
Net Profit	59,687

City B

Year Three

Net Sales	$ 2,995,355
Material Costs	
Copper	190,181
Steel	753,497
Other	93,288
Direct Labor	411,255
Burden Accounts	
Indirect Labor	23,040
Supplies Expense	75,711
Repairs	19,018
Assembly Costs	55,759
Product Shipping	474,314
Other Controllable	
Overtime Expenses	42,174
Lift Truck Rental	5,060
Fixed Expenses	
Clerks	42,854
Property Tax	110,135
Depreciation	51,885
Fringe Benefits	74,425
Utilities	21,320
Total Operating Costs	2,443,916
Gross Profit	551,439
Selling and Administration Costs	209,675
Net Profit	341,764

City B

Year Ten

Net Sales	$ 12,216,711
Material Costs	
Copper	775,664
Steel	2,972,190
Other	355,302
Direct Labor	1,735,500
Burden Accounts	
Indirect Labor	97,145
Supplies Expense	303,677
Repairs	77,567
Assembly Costs	219,942
Product Shipping	2,834,000
Other Controllable	
Overtime Expenses	177,193
Lift Truck Rental	19,300
Fixed Expenses	
Clerks	178,100
Property Tax	219,631
Depreciation	75,423
Fringe Benefits	313,247
Utilities	92,921
Total Operating Costs	10,446,802
Gross Profit	1,769,909
Selling and Administration Costs	855,170
Net Profit	914,739

City B

Capital Requirements

Land	$ 30,000
Building and Site	847,701
Equipment and Installation	498,805
Additional Equipment	163,933
Total	**1,540,439**

City B

Capital Investments

Year of	Investment	Amount	Annual Total
0	Land	$ 30,000	
0	Building & Site	500,000	
0	Plant Equipment Installed	200,000	$ 730,000
1	Additional Equipment	42,000	42,000
2	Building & Site	165,375	
2	Plant Equipment Installed	110,250	
2	Additional Equipment	22,050	297,675
3	Additional Equipment	34,729	34,729
4	Building & Site	182,326	
4	Plant Equipment Installed	121,550	
4	Additional Equipment	12,155	316,031
5	Additional Equipment	25,527	25,527
6	Plant Equipment Installed	67,005	
6	Additional Equipment	13,401	80,406
7	Additional Equipment	14,071	14,071

City B
Capital Depreciation

Capital	Amount
Land	$ 30,000
Building & Site (Year 0)	500,000
Plant Equipment (Year 0)	200,000
Additional Equipment (First Year)	42,000
Building & Site (Second Year)	165,375
Plant Equipment (Second Year)	110,250
Additional Equipment (Second Year)	22,050
Additional Equipment (Third Year)	34,729
Building & Site (Fourth Year)	182,326
Plant Equipment (Fourth Year)	121,550
Additional Equipment (Fourth Year)	12,155
Additional Equipment (Fifth Year)	27,527
Plant Equipment (Sixth Year)	67,005
Additional Equipment (Sixth Year)	13,401
Additional Equipment (Seventh Year)	13,401

Estimated Life	Annual Depreciation
Indefinite	0
20 years	25,000
20 years	10,000
20 years	2,000
20 years	8,269
20 years	5,513
20 years	1,103
20 years	1,103
20 years	9,116
20 years	6,078
20 years	608
20 years	1,276
20 years	3,350
20 years	670
20 years	704

City B

Investment and Cash Flow

Year	Investment	Amounts	Annual Total
0	Land	$ 30,000	
	Building	500,000	
1	Plant Equipment	200,000	$ 730,000
	Additional Equipment	42,000	
	Inventory	116,250	
	Receivables	115,000	
2	Building & Site	165,375	273,250
	Plant Equipment	110,250	
	Additional Equipment	22,050	
	Inventory	5,813	
	Receivables	7,750	
3	Additional Equipment	34,729	311,238
	Inventory	163,209	
	Receivables	217,613	
4	Building & Site	182,326	415,551
	Plant Equipment	121,550	

	Additional Equipment	12,155	
	Inventory	74,171	
5	Receivables	98,894	489,096
	Additional Equipment	25,527	
	Inventory	253,172	
6	Receivables	337,563	616,262
	Plant Equipment	67,005	
	Additional Equipment	13,401	
	Inventory	105,293	
7	Receivables	140,391	326,090
	Additional Equipment	14,071	
	Inventory	105,248	
8	Receivables	140,327	259,646
	Inventory	186,793	
9	Receivables	249,057	435,850
	Inventory	98,145	
10	Receivables	130,860	229,005
	Inventory	55,405	
	Receivables	73,873	129,278

City B

Book Value

Year	Annual Depreciation	Capital Investment	Book Value
0	0	$ 730,000	$ 730,000
1	$ 35,000	42,000	737,000
2	37,000	297,675	997,675
3	51,885	34,729	980,519
4	53,621	316,031	1,242,929
5	69,423	25,527	1,199,033
6	70,699	80,406	1,208,740
7	74,719	14,071	1,148,092
8	75,423	0	1,072,669
9	75,423	0	997,246
10	75,423	0	921,823

City B

Year	Cash Flow	Amount	Annual Total
1	Profit and Depreciation	$ 114,742	$ 94,742
	Start Up	20,000	
2	Profit and Depreciation	96,687	96,687
3	Profit and Depreciation	393,649	393,649
4	Profit and Depreciation	451,950	451,950
5	Profit and Depreciation	773,355	773,355
6	Profit and Depreciation	813,797	813,797
7	Profit and Depreciation	980,223	980,223
8	Profit and Depreciation	1,035,130	1,035,130
9	Profit and Depreciation	912,060	912,060
10	Inventory	1,163,497	
	Receivables	1,551,328	
	Book Value of Equipment Building and Land	921,823	
	Profit and Depreciation	990,162	4,626,810

Cash Flow Discounted to Present

Year	Cash Flow Out	Cash Flow In	Net
0	$ 730,000	$	$ (730,000)
1	273,250	94,742	(178,508)
2	311,238	96,687	(214,551)
3	415,551	393,649	(21,902)
4	489,096	451,950	(37,146)
5	616,262	773,355	157,093
6	326,090	813,797	487,707
7	259,646	980,223	720,577
8	435,850	1,035,130	599,280
9	229,005	912,060	683,055
10	129,278	4,626,810	4,497,532

Return on Investment 24.3%

The numerical examples have been presented in some detail to illustrate that the basic procedures are not really so difficult, though the arithmetic is substantial, and that reasonable projections on a host of variables are critical. The complexity of the analysis increases with the number of variables. For this reason, advocates of capital budgeting techniques stress the need for prior sensitivity analysis. Sensitivity analysis provides decision criteria for eliminating minor variables or those which do not vary significantly over time or space, thus reducing the discounting problem to manageable proportions. Discounting procedures are especially sensitive to profit forecasts.[17].

The presentation in this chapter certainly does not exhaust the items which should be considered in capital budgeting analysis. It is beyond the scope of this volume to do so. The interested site selector may make good use of the voluminous literature in this field; for starters, the chapter references are suggested. Good use also can be made of the expertise of intra-company financial experts who routinely make investments analysis but rarely apply their talents to location problems.

As indicated at the outset of the chapter, discounted cash flow analyses offer considerable advantages to the site selector. They provide useful indicators for screening out unworthy locations and for deciding on the preferred. They prevent over simple and incorrect conclusions based on considerations of only part of the profit matrix (e.g., focus only on costs) and on immediate returns. They place at least part of the location analysis in format familiar and acceptable to management. But they are not sufficient unto themselves. "These techniques can be used only to the extent that the facts of a proposal can be reduced to dollar amounts for investments and earnings. For many proposals, nonquantitative considerations are dominant, and the techniques are not applicable. In nearly every problem there are some nonquantifiable considerations, and these must be used to temper the numerical result."[18]

Notes and References—Chapter 9

1. Cohen, K.J., and Cyert, R.M. *Theory of the Firm: Resource Allocation in a Market Economy.* Prentice Hall, 1965, p. 329.
2. The specific terminology for the several discounting techniques varies among authors.
3. Conway, H.M., and Liston, L.L. *Industrial Facilities Planning.* Atlanta: Conway Publications, 1976.
4. Blyth, Howard A. "Justifying Expansion," *Industrial Development,* August, 1961. (In *Industrial Facilities Planning, op. cit.,* pp. 45.47.)
5. Nieman, John S. "Centralize Capital Assets Acquisition to Promote Efficiency, Expertise," *Industrial Development,* July/August, 1972. (In *Industrial Facilities Planning, op. cit.,* p. 27.)
6. Hawkins, Clark A. "How to Tackle Capital Budgeting Decisions;" *Industrial Development, Sept./October, 1969. (In Industrial Facilities Planning, op. cit.,* pp. 16-19.)
7. Petty, J.W., Scott, D.F., and Bird, M.M. "The Capital Expenditure Decision-Making Process of Large Corporations;" *The Engineering Economist,* Vol. XX, No. 3 (Spring, 1975), pp 159-172.
8. Carran, R. Drew. *Financing Business and Industry.* Newton Abbott, U.K.: David & Charles, 1971, p. 70.
9. Anthony, Robert N. *Management Accounting, Text and Cases.* Homewood, Ill.: Richard D. Irwin, Inc., 1970, p. 645.
10. See Townsend, Edward C. *Investment and Uncertainty, A Practical Guide.* Edinburgh: Oliver and Boyd, 1969, p. 37.
11. Petty, J.W., Scott, D.F., and Bird, M.M., *op. cit.,* p. 169.

12. Adapted from Carran, R. Drew, *op. cit.,* pp. 71-75.

13. Anthony, R.N., *op. cit.,* p. 651.

14. The assistance of Deborah Mariner and Gregory Trygg in preparing the examples of Section B is gratefully acknowledged.

15. Horngren, Charles. T. *Accounting for Management Control.* Prentice-Hall, 1974 p. 605.

16. Black, H., Champion, J.E. and Brown, E.G. *Accounting in Business Decisions.* Prentice-Hall, 1967, p. 875.

17. Townsend, E.C., *op. cit.,* p. 99.

18. Anthony, R.N., *op. cit.,* p. 653.

Part IV Summary
And Advice

X Judgmental Location Decision-Making

X
Judgmental Location Decision-Making

Building a new plant is a major, long-term investment for any manufacturer. Deciding where to put the plant is a critical component within the total investment decision. As such, industrial location analysis is big business, whether measured in terms of investment dollars, or decision-makers involved, or employees affected, or the economies of areas influenced (Chapter 1). The exact nature of the decision-making mechanism remains an enigma.[1] It varies from manager to manager, firm to firm, industry to industry and area to area. Keeping in mind the variations, it is possible to suggest some of the common elements in the location decision-making process (Chapter 1) and to provide some between-firm comparisons (Chapter 2).

In common with other types of investment decisions, choosing a plant location involves the integration of both objective and subjective information. Incomplete data about the past and present and, especially, uncertainty about the future mean that locating a plant necessarily requires judgmental decision-making (Chapter 1).

There are no perfect sites.[2] Even if there were, there would be no sure way to know them. All locations involve compromises (Chapter 1). However, the facts that there are no perfect solutions and there is always uncertainty do not mean that locational decision making is irrational (Chapter 1), nor that it cannot be improved. The best location for a plant must be thought of in terms of both known and probable states of affairs, in terms of alternatives between logically feasible locations, and in terms of the very real limitations of time and resources on the search. Choosing an industrial site is a complex research problem.

A. Research

Problem solving in any field of endeavor involves similar elements of research design. These may be outlined as follows:

1. A clear and concise statement of the problem.
2. Specification of the factors thought most relevant to the problem. A model of the process involved may be constructed. Significant variables are stated in the form of hypotheses, with supporting rationalization for their inclusion.
3. Statements of operational definitions.
4. Collection of data on the relevant variables necessary to calibrate the model and to test hypotheses.
5. Analysis.
6. Evaluation of results and the specification of new lines of inquiry suggested by the analysis.

These standard research design steps may be translated more explicitly into a typical industrial location context:

1. The problem. "Where should a plant of type and size X be located?"
2. Construction of the model which specifies the relevant locational influences. Standarized checklists[3] commonly include the important factors, but the relevance and weighing of each will vary for each specific situation. The significant variables, and the rationalizations for their inclusions, are most likely those discussed in Part II (Chapters 2, 3, 4, 5 and 6). A powerful method is the use of firm and industry analogs; that is, the use of previous experience. However, care must be exercised to separate out anecdotes and personal biases from the wisdom contained in past successes and failures.
3. Operational definitions. The type and size of a plant must be defined. The primary areas of search should be made explicit, as should the reasons for such spatial limitations. All factors (variables) require operational definitions.
4. Collection of data. All good sources of data should be explored. These include company data, industry data and information about the economy and society at large. Some factors can be

measured fairly objectively, making such data especially attractive, but more subjective information can and must be utilized. Particuarly important, and particularly troublesome, is the collection of "future data." Some forecasting issues are discussed in Chapter 3.

5. Analysis. In reality, the analysis process permeates the entire research process. The very nature of the problem statement and each subsequent research decision has an influence on the results. More specifically, however, the analysis requires the employment of methodologies to put the disparate pieces together to produce comprehensible answers. Most commonly utilized and relied upon is a Cost Analysis.[4] To be of maximum utility, the standard cost analysis should be expanded into a comparative analysis of both costs and revenues, as shown in Chapter 7. Other methods include the useful Linear Programming/Operations Research and Capital Budgeting techniques discussed in Chapters 8 and 9.

6. Evaluation of Results. The results of the research process will be invaluable in industrial site selection. The process will preclude the hit-or-miss, throw the dart at the map, approach with its very large potential for egregious error. Of course, no firm really ever operates totally by the hit-or-miss approach, since all have at least some intuitive notions about where they should be; but making explicit what is implicit and examining it for completeness, logical consistency and bias can greatly enhance the site selection process. On the other hand, no analysis will produce completely unequivocal answers; it is at this point that managers must truly manage and be most clearly engaged in judgmental decision-making. Is the site selection to be made from among the examined alternatives, or is further research warranted?

B. Risk, Uncertainty and Decision Rules.

How management exercises its judgment is conditioned by the quality of its research. Managerial judgment is also conditioned by how it deals with uncertainty and by the decision rules adopted. In a circular manner, the decision rules and attitudes toward uncertainty can influence the research process.

A distinction can be made between "risk analysis" and "uncertainty analysis." "Risk analysis" involves the use of subjective probabilities, while "uncertainty analysis" operates when subjective probabilities cannot or will not be used. The distinction has implications for methods of forecasting and for modes of analysis. A situation is characterized by risk if the probabilities of alternative, possible outcomes are known; in such a situation the analysis may proceed via statistical decision theory. But clearly such situations are rare. Most investment decisions take place under conditions of uncertainty. If subjective probabilities can be used to construct a payoff matrix, game theory can be utilized. When subjective probabilities are inadmissible, recourse is to mechanistic, simulation techniques.

How managers perceive the hazards involved in the locational decision may well condition the selection of the site. If, for example, management concludes that the risk is low, it may opt for a maximum promised return decision rule, in which the return may be measured by a variety of indices, such as profits, growth of the firm or executive convenience (Chapter 1). Conversely, if risk is thought to be high, management may behave more pessimistically and adopt either a minimax or a minimum regret decision rule. Obviously, the decision rules invoked will condition the final site selection. The decision rules should be as carefully examined as any of the traditional locational variables.[5]

C. Consultants and the Involved Management

Many companies do not fully appreciate the importance of their geography. However, there is evidence that the geography of the firm and the astute management of spatial factors are being increasingly recognized as critical elements in the well being of the manufacturing enterprise. The current trend in industry appears to be toward more explicit and open site searches.[6] As manufacturers realize both the importance and complexity of selecting good locations there is a growing awareness that a company will probably not possess internally all the necessary data, analytical techniques and insights. Management is often too close to the problem, and usually lacks extensive site selection experience. Thus, "numerous industries are drawing on the outside expertise of consultants, area development organizations and government agencies for assistance with gathering data and analyzing it."[7]

A recent survey[8] revealed that when management does go outside for assistance, the most frequently utilized sources are the utilities operating in the regions of interest. Of the firms surveyed, 55 percent asked local utilities for help in selecting a manufacturing site. Second most utilized for help are the state development agencies, used in 47 percent of the searches. Following these, in descending order of magnitude, are the local development agencies and chambers of commerce (41 percent), the railroads (27 percent), developers, realtors and brokers (24 percent), banks (12 percent), and, lastly, consultants and research groups (5 percent). The survey also asked the corporate real estate managers which sources of outside assistance they find most effective in site selection. Deemed most useful were the utility companies and the state and local development organizations. Banks, developers and consultants were judged to be generally only somewhat useful, and railroads most often were put in the "not useful" category.

Companies most often turn outward for assistance in obtaining specific data on areas of interest and in determining the availability of adequate sites. They much less frequently seek help in the broader realms of management and judgmental decision-making, in spite of the fact that site selection is a relatively rare event for many firms and is thus a management area in which expertise is typically lacking. The reluctance, or absence of perceived need, to engage outside managerial decision-making help is suggested by the low frequency of use of consultants and research groups and by the only somewhat useful categorization of the services rendered. These points demand further consideration.

Several possible reasons for the relatively infrequent use of consultants, and the relatively poor rating of consultant's work, may be hypothesized. First, it is likely that many firms do not think to engage consultants, or are reluctant to pay for their services, because the location decision is incorrectly viewed as an easy straight forward task. It is too often viewed as a rather unimportant task within the context of the firm's total operations. Second, there is no doubt some degree of dissatisfaction with results produced by consultants. In part, this is because consultants do not always do a thoroughly competent, professional job. Since consultants are also businessmen, there is always a great pressure of time, sometimes leading to hastily produced reports. Problems can be exacerbated by the client firms who try to get off cheaply, leaving the consultant with insufficient resources to do a complete study. For these same reasons, consulting agencies may assign inexperienced staff to the job; this situation may lead to the firm complaining that the consultants simply repackage and give back that which they already knew. However, in all fairness to consultants, it must be recognized that many of the difficulties stem from the company itself. Sometimes, for example, the company cannot even do a good job of defining the problem.

This last point suggests a more fundamental truth: A company cannot turn its locational problems over to consultants and simply sit back and wait for the good answers. Company management must be involved from beginning to end. Since any locational decision is judgmental, containing large degrees of uncertainty, there is the very real danger that an uninvolved management will subsequently blame all shortcomings on "those outsiders."

Companies can use consultants to good advantage, but on a partnership basis. Although consultants may function as data gatherers and analysts, they are most profitably used as participant-observers. Consultants should facilitate intra-firm communications. They should advise in setting agendas, and in pointing out issues overlooked, as well as steering inquiry away from unproductive avenues. Finally, consultants may be most useful precisely because they are from outside the firm and have no internal vested interests. They can be effective adjudicators of the inevitable intra-firm debates.[9]

As pointed out in Chapter 1, it is those managements which have been actively engaged in the site selection process who most fully appreciate the difficulties of locational decision-making and who are most appreciative of the necessary compromises. The managements who have gone through the psychologically severe initation process are also those who are most happy with the final location decision. This in turn tends to lead to a self-fulfilling prophecy: happy managers manage successful plants. Probably the surest key to successful plant location is the active participation of an enlightened, knowledgeable and concerned management, including not only the actual site selectors but also those who must finally ratify the location decision.

Notes and References—Chapter 10

1. Conway, H.M., and Liston, L.L. *A Composite Case History of a New Facility Location.* Atlanta: Industrial Development Research Council, 1978.

2. *Ibid.*

3. See, for example, "Checklist of Site Selection Factors," *Site Selection Handbook,* Vol. XXIII, No. 1 (February, 1978). Atlanta: Conway Publications, pp. 59-71.

4. *A Composite Case History of a New Facility Location, op. cit.*

5. See Love, Charles A. and James G. March, *An Introduction to Models in the Social Sciences,* Harper and Row, 1975, for an introduction to decision making and decision rules.

6. *A Composite Case History of a New Facility Location, op. cit.*

7. *Ibid.*

8. "Corporate Real Estate Management: An Influential and Financially Rewarding Profession;" *Site Selection Handbook, op. cit.,* pp. 2-4.

9. Similar advice is given in Rabin, Sol "Tackling Corporate Real Estate Assignments. When to Build Staff and When To Use Consultants," *Industrial Development,* November/December, 1979, pp. 20-22.

Index

Industrial Facilities Planning

Over 100 of the most outstanding articles from *Industrial Development's* 25-year history were selected and reproduced in this "how-to" manual for planners and developers. Topics highlighted include such critical planning areas as establishing criteria for new facilities, financing and taxes, community factors, environmental regulation, energy availability, corporate growth planning and site selection techniques.

Other reports in the book focus on specific aspects of facility planning: appraising, capital assets, leases, mineral rights, employee relocation, warehousing, plant security, capital budgeting, project scheduling, control of construction costs, new vs. old plants, construction contracts, plant start-ups, project feasibility and surplus properties.

Companies represented by the authors of *Industrial Facilities Planning* include General Motors, DuPont, Westinghouse, Ford, Alcoa, Honeywell, IBM, Xerox, RCA, Consolidated Foods, TRW, E.R. Squibb, B.F. Goodrich, Owens-Illinois and Armour and Co.

Outline of Contents

Industrial Facilities Planning

330 pp. 8½ × 11. Soft cover. U.S. $35.00
ISBN: 0-910436-05-3

Conway Publications, Inc.

1954 Airport Rd., N.E.
Atlanta, Ga. 30341
(404) 458-6026

New Project File And Site Selection Checklist

Providing a systematic approach to location decisions, the checklist presents a logical sequence of events from determination of need for a facility through disposition of the plant as surplus property after it has served its useful purpose.

The result of more than two decades of additions and refinements, the checklist includes more than 1,700 items arranged in a loose-leaf binder format, tabbed with major headings. This enables the user to insert his own project notes in the binder to custom-fit the checklist to each project.

Major subject headings....

Company Organization and Preparation For Expansion Planning

I.Corporate Strategy
II.Company Organization Structure
III.Criteria for Site and Facility

Location and Site Analysis

I.Market and Demographic Data
II.Work Force, Wages and Productivity
III.Transportation
IV.Energy and Utilities: Electric, Gas, Communications
V.Materials, Supplies, Services
VI.Government Programs: National
VII.Government Programs: State
VIII.Government Programs: Locai
IX.Water and Waste Systems
X.Ecological Factors

XI.Quality of Life Factors
XII.Climate
XIII.Specific Sites—Planning Factors
XIV.Buildings: Office, Warehouse, Industrial
XV.International Projects

Decision-Making

I.Facility Feasibility Analysis
II.Financing
III.Lease vs. Buy

Construction Start-up, Property Management

I.Construction and Implementation
II.Property Management

New Project File and Site Selection Checklist

84 pp. Looseleaf Binder. U.S. $35.00
ISBN: 0-910436-12-6

Conway Publications, Inc.
1954 Airport Rd., N.E.
Atlanta, Ga. 30341
(404) 458-6026

Disaster Survival
How to Choose Secure Sites and Make Practical Escape Plans
by H. McKinley Conway

There is overwhelming evidence to prove that industrial plants and other facilities are exposed to sufficient risk from either man-made or natural disasters to warrant giving thought to methods of preparedness. *Disaster Survival* is a practical guide to finding safer sites for facilities and helping personnel prepare for emergencies. The report divides disasters into two main categories—natural disasters and man-made disasters—and provides a pre-disaster plan to minimize risk and a post-disaster plan for response and recovery for both individuals and corporations.

Over 200 maps, charts and photographs, including 50 state maps, aid the facility planner in evaluating the natural risk potential and man-made hazard possibilities for each locality of interest. A summary of federal disaster assistance programs and suggested contents of a remote emergency medical supply are also included in the appendix.

Outline of Contents

I. **Introduction**

II. **Natural Disasters**
  A. Astronomical Phenomena
  B. Cold Waves and Blizzards
  C. Droughts and Heat Waves
  D. Earthquakes and Volcanic Eruptions
    1. Earthquakes
    2. Volcanos
  E. Ecological Phenomena
  F. Floods
  G. Land Sinks, Slides, Avalanches and Soil Expansion
  H. Wind Storms: Hurricanes, Typhoons and Cyclones
  I. Thunderstorms, Tornados and Related Phenomena

III. **Man-Made Disasters**
  A. Fire and Explosion
  B. Transportation and Travel
  C. Structural Failures
  D. Nuclear Radiation
  E. Ecosystem Mismanagement
  F. Terrorism
  G. War: The Ultimate Man-Made Disaster

IV. **Evaluation Of Risk Potential**
  A. Scope of Disasters of Various Types
  B. Comparing Risks for Nations, States and Localities
  C. State Maps Indicating Potential Risks
  D. Risk Potential at Specific Sites
  E. Combinations of Risks
  F. Finding the Intelligent Compromise

V. **Survival Planning: Site Hardening And Escape Contingencies**
  A. Household Survival Plans
  B. Corporate Survival Plans
  C. Planning New Facilities for Survival
  D. Personal Action Plans

VI. **Public Policies And Survival**
  A. What Government Can Do
  B. Where Government Falters
  C. The Future: Will the Odds Improve?

VII. **Appendix: International Disaster Risk Data**
  Bibliography
  Index

278 pp. 8½ × 11. Cloth. U.S. $48.00
ISBN: 0-910436-17-7

Conway Publications, Inc.
1954 Airport Rd., N.E.
Atlanta, Ga. 30341
(404) 458-6026